Acting Up

– A diary –

by the same author

plays
PLAYS ONE
(Slag, Teeth 'n' Smiles, Knuckle, Licking Hitler, Plenty)
PLAYS TWO
(Fanshen, A Map of the World, Saigon, The Bay at Nice, The Secret Rapture)
BRASSNECK (with Howard Brenton)
THE GREAT EXHIBITION
PRAVDA (with Howard Brenton)
RACING DEMON
MURMURING JUDGES
THE ABSENCE OF WAR
SKYLIGHT
AMY'S VIEW
THE JUDAS KISS
VIA DOLOROSA

adaptations
THE RULES OF THE GAME by Pirandello
THE LIFE OF GALILEO by Brecht
MOTHER COURAGE AND HER CHILDREN by Brecht
IVANOV by Chekhov
THE BLUE ROOM from *La Ronde* by Schnitzler

screenplays for television
LICKING HITLER
DREAMS OF LEAVING
HEADING HOME

screenplays
WETHERBY
PARIS BY NIGHT
STRAPLESS
PLENTY
THE SECRET RAPTURE

opera libretto
THE KNIFE

prose
WRITING LEFT-HANDED
ASKING AROUND: Background to the David Hare trilogy

DAVID HARE

Acting Up

A diary

faber and faber
LONDON·NEW YORK

First published in 1999
by Faber and Faber Limited
3 Queen Square London WC1N 3AU
Published in the United States by Faber and Faber Inc.
a division of Farrar, Straus and Giroux Inc., New York

Photoset by Faber and Faber Ltd
Printed in England by Clays Ltd, St Ives plc

Lines from Sylvia Plath's 'The Applicant', from *Collected Poems*, published by
Faber and Faber, are reproduced by kind permission of Faber and Faber Ltd
and HarperCollins Ltd
Lines from *Collected Poems of Anne Sexton*, published by Houghton Mifflin
Ltd, are reproduced by kind permission of Sterling Lord Literistics
Lines from 'Poem XVIII, Section 12', from *The English Auden, 1931–1936*,
published by Faber and Faber, are reproduced by kind permission of Faber
and Faber Ltd and Curtis Brown Ltd
Lines by Maurice Hare from *The Penguin Thematic Dictionary of Quotations*
are reproduced by kind permission of Penguin Books Ltd
Lines by Margaret Atwood from 'Heart', © Margaret Atwood, 1997,
reproduced by kind permission of Curtis Brown Ltd

David Hare is hereby identified as author of this
work in accordance with Section 77 of the Copyright,
Designs and Patents Act 1988

A CIP record for this book
is available from the British Library

ISBN 0–571–20135–0

2 4 6 8 10 9 7 5 3 1

For Nicole, Joe, Lewis, Darcy and Candice

Contents

Anyone who does not lose his reason over certain things has no reason.

GOTTHOLD LESSING

Foreword

In November 1997, I first went to Israel and Palestine at the request of Elyse Dodgson, the director of the International Department at London's Royal Court Theatre. Elyse hoped that I would be one of three writers – one English, one Israeli and one Palestinian – who would all write plays about the period of the British Mandate in the 1930s and 1940s. On my return, however, I told Stephen Daldry, who had just resigned as the theatre's Artistic Director, that I wanted to write a monologue for myself to perform. I also insisted the subject matter be contemporary. It is to Stephen's everlasting credit that he received the idea of my acting my own work without a second's hesitation. A look came into his eye which would even have passed for relish.

Stephen had recently handed over responsibility for the Royal Court's programme, but he had retained the task of moving the company back from its temporary quarters at the Duke of York's Theatre in the West End to its famous home in Sloane Square. Stephen's remaining task was to supervise the new building while he got on with originating his own film directing career.

The first draft of *Via Dolorosa* was finished in February 1998. In April Stephen and I examined both the text and my ability to perform it in a couple of weeks of workshop. During this period and then later, substantial changes were made to the text of the play. It was rewritten again before I gave over the month of May to the task of learning it.

Because I felt that this sudden change of profession might prove interesting, I started keeping a diary. I wish I had started earlier. This text dates only from the beginning of formal rehearsals in August. For me, the diary was not just a record. It was the essential means of trying to understand what was going on. Knowing I would sit down every morning to lay out the previous day's trials gave the experience calm and order. In a profound way, the diary got me through.

All published diarists face the question of how much to revise. I have had to obey a few legal restraints, but the balance of my judgments has been against editing and in favour of retaining the heat of the original moment. I have worked on the principle that what I felt at the time is more valuable than what I feel now. Some of my sentiments are sometimes unfair. If the effect is raw, then this is the price you must pay for learning what it's like, trying to do something when you don't know how.

Acting Up is a diary of learning to act.

PART ONE

An End to Tim and Jim

4 August 1998 First day of rehearsal in the room at the top of the Old Vic. I first worked here in 1971 when I adapted the Pirandello play *The Rules of the Game* for the National Theatre. I remember the excitement of listening to Paul Scofield say lines I'd had half a hand in writing. And I last worked here in 1973, when I directed Fulton Mackay in the touring version of Trevor Griffiths' play *The Party*. The room was charged with the ghost of the just-departed Laurence Olivier.

Stephen Daldry arrives an hour late, thinking we're starting at 12. There's a whole group of us – publicity, stage management and so on – who've been there since 11. Stephen tries to be boyish and charming about it but nobody's charmed. I'm already exhausted from talking to a whole lot of people I don't know. It's the worst possible start. I find that doing anything except the play itself is impossible. On Thursday I'm meant to attend the Royal Court Summer School, to talk about the play to student directors and writers. I don't want to do it.

At the end of the day I feel horrible. We got through only two pages because most of our time was spent trying to establish a working language. I'm self-conscious anyway and find acting unnatural. Stephen wants me to walk on very slowly, and I feel a nelly. I keep asking him to get up and do it in order to show me what it looks like from the outside. When he eventually does, after two hours of refusing, only then do I understand what the effect of what he wants is.

At a couple of points in the day I get very angry. A real white rage: a function of my own incompetence. Once it is quite simply because there are three people behind the table – Rufus (the assistant director), Lesley (the stage manager) and Stephen. Rufus and Stephen are giving me contradictory notes at the same time. I can't cope. I get even angrier when Rufus starts telling me that each line must be reduced to an action. 'What are you doing? Are you seducing? Are you tickling? Are you provoking?' This approach, to me, is irredeemable bullshit, because the style of my writing is do all three at once, and with the same line. I found the experience of being taught this so-called method of work as if it were enlightening just incredibly annoying and unhelpful – and slightly insulting. I found adjectives unhelpful. Stephen wanted me to be 'mischievous', he said. But the word seems inadequate to the text. 'Mischievous' just won't do, as a word. I am confused by a mix of feelings brought on by direction about something I understand better than anyone in the room, i.e. writing, and something I do worse than anyone in the room, i.e. acting.

I realize the purpose of my acting is to make me a better director, to understand acting better.

There is no doubt that my entrance will be crucial. How I come on. What effect I have by coming on. And how I keep the audience wanting to know what comes next. I learn two useful things today. First, not to rush straight from the end of one line on to the next, but to allow the end of the first line to do its work before I proceed. Second, not to look away from a particular member of the audience before the end of the line, since this creates the impression I don't trust it, or am ashamed of it.

Stephen says at one point that my tendency is to undersell the writer's work, as if I were embarrassed by it. This is a first-class note.

The physical is important. I can't work with keys or wallet in my pockets. I need to feel I'm naked. The work tails out inconsequentially because we have to go and do something called 'doughnuts'. This means meeting the staff of the Royal Court at the Duke of York's. There, I take Stephen aside and request that I never again get contradictory notes from two directors at the same time. If I were Judi Dench, I would be able to offer two readings to satisfy both directors. But I'm not and I can't. It freezes me up. Stephen says 'My God, I'm sorry. You should have said at the time.'

In the evening, I go to Renoir's film *La Grande illusion* with Nicole, my wife. The last half hour is unbearably moving. I ask Nicole why. 'Because it shows human beings behaving at their best.'

4

5 *August* I've been awake in the night, but I realize, tossing and turning, what the day's profit has been. I no longer think of the text as something to explain, but as something which expresses emotion. If this is right, then the pain of the first day has been worth it.

Luckily, Stephen is alone when I go in, so I can get my doubts off my chest. I tell him I don't want to go home feeling terrible again, because that isn't helpful to me. We mustn't leave work unresolved. I also said I wasn't going to talk to the International Summer School, because it was the thing that would most fuck me up at this point. My worst tendency is to explain the text, rather than to act it. To make me go back to explaining it to young people will take me in quite the wrong direction. Stephen accepts this and we cancel the session. Frankly, I also don't want to have to listen to everybody's views since, based on an ignorance of the overall text, they are only going to be prejudices anyway. Of which, with this subject, there are too many already.

The day's work is much better. We have some interesting problems. Most importantly, Stephen tells me I go too fast. I tell him there are two reasons. First, because subconsciously I think the play is too long and I am worried it will be boring. He says it most certainly will be boring if I go as fast as I do at the moment. And secondly, I think that all plays are too slow. Whenever I go to the theatre I sit there thinking 'For fuck's sake get on with it.' When I directed Wally Shawn's play *The Designated Mourner* I had to ratchet Mike Nichols up day by day. The slower people speak the harder they are to understand. Dialogue is rhythm, and there is some scientific rhythm which I believe corresponds to the natural pace of activity in our brains. Mike, himself one of the world's most experienced directors, kept complaining. 'Nobody can understand this at the speed you want it.' But I believe I was right. Why am I not right this time?

Audiences move at the speed of their brightest member – not their thickest. Frank Capra proved this by a famous demonstration. If you make a film, sit alone and watch it. You will believe that the story is going at a comfortable speed. Watch it with five other people and the film will seem a bit slow. Watch it with fifty people and you will find it has suddenly become very slow indeed. Watch it with five hundred people and you will be screaming in agony at how snail-paced it is. The more people present, the quicker you have to be.

Speed is not our only disagreement. So is size. It's a mark of my trust in Stephen that I now dare mention this, but I am aware that some of Stephen's productions are a little bit heavy on the acting. For my taste, they're over-pitched. Stephen just laughs when I remark that I don't want to come over like Fiona Shaw in the Sophie Treadwell play *Machinal*, belting it out to the back wall. This is what he calls 'playing baseball', i.e. trying to hit the ball out of the fucking park. Stephen, needless to say, rather likes this style. He remarks that I am more like Barbara Leigh-Hunt, who refused to shout in *An Inspector Calls* because she'd been taught at drama school that shouting on stage was wrong.

We settle a happy medium. I agree with Stephen that my pitch will be higher than Barbara Leigh-Hunt's but lower than Fiona Shaw's.

What is good is that today it *is* a performance. How many times have I said to actors 'I don't want you to be playing the line. I want you to be expressing an overriding feeling, and then to watch your mouth move independently underneath your forehead. Disconnect the line from your brain'? And here I am, now doing it myself – concentrating on the feeling above the line, rather than the line itself. It's incredibly liberating. Mouth's moving, brain's somewhere else.

Tonight Nicole and I watch *La Règle du jeu* on video, to complete our short Renoir season. A flop on its release, because of what it is saying. Like all artists Renoir's a bit of an opportunist: *La Grande illusion* is pro-aristocracy, *La Règle du jeu* is anti-. Whatever produces the best work.

6 August I'm not sure why I'm so depressed this morning, since we had what's called a good day yesterday – speeding through from my arrival in Tel Aviv, all the way to Benni Begin without too much difficulty. Stephen wants to choreograph and inflect every single moment, tying me down into specificity. Say this, look there, pause, don't breathe here, etc. This suits me fine. The more fixed it is the better. I have no fears about this at all. At one point by telling me to stop and count to five in silence, Stephen liberated a passage which had been giving me trouble. This is the kind of direction I like.

In its form, the play is a travel diary of Israel and Palestine, which dramatizes my meetings with politicians as well as the less formal, everyday encounters I had. In its aim, however, it hopes to be somewhat more than that. It is the story of a Westerner trying to understand two societies where belief is at the centre of the way of life. It is about the wrenching effects on a person apparently without faith of meeting a whole lot of people who have only faith. Its shape has been extremely hard to arrive at, and has involved endless rewriting. It has to seem artless, natural. That, as we know, is the most difficult effect of all to achieve in writing, as in everything else.

A lot of time today is spent searching for a parallel artlessness in my style of delivery. Stephen invents a technique to make me seem to be speaking to only one individual in the audience, and to no other. It's a technique he's seen preachers use. I christen it my Jerry Springer technique. By focusing down on to one person in five hundred, we discover we can convey sincerity. We develop this technique for passages which need special credibility.

The most interesting problem was with the design. I'm to walk along a gangway to a stage built over an abyss. If I fall off the walkway I will die. This does not particularly bother me. For some reason I assume it's not going to happen. But what does bother me is the idea that the structure may not be completely solid. Simon Callow said he never felt comfortable in my production of Christopher Hampton's play *Total Eclipse*. His chair was on a revolve, so the ground didn't feel firm beneath his feet. After three days I have exactly the same feeling – that when I put a foot on the ground, the ground must not respond to my foot. I know I won't be able to act if it does.

At the end of the day we discussed costume. I enjoyed this very much since, for once in my life, it's up to others to woo me. I don't have to do the wooing. Like all writers and directors, I've spent my life being the persuader. You're always the school prefect, coaxing and imploring – 'come on, chaps, please do what I ask you, it's going to be fine.' Now the boot, spectacularly, is on the other foot. Ian McNeil, the designer, comes to me and says he hopes that I'm going to like his ideas. He even looks a little nervous. This is terribly refreshing. Best fun of all is keeping out of crucial decisions. There is to be a vision of Jerusalem at the end of the play when a model hillside will rise up out of the stage. It was a pleasure to walk away and let Ian and Stephen decide exactly what form it should take.

Dinner with our French actor friends, Yves Lefèvre and Sabine Haudepain. Sabine was the little girl in *Jules et Jim* – her first role, at the age of five. The extraordinary thing is that she says she can still remember every day of the filming. They all lived in the house where the film is set and Jeanne Moreau cooked for them. Now, she says, she is the only actor she knows who goes home after a show. The rest all eat out, have bread and butter and wine and steak and chips. She watches them get bigger as the run goes on.

9 August For the weekend I went to Malvern to see *Phèdre*. I spent most of my time trying to work out why Barbara Jefford, classically trained at the Old Vic in the 1950s, is presently so much better than anyone else. What is this thing some actors have – absolute simplicity, absolute authority? Dinner afterwards was very disturbing. I was shocked first of all by the hostility some people showed to the idea of Nicole Kidman appearing in *The Blue Room* – a Schnitzler adaptation I have just done for the Donmar, and which is rehearsing concurrently with *Via Dolorosa*. They resent the idea of Nicole swanning in from Hollywood and taking a job from our local actors. It is very rare to feel you are working on a project that everyone wants to fail. When conversation then turned to my own acting debut, the actors at dinner were not hostile, but everyone else was. The form the hostility takes is for everyone to tell me how 'brave' I am being by doing it, how difficult one-man shows are, how impossible it is to remember your lines, how contentious the subject is, etc.

It reminds me of Wally Shawn's story in his film *My Dinner With André*. When he was going to act for the first time, as it happened as a cat, in *The Master and the Margherita*, everyone told him how impossible it was to act in a cat-suit, how you can't breathe in cat-suits, how you become disoriented, and so on. Wally thought, do these people *want* me to fail as a cat?

However, the most positive sign of change was when I made a short speech introducing the old Joan Crawford melodrama *Mildred Pierce*, which I had chosen for a screening at the Malvern cinema as part of the festival. Afterwards, Nicole asked what had happened to me. My manner had changed completely. My nervousness had gone and I spoke fluently. I said I'd been using this occasion as a sort of rehearsal, to see whether I could make a public appearance using the techniques I've learnt. The only problem? Nicole told me I still twitch my nose.

Also, Friday had been encouraging. For the first time, I flew. I took the material where Pauline talks in the boarding house in Gaza about the tendency of Palestinians to be delighted when things fuck up. I asked Stephen, 'Does it worry you that Pauline has no particular motive to be as passionate as this?' He said, 'Not in the slightest.' At once I let rip. The following section, which leads us to Birzeit University, suddenly became malleable. There was that feeling of meltdown you get in all proper theatre when the material ceases to be about its supposed subject (in this case, Israel and Palestine) and instead becomes about something else entirely (faith and conviction).

Stephen and I were both amused because we had independently come to the same conclusion. It's fine for Pauline to be passionate because, in some mad way, I *am* Pauline. The end of the day was therefore exhilarating, with me feeling for the first time I was acting. What does this mean? I ceased to be me.

10 *August* Not a great day. It was 93 degrees and the sun beat down on the glass roof of the Old Vic rehearsal room. I got a parking ticket in the middle of trying to do a particularly complicated passage, where, rather like Rod Hull and Emu, I have to impersonate George Ibrahim talking to Hussein Barghouti. Stephen had come off a plane. He had been fundraising for the Royal Court in Cap Ferrat ('*Quelle vie, quelle existence!*') and he seemed unfocused and bored. It occurred to me that maybe he has given me all the notes he has. When we went back to the beginning of the text he seemed to have remarkably little to say.

I think it is very hard for him. Listener-fatigue must set in when you have only one voice to listen to all day. It's very easy to find your judgment going, particularly in the stifling heat. The sound designer, Paul Arditti, needs to hear some of the show today. We agreed it couldn't be the whole thing because that would be too much for me. But then I left a message for Stephen after rehearsal saying I would prefer to do the whole ninety minutes. My true reason is I think it might stimulate Stephen. To get the best out of my director, I feel I have a duty to keep him entertained. We have to proceed in a way which allows him regularly to hear things fresh, or he will become too implicated, by habit.

We have decided that we will preview the play to invited audiences before we open at the Royal Court.

The best part of the day was spent in the morning with Patsy Rodenburg, the National Theatre's voice coach. I have known Patsy a long time. She operates throughout the British theatre as a kind of paramedic, an angel of expertise, rushing in wherever she's needed. Her books about how to speak are huge bestsellers because she has the gift of being able to address the specialist and non-specialist alike. She's the Delia Smith of the vocal chords.

Once, when I was going to Japan, Peter Brook gave me an introduction to meet his favourite monk in Kyoto. I approached the old man with appropriate reverence, hoping he might pass on some special wisdom. He turned out, in his youth, to have been a student at the London School of Economics. We sat in a grey pebble garden in silence for some time before he said, 'I can't say I've learnt a great deal in seventy-five years, but I do know a little bit about breathing.' As the years have gone by, I have realized that to know a bit about breathing is a considerable achievement.

Patsy started by saying that I spoke from my shoulders – far too high up – and that my tendency was to think so fast that I rushed to my next thought before I had even completed the last. Her advice was so similar to Stephen's that I suspected collusion, which was hotly denied. Patsy showed me a series of exercises to lower my voice into my diaphragm, and to release the top half of my body. They were so good that not only could I feel the pressure coming off my voice, but I also found myself standing differently all day.

Both she and Stephen have taught me about the act of trust. Take one sentence at a time, invest that sentence with its full meaning. And *trust* that the next sentence is going to appear. 'You know it,' says Patsy, 'so it *will* pop up. Think of it in advance and you will destroy the performance.'

Patsy sums up my whole dilemma. 'It's odd to say this to a writer, but what I shall be trying to teach you is to put your own rhythms aside so that you can find the writer's. All my teaching is to free the actor from their own voice in order to express the writer's. And so it's essential that you feel them as two different things.'

I am beginning to realize this experience is going to help me not just in the month of September, but for the rest of my life.

At the end of the day, Ian McNeil and his assistant – everyone has assistants except me – came in and looked fairly bored as I worked. But I have toughened enough that it doesn't any longer affect me how bored or otherwise visitors look. Fuck 'em.

11 *August* The precipitated run-through turned out to be useful because, for a start, we found that at Stephen's pace the play is 1 hour 50 minutes long. Which is impossible. It used to be 1 hour 30 minutes when I learnt it by myself. I want to cut savagely into the opening material, which I feel is unwieldy. David Grossman and George Steiner look ripe for the axe, because – to adopt the criterion which Stephen has made familiar to me – they deal in ideas rather than feelings. The weird thing was that even I, this time, felt that I was rushing the opening. Stephen has given me a reliable lock on the first twenty minutes, so that I know exactly what speed I should be going at, and I am now aware when I go off on the timing. The rest of the piece is more free-fall, because we haven't planned it in the same detail.

I made one disastrous mistake. I said that I *realized* that the Jews did not belong in that part of the world, rather than saying that it *momentarily occurred* to me. The result, as I pointed out afterwards, would have been to change, and ruin, the meaning of the whole play. It would have turned me into an anti-Zionist. Stephen sweetly said, 'Well, you won't make the same mistake again.'

For most of the time, I was like a man frantically running along to catch a train. I hit a couple of good passages – most notably when I was with Sarah walking in the settlement, and my Shulamit Aloni was pretty shit-hot – but otherwise I was wobbling about, panicking and trying to climb back on and feeling pretty humourless. When I said at the end, 'Do I really need to be this big and work this hard?' Stephen replied, 'Bigger. Harder.' To my astonishment, when he went out of the room, Lesley and Rufus agreed. Lesley said, 'It's such fun to watch you work so hard.'

Fun it may be, but the sweat was pouring off me. I am allowed two drinks in the show, and they both came straight off my brow within ten seconds. The heat was terrible.

I feel unsupported outside the rehearsal room. The bloke doing the programme sent me a few illegible scraps by fax, and this really pissed me off. The content of the programme will provide the context for the whole play. I can see that the Court's employees have a problem relating to the play, because none of them has read it. I have wanted to keep the control group down to the smallest possible number while I am so vulnerable. The result is that the rest of the staff feel uninvolved.

The problem has been made worse because the theatre is in a handover period. For five years it has been run by Stephen, who is a forceful figure. It's now in the hands of Ian Rickson, whose manner could hardly be more different. I've known this situation before and it's never easy. *Via Dolorosa* is the project of the outgoing director. Few people in the theatre – there are exceptions – seem to feel much obligation to put it near the top of their priorities. It's the new man they're working for.

12 *August* Terrible day. It started brilliantly with Natalie, my new exercise teacher, who comes from Martinique. Stephen insisted from the start that I get a trainer, and I came up with Natalie, who has been helping a friend of mine. She's never worked in the theatre before, or even with actors, although she herself was once a dancer. She's in her early thirties and formidably confident. She gave me a look-over and followed it up with lightning analysis, shaking her

head all the time and drawing the air in between her teeth at the horror of it all. The problem with my body, she says, is the same as the problem with my mind, i.e. I get ahead of myself. I'm where I want to be before I can be bothered to go through the dreary business of getting there. I dart ahead. I lean forward. I incline. I grinned as she developed her view of my terrible physique but, as we began to work, she warmed up. Most teachers start out by telling you how fucked you are, so as to impress you the more with the progress they then make. I have some memory of Bette Davis in *The Corn is Green* impressing on the young Welsh boy that he's useless. Then us all being in floods of tears when he goes on to make spectacular progress – thanks to her, of course. In my memory, *Top Gun* works on the same principle. Natalie wants my shoulders to be suspended permanently in the form of coathangers. She tried to teach me to walk. It's surprisingly hard.

Things went downhill from there. Stephen and I went through the text looking for cuts. Eventually we came up with a list of twenty-four. I was getting so overwhelmed by them that I said I needed to make a list of them on paper. Stephen said, OK, then the rest of us'll go off for lunch. I started to work transcribing the text. Nobody offered to go and get me a sandwich, even. So I went to get one for myself, came back, and resumed making the list while everyone else sat around, doing nothing.

Stephen then insisted on working on the Grossman passage, which had gone dead on us. I pointed out that in its shortened version it was no longer a scene. The dialectic had gone, so that instead of it being an argument between me and another character, it had been reduced simply to a passage conveying information. It was so quick now that there was no tension. As a result it seemed tedious, although it was much shorter.

Stephen could see this was indeed the problem, so I said I would rewrite it. We went back to my original research and I came up with the idea of showing Grossman in a different light, so that he becomes someone who knows so much about Israel that he can barely bring himself to listen to questions about it. Their crudeness offends him. I made a painful comparison. It's like when I have to listen to people lecturing me about the theatre. After thirty years of thinking of little else, I tend to tap my fingers impatiently, or be elaborately polite when confronted with people who want to tell me how plays work. The innocence of their thinking often seems unbearable. I suggested we should multiply this effect for Grossman. He should find it tough being the world's greatest expert on Israel.

To do this, of course, it will be necessary to make me stupider than I actually was. If Grossman is to play the part of 'man who knows everything' then I, as narrator, will have to pretend to be 'man who knows nothing'. This is the only way we can develop some edge between the two of us. Nothing is more boring on stage than two characters who know the same things. Stephen has always been keen on anything which makes me appear stupid or clumsy because, he says, audiences side instinctively with anyone who shares their own ignorance.

He then asked what we should do for the last hour. I said I needed to go through the 24 cuts. One of the first cuts came at a place where I take a drink of water. There was no glass and no water in place. The three of them watched as I crossed the room to the fridge, found the glass (which I had brought in that morning because there were no glasses), poured my water and returned to my place. Again it seems not to occur to anyone that it might possibly be their job to help the actor. The rewrites were foully difficult, because they changed the rhythm of everything. Lines that I had previously found perfectly easy to remember became impossible, and yet they weren't even in passages that had been touched. What has been disturbed is the overall music of the whole piece.

We made one useful discovery. The feeling that I am shouting or overacting is fine when I am animating other characters. It is wrong when I am playing myself. I said I most hated those places where I had to boom sonorously as if the work were by some historical writer of the fifties. Stephen said these were the places where, indeed, I had to be more like myself. Rufus came up with a brilliant way of playing a passage which had particularly bothered me. The play begins with me making the rather pompous generalization: 'For as long as I can remember, people have told me that in England we lead shallow lives.' Rufus suggested we change it to the far more throw-away 'People always say, in England we lead shallow lives.' At once it came to life. It stopped being pretentious and became snappy.

At the end of the day we had a costume try-out. This was rather self-consciously in a small room at the side, since I had complained to Ian that last time about ten people stood and stared at me, as if I were cattle. Again, nobody had noticed that I would prefer to do this quietly. When we had finished, Stephen apologized for the need for the rewrite. I said, obviously if it would help the play, I would be stupid not to do it. He said he would give me one note as we walked out together. He said he was not sure if he knew me well enough to give it. He said that I would have to learn to listen to myself as I spoke, and to do that, I would have to learn to listen to others.

We were walking down Waterloo Road for an *Evening Standard*. I jokingly said I couldn't do that because I knew what people were going to say half way through saying it. Stephen finished my sentence for me 'And you don't want to listen to their crappy thoughts.' When he said this, I suddenly felt myself go stone cold with anger. 'No. On the contrary, I don't think their thoughts are crappy. It's because I actually respond to what people say that I tend to seize on things even as they're saying them.'

I walked away. I have been white with fury all night.

13 August I left Stephen a telephone message saying I was too angry to write or act. I went to rehearsals of *The Blue Room*, shaking with jealousy when somebody offered to order in a sandwich for lunch, or stepped forward to give Nicole Kidman a pencil when she needed one. The director, Sam Mendes, was lounging around, tipping back his chair in his usual easy-going manner. He has a big Tupperware box of sweets into which he dips frequently. It was just a normal rehearsal atmosphere – pleasant and friendly. I drove to work, and found Stephen parking his bicycle in the street outside the Old Vic. He had got my message, and had a bunch of flowers in his hands. He wanted to apologize, but I went berserk, shouting at him in the street, not caring who saw us. 'You have the fucking cheek to accuse *me* of not listening, when for ten days I have been working in a rehearsal room where not one single person seems to have any sensitivity to my needs or difficulties.' I raved on about how it shocked me how little Stephen must understand me if he thought that I never listened. If I was an arrogant twerp, what the hell was the point of working with me? And so on.

He said he had had no idea how badly he had hurt me until this morning when he got my message. He had meant it as a stupid joke but he could see that it was both badly timed and not funny. He asked me to forgive him. Which I did. And we then went upstairs and had a sort of rational discussion about why it seems to be part of Royal Court culture not to be seen to want to be too helpful to the actors. Stephen said it had driven him mad when he was running the theatre. It was a phoney idea of democracy. I said perhaps we had compounded our problems by being so secretive, by going off and doing our work by ourselves without anyone seeing a script. Stephen didn't accept this. I suggested we should do a show at some point for the staff, so they can see what we are working at.

Stephen had asked Rufus and Lesley not to come in for an hour, so we had the luxury of being alone. The conversation slipped naturally to my saying that I was very uncomfortable with the opening of the show where I have to walk on and look at the audience with a sort of conspiratorial smile that I just don't feel. I asked him if I could be on stage already, coming on five minutes early to put water in place, and so on. Then just sitting in a chair and starting when we're ready.

At once Stephen got fired up, and began to see the production. He introduced a couple of tables and chairs with objects on them – including my script. And I just eased into the opening, telling him that I didn't want the house lights to go down until I was ready to tell them to go down. At once the whole metaphor of the evening – that it is both theatre and anti-theatre – came alive.

Up till this, I had taken no real part in the production ideas. I thought that since I was actor and writer, that was enough. I should let Stephen get on with the directing. But in fact by beginning to contribute to the production itself, I only stimulated Stephen to have better ideas.

I realize how stupid I've been. I've had a completely false idea of what an actor is, or does. I've thought: 'I'm an actor. It's not up to me to take responsibility for the whole production. I'm here to be told what to do.' In a moment of blinding revelation, I realized what a patronizing and silly view of acting this is. All the good actors I've known do indeed make the whole production their business. They just don't make a song and dance about it. As a director I always invite a dialogue with the actors. Why on earth have I been denying that dialogue to my own director?

The work we then did was to give the evening shape. The lights going down later, so you are five minutes in before you feel the show beginning. A sound effect to tell the audience I have gone to Israel. A moment where I effectively back out of the show altogether because my wife has been so insulted in the settlements. And best of all, the idea that the model of Jerusalem should appear not for the epilogue, but when I go to Jerusalem. All these ideas will have three effects: (1) They will give the play shape and make it seem shorter, (2) They will play with the theme of theatre itself, and (3) They will make my own character much easier for me to play, and much less forced. I no longer have to boom out lines in a way which seemed grandiloquent and false.

Just to be able to sit at the side of the stage while the audience comes in, and to sit again when I reach the line 'I've reached a low point, it's obvious' seemed completely liberating for me. A lot of this rehearsal was therefore spent discussing Brecht. It's one of the things I like about Stephen. He's one of the few intellectual directors around. He's interested in what theatre *is*. We have both noticed that at various points I have to both embody and comment. So we discussed how bad Brechtian acting is always demonstrative. The good stuff seems to come from a place where you can't tell if the actor is the character or not. You can't easily find the attitude. A Stanislavskian actor takes the word 'sincere' as a compliment; but a Brechtian actor prefers to hear the word 'clever'.

The perfect example was Laurence Olivier playing Archie Rice in *The Entertainer*, doing the damn stupid dance, looking down at his feet as if to say, 'This is tacky and stupid', and yet at the same time executing it perfectly. It was the most beautiful knife-edge Brechtian acting I've ever seen. *That's* where I have to head. To a place where I am doing a huge amount, but you can't quite tell where 'I' am inside all this.

Stephen said, 'Well, we've had our first row.' And, in the way of things, the day was hugely productive and worthwhile. There's a message from him on my answering machine, thanking me for forgiving him and apologizing again for being a cunt. The message couldn't be nicer.

14 *August* End of the week. Bit depressed. Yesterday was so exciting it was inevitable that today would be rather dull, and probably tired as well. But I could feel Stephen's attention wandering. There was an awful lot of talking on the mobile phone and waiting for the rehearsal to end. And, sure enough, as we talked through the arrangements for the next few weeks, he admitted he wouldn't be around to direct the radio version he has set up because he has a small film to make that week. In other words, he's typically dodgy, like all directors. They're all the same. They always have another pot cooking on another stove. One of the reasons I loved Louis Malle was because he was the only director I ever knew who cooked one dish a time. While you were his, you were his alone. But today we reached that familiar moment where something in the rehearsal period makes you realize, 'Oh I see, it's just one more show, like any other. It won't change my life.'

This moment always comes on any play. It's just come early on this one.

Natalie came in the morning, with her series of exercises. I am beginning to learn a little about her. She takes posture so seriously that at one point she had a nervous breakdown, brought on by her daily journey from Brixton. She could not longer bear how badly people moved on the street and on the Underground. Their sloppiness offended her to a point where she simply couldn't take it any more. She reminds me of a composer friend who is tortured by muzak. Once, in a restaurant, he asked for it to be turned off. The waiter said, 'Why? Don't you like music?' He replied, 'No. On the contrary, it's precisely because I do love music that I want that noise turned off.' He then said to me: 'Imagine if in every restaurant you went to, you had to listen to bad dialogue.' I said, 'But I do.'

I had got up early to rewrite the Grossman passage to restore the dialectic, so I was pretty tired by the time Stephen rolled in at 12. We worked for two hours on the epilogue, teasing out what it means and trying to see how it should be staged. I argued at first for a Peter Brook-like kind of anti-theatre. It's the old dream, which has haunted my theatrical generation from the sixties onwards: the empty space. Rather than put me in a spotlight and intensify the theatricality of the ending, Stephen should instead bring all the lights up and let me be a person on a huge empty stage, doing my magic with no resources. The moment I tried it I knew it was a terrible idea. It usually is. Stephen replaced it with a better one. At the end I should go offstage and you should see normal life outside the door – stage managers going about their business, even me chatting to them – so that it is clear that the Via Dolorosa leads back to normal life. Much better.

We then worked on the settlement material. I have the problem I know too well when I get to Benni Begin. I want a tone which is patient, lucid, clear like water, which – as I have said ten thousand times to actors doing my work – 'just explains the facts with utter conviction.' I can't find this tone any more than they ever can. Whenever Begin talks about his historical sense of Israel he always sounds as if he's trying to persuade me, to argue from a position of weakness. Stephen suggested I lower my voice. Disaster. I sounded pompous. Rufus said I should be like an enthusiast. I said that's what I was doing, I just always came out unconvinced. I said I'd go away and practise by myself. However, we did manage finally to introduce a prop into the play, in the form of a handkerchief I will take out before Benni Begin. It was curiously satisfying to handle this thing and plan its little appearance, and then to slip it back into the right place at the right dramatic moment. Pleasures of being an actor.

The rewrite of Grossman was a triumph. We have a dialectic by the usual tactic of my pretending to be stupid. Stephen rather generously asked me whether I minded painting myself as stupid and ignorant quite so frequently. I said if that's what I needed to do for the good of the show, then so be it.

The atmosphere of the rehearsal is better, much politer and sometimes even nudging towards warm. Press and publicity are still a bit of a nightmare, again because of interregnum problems. Anne Mayer, the press person, used to be full time at the Court. She then left and has just agreed to do this one show for Stephen, I guess for old times' sake. Tonight, she wouldn't meet me at 6 p.m. because she had to go to *Oklahoma*. Note 'had to'. I think I'm depressed because I feel very slightly farmed out, as if the director now thinks that the coming work is containable and limited; not, as it has been these past two weeks, capable of infinite expansion. Sad.

17 August Some bad news, some good. The worst is that bookings are poor. Of course, we always knew bookings would be poor. Firstly, everyone is away and won't book until they come back. Secondly, there's no publicity possible now. And thirdly, the subject matter. But it's like what I always say about suffering. You think 'Oh, I'm bound to have to suffer,' but then when you do, you think 'Hey this is actual suffering. It's horrible.' Jonathan Kent rang at the weekend. He is directing *Phèdre* for the Almeida's season at the Albery. He rang to say that he found Racine very difficult. I pointed out that everyone knows that Racine is difficult. He said it's one thing to know it, another to experience it.

Proust says you should only ever go to a doctor who has actually had the disease you have.

I find the Duke of York's a gloomy theatre, and not only because of the box office sitting there doing no business. I think it's the brown seats and the black proscenium. We are revealing the opened-up stage for this production – I went to look at the end of the day – and looking into the fly tower I asked whether anyone used it. Stephen said, 'Never. Flying's out of fashion.' It is strange. The Royal Court's artistic practice is to do little plays which sit on the forestage, and to ignore the language of theatre behind. The studio aesthetic is transferred to the main stage.

This is the outstanding problem of British theatre. There's been a crop of gifted young writers who know how to handle small spaces, but who have no experience of commanding the technical resources of a proscenium arch. Maybe they don't want to. But, for me, it's as if they're robbing themselves of the glorious articulation which a great stage provides. They are also denying themselves what Arthur Miller called 'the general audience' – the one that is big enough to contain as many sorts and differences of people as possible. It is one of the strengths of British culture that, since Shakespeare, there has always been a middle way. To one side of society lies the academy, the university, with all the attendant dangers of aridity and isolation. To the other lies what is now called the media, with all its potential for stupidity. In the middle you find the theatre, the place where, traditionally, through a distinctive mixture of practicality and highmindedness, people (again, like Shakespeare) have been able to develop their own education. The theatre is what the British have always been good at. It's worth fighting for, precisely because it's auto-didactic. It puts things under the microscope and people learn for themselves. Art teaches in a way instruction never can.

Like the current generation, I started out on the fringe, doing plays out of vans, on any kind of available surface. But when Richard Eyre asked me to write a play for the Nottingham Playhouse, I found the proscenium arch a welcome discipline. It forced me to examine my own failings as a playwright. Things I'd got away with in happy little rooms looked horribly exposed on a stage. The frame, far from containing a play, consistently revealed it – and revealed its faults. It was an essential step in my learning. But this transit into larger theatres now seems less easy to make, largely because the regional houses are suffering an aggravated crisis of funding. Meanwhile, the Royal Shakespeare Company is under critical attack for having lost its sense of classical purpose. Far more serious is the fact that it has effectively abandoned large-scale new writing altogether. One of the two theatres best equipped to develop ambitious plays is too lazy to do so.

At rehearsals we discussed the long history of the Royal Court fucking up people's lives. We have given up on our original plan, which was to preview the play in front of the public – I'd even had a mad idea to turn up and do it at the Edinburgh Festival un-announced. Instead, we've decided to invite small groups of people into the rehearsal room to see work in progress. By chance, Gita Sereny had asked Stephen if she could come to Friday's run-through. I found this a daunting prospect because her life of Albert Speer is one of my favourite books. So we found ourselves fantasizing the list of people we would be most scared to see at one of these invited run-throughs – V. S. Naipaul and George Steiner for me. Stephen chipped in with Doris Lessing. I said that if you read Lessing's biography you will find that she wanted to be a playwright, but that the Royal Court directors managed to convince her she was no good. Or rather, they tried to fuck her and then sought to convince her she was no good.

I asked if the Royal Court was still as good at demoralizing writers as it used to be. The question was directed at Rufus, in fact, but before he could answer, Stephen jumped in quickly with a firm 'No'. When I pointed out it was Rufus I'd asked, Rufus said, 'Stephen is so nice that he always tells writers kind things. But writers are still destroyed, not by the Royal Court's words, but by its actions.' Or inactions.

It was a decisive day's rehearsals. I came in with a new text I had assembled at the weekend. I have two rules about the script itself. (1) Never write on it. (2) Never look at it. I have always believed the play should exist in an actor's head. Staring at bits of paper is the wrong action. The correct action is to go into your brain and heart, which is where the play's language, movement and meaning should be lodged. Nothing so far has changed my mind about this theory, and I don't see myself sitting in cafés in St Martin's Lane checking my lines before a performance. In fact, I never think about them unless I have to. I certainly never rehearse outside rehearsal hours. I am mystified when I hear that a terrific actress like Helen McRory spends three hours staring at her manuscript before each perfor-mance. What on earth can she be doing?

However, we did start by doing some line-bashing with Lesley. Then I showed Ian the way I used the set, so that he could decide whether to make the little tables at the side a step down from the main arena. At the time, I thought not. By the end of the day, I thought so. We found another place for me to dip out of the show. I go to the side and appear to foreswear performing altogether during the passage when I explain why some Jews believe that fiction and theatre themselves are morally wrong. The move to duck out of the play feels dead right.

Then I performed the first half, up till Benni Begin – about forty minutes. At the end Stephen leapt up and said, 'What happened to you at the weekend? A lot of that was like, well, like proper acting.' I had made a qualitative leap, for all sorts of reasons – because the idea of the staging is now right. It's Brechtian. I slip in and out of character, because the Grossman passage now frees me up, because I no longer feel I'm fighting the clock. And, most important, because I am trying to look as if I actually enjoy it. The rule is: never look back. I would rather come off stage and be told by Lesley that I've cut three pages than realize at the time. Because as soon as I realize, I'm dead. But I knew I was cooking. I was riding the burning hot bicycle across the wire.

As I walked home, I was quite frightened. I was passing Hampstead Cemetery. It's always my favourite part of the walk because I like saying hello to Hugh Gaitskell and Anton Walbrook. Some days I even blow a kiss at Kay Kendall. Then I suddenly realized that the strange tightness in my stomach was fear. I think I'd always imagined that I would 'do' the play, but it never occurred to me that I could be seriously good in it. That wasn't on the agenda. But now I can feel it is, and so it scares me. Whatever I thought performing was going to be like, I was wrong.

18 August Stephen is always working at the framework of each encounter in the play, making sure there is a dialectic. He sits with a frown on his face, staring at the text in often rather schoolmasterly gloom, while I spark around like a fairy filling in the silences, just to make sure the whole afternoon doesn't go by in a knot of wordless concentration. He didn't know why the Begin passage wasn't working, why I couldn't find a tone for it. So he managed to get me to do a small rewrite which ensured that it was a surprise that Begin was writing an archaeological treatise. I used to have a line 'Before he was a politician, Begin was a geologist.' This meant that you were ready for the fact that he studied Ancient Hebrew messages on stones. Stephen got me to take that mention of his previous profession out, and then it became weird and interesting – a *politician* who can read old stones?

For the moment, Stephen's method is apolitical. For now, he's put his theoretic interests to one side and is simply doing what he can to introduce dramatic shape and structure where it's missing – occasionally with cavalier disregard for the politics. Today he even suggested we cut a bit explaining that half the Palestinians live in refugee camps – a fact I insist on thinking rather important.

We did a run-through. As he had asked, I shouted Eran Baniel's line: 'The obscene spectacle of Jews sitting by their swimming pools while the Palestinians carry their drinking water round in jerry cans.' Not only was it dramatically inept – Eran didn't shout, so why did I? – but it also made the piece offensively anti-Zionist, because the audience thinks: 'Oh, whenever there's an anti-Israeli sentiment, he shouts it.' In fact, when I said the whole piece was getting too anti-Zionist, Stephen replied, 'I'm not going to rule on anti-Zionism at all in the next few days, I'm just going to make the piece work theatrically.' He pointed out, which is true, that the piece is harder, if anything, on the Palestinians. But is that the point? I am resolved to remove some lines at the end of the play which I think take things too far. Sigal's sister is currently quoted as saying that the Jews don't belong together in one country. It's too much, and anyway it isn't what the play is trying to say.

Apparently I mispitched the run. Stephen and Rufus both said I was working too hard for the first half hour. What is alarming is I had no sense of it. This problem of overall pitch is the most difficult thing in the show. When I get to Sarah in the settlements, then I always subside into a natural conversational tone, but we still don't have the overall crescendo of the piece which should be as follows:

Bloke announces he can't act.

Bloke tries a bit of acting but basically just talks.

Bloke begins to act more and more when impersonating other people but remains himself.

Bloke starts to act brilliantly.

I found the run less exhausting which, to me, is a good sign. It lasted 1 hour 43 minutes – down nine minutes from last time. I didn't feel knackered afterwards. A real surprise, because Natalie had done a punishing session with me before. I need to perfect an approach to the evening which puts me both physically and mentally in the right place to perform. What is slightly depressing is that I felt very good as I started and thought, this is going wonderfully. But it wasn't.

I did, however, feel some marginal relief that I could remember the play at all. Like most ageing men, I have a terror that I can't remember anything. When I was forty, I set myself the task of learning an Auden poem as pure exercise, to see whether my memory functioned at all. I failed ignominiously.

Love had him fast, but though he fought for breath
He struggled only to possess Another
The snare forgotten in the little death . . .

I was, I decided, insufficiently motivated. Coming nervously to *Via Dolorosa*, I borrowed a specialist line-basher, a young man whose profession has been to sit helping actors repeat their lines over and over again. Then I went to France where I sat alone for a week on rocks in Cassis for six, seven, or even eight hours at a time, with luck annexing two new pages a day. It wasn't any easier to learn because I had written it myself. But because I knew my own rhythms, once learnt it was easier to retain. The first performance of the play was given in louring weather to a choppy, indifferent Mediterranean.

After yesterday's run-through I had dinner with Tony Bicât, with whom I started Portable Theatre thirty years ago. We went to that weird place in Clerkenwell called St John where they give you bits of cooked animal tail or nostril. We both like it because it isn't like the ten thousand identikit restaurants that you now find in every Western capital. Tony pointed out to me how whenever an actor on film says '*That's* the take', they're wrong. Whenever they want one more take for themselves, it's crap.

19 *August* I hate the days after a run-through, because they always turn into two-hat days – where I have to be writer *and* actor. I was in a foul mood today, because I'd had to be a writer all morning with *The Blue Room*. I had warned Sam Mendes from the start that it was the kind of material which would need infinite adjustment. Schnitzler's ten scenes represent ten different sexual liaisons. Each one has a new character in it. Underneath each encounter lies a huge amount of subtext. The play is a mosaic. Every colour has to be exactly right for each other colour to shine. Sam, whose defining characteristic is his astonishing confidence, kept saying 'Oh no. The text is exactly how I want it. There won't be any need for much work when we rehearse.' Anyway, on this occasion, I turn out to be right. The play needs ceaseless fine tuning. You need to vary tones and levels of sincerity all the time.

The *Blue Room* rehearsals always seem sweet and easy compared to ours. Iain Glen and Nicole Kidman look such a handsome couple, scampering about laughing and making jokes. Then Nicole Kidman opens the little Tupperware boxes in which she now brings all their lunches. The whole thing is like summer camp, charged with a nurturing pleasantness. Then, of course, I have to go to the Old Vic, where the atmosphere is more like National Service in the provinces in the 1950s. It's my fault. A fish rots from the head. A rehearsal takes its tone from the leading actor who, in this case, is a distinctly humourless figure. Or he is when he's acting.

Today I wanted to try to make more cuts. I cut mention of Sigal's sister who claims that Israel is a failed experiment. It was simply too bald and too prejudicial. Martin Sherman, the American playwright, told me he is planning a monologue in which he is going to say Israel is a historical mistake. I said, 'You can say that. You're Jewish. But I have no right to make that kind of judgment. And anyway, it's not what I want to do.'

I then tried to cut Aghazerin's story about roadblocks and checkpoints, but I found the reality it gives the play valuable. It reminds you that the Palestinians are effectively occupied. The easiest cut would be a passage about the Israeli equivalent of the Oscars, but I love it because it shows the audience that the author is not a complete egghead – I'm interested in Oscars as well as politics. Instead (and against Lesley's wishes – we all vote on these things) we cut a passage which pretends that it was David Grossman who inspired me to go to Palestine as well as Israel. It contains one important phrase 'to walk through the mirror', but I have managed to salvage it by putting it elsewhere.

I was late, so I had a haircut in Dressing Room 10, and then looked at the model. I pointed out that if I step back too far I have a dead drop into the pit behind me. Ian agreed to think up some protection. We then began with quite a bad-tempered rehearsal of the Eran Baniel passage. I made a list of the characters I have to 'play' in the show and there are thirty-three. Eran lacks definition, but when we discuss him he's the only one we really disagree over. Stephen has a view of Eran in real life because he knows him much better than I do. So we were in the unusual position of having to juggle three different Erans – the one Stephen knows, the one I know and the one who is the character in the play. No wonder we got ourselves into a dismaying mess.

Stephen wanted me to fiddle with the frame of the encounter to imply that Eran had a *shtick* about Israel which he was going to give to impress the visiting foreigner. I refused to do this because I like Eran and feel it is unfair to suggest that he was anything but honest and spontaneous with me. It might make for 'better' drama, but it would be wrong. Meanwhile, a small rewrite ensured that it is not *me* who thinks it 'obscene' for Israelis in settlements to sit by their swimming pools while Palestinians hump their drinking water round in cans, but *him*. This enables me to raise my voice and give the passage plenty of attack without seeming to be outraged myself. Vital.

I suspect that at some level Stephen is quite bored with the play, and with me. The row we had last week was not entirely a good thing. Like all rows, it cleared the air, but it also subtly changed the atmosphere. As I have discovered before, there is something ignoble about getting your way by raising your voice. Before, Stephen was insensitive to me, but the advantage was that he therefore dealt with me very directly. Now he 'manages' me, is 'careful' with me, prefaces direction with 'You're going to hate me for this but', and generally treats me as if I were someone who had to be 'handled' – with all the contempt that suggests. And at times I am such a person. When I found myself telling him what my exercise teacher thinks I should do about my upper body, or how mucus collects in my nose when I lie down, I do think I have turned into a classic thundering bore – or actor, as one might call it. Or rather, to be fair, I have turned into one of those actors who is always telling you how incredibly difficult what they do is. Which it is. It would just be cleverer not to go on about it. Put it another way: the day after a run is hard, because the exhilaration of getting through it wears off, and you just feel angry at yourself for all the little bits and pieces which you ought to be able to get right, and can't.

However, we did redo the opening. It was much less forced. I said to Stephen that yesterday was the first day he had ever given me a note asking me to quieten a passage down. I remembered the story of how Ken Cranham, in Stephen's production of *An Inspector Calls*, used to go round the back of the little house. From the stage he could see Richard Pasco in the wings, with his head in his hands and Barbara Leigh-Hunt with her arms round him, saying 'You can do it this big, Dickie. You *can*.' At times I have known how he felt. So I say today that I want to lighten those passages where I feel strained or forced. We agree to do this.

Afterwards Ivan Kyncl comes with photos to help us choose a front-of-house display. I have known Ivan for some time. He is not the most tactful of theatre photographers. At dress rehearsals he has a habit of leaping up on stage and getting himself between the actors during their most intimate moments. But it's his photos which have made the image of the Almeida Theatre seem so distinctive and sophisticated. As a Czech exile who always wears the same pair of jeans and the same scruffy ginger beard he seems an unlikely person to have been asked to be ambassador for his country when Havel became president. He says he turned the job down because he couldn't face wearing a suit. That part isn't hard to believe.

Anne Mayer, the publicity person, is panicked by the lack of coverage. I am therefore being told that I must talk to Michael Billington, who will do a piece for the *Guardian*. This evening I speak to David Nathan from the *Jewish Chronicle*. When I tell him I have to play thirty-three characters, he says, 'Well, Stephen Daldry is a great director, but that's sure going to be an interesting test of his greatness.'

Max Stafford-Clark comes in to where we are doing the interview. I say it's a classic Joint Stock show – which it is. Elucidation, instruction and enlightenment. We talk about how many openings there are next month. I say, it makes no difference. He says 'That's right. There are always three hot shows and everyone wants to see them and that's it.'

This remark chills me because we are so plainly not one of them.

20 *August* This was my third run-through. I was very nervous. I'd woken in the night overwhelmed by the mass of small changes we'd made in the last forty-eight hours, and needing them to stop. When I saw Stephen, we agreed we had to lock the show off very quickly in order to build my confidence.

As soon as the run began I felt myself in trouble. The first thirty minutes seemed nightmarish. There was an extra person in the room – Simon, the ASM – and it was interesting how the atmosphere was changed by a stranger's presence. Just one person tipped the balance. I felt foul through the opening passages, then worse as I did Eran Baniel and the passage about the Cameri Theatre. In front of me, I could see *two* fucking directors, each taking notes, which, in a paranoid way, I assumed to be about passages I had just fucked up. Since the one essential principle of these performances is that you must always forget your mistakes and move on as soon as possible to rebuild your confidence, the sight of *two* people recording my failings had the wrong effect. It dragged my mind backwards to what I should have been forgetting.

Rufus was right in my eyeline, writing notes. I tried to struggle on, signalling to him that he should stop. Eventually, I came to a halt and told him please to stop writing. I can see the purpose of one director writing notes. Two hanging judges is crazy. Anyway, I

29

started again, and I was shaky for a while through the settlements, but as I moved into Benni Begin I began to get good. Basically, the second half felt great, with me going all the way through the big bravura passages, which were right off the scale.

At the end, I apologized to Rufus, though, to be honest, I had nothing to apologize for. It was insensitive to make notes in my eyeline. The reason I was upset is that stopping is a form of cheating. In a way, it was easy to relaunch the piece from a less paranoid platform. So I was furious that I had, in effect, broken the rule – which is that I must always find my own way back, however dreadful I am feeling.

I know that I have always had a problem with assistant directors. I can't see any point to them. I like people to have functions. This person tells you what lens to use, this person hangs the lights, this person plays the waiter and this person directs. What the fuck does the assistant director do, except wield power without responsibility? In the arts, opinion is cheap. Only people who are risking something on the outcome have the right to shape the performance.

All this is not against Rufus. On the contrary, he's an excellent assistant. When he had a function, he performed it brilliantly. But anything that struck him in the run-through should have been committed to memory. This is, after all, what the rest of us have to do. If anything about the performance is really that important, the chances are you'll remember it.

Of course, I can see I was projecting my own anger at myself on to Rufus. Stephen, surprisingly, said I wasn't too bad in the first twenty minutes until I became distracted. This really worried me because I said I still had no way of monitoring, so we embarked on another very precise rehearsal. Stephen marked lines I was to take loud and ones I was to take soft, and exact places where I was to take my hands out of my pockets. Once more this kind of tracking, far from being rigid, was incredibly useful. The more precise, the better. Once I get into the second half, then inaccuracy matters less, because emotion takes over.

If I hadn't insisted, we wouldn't have reviewed the whole performance. Stephen wanted to go on to the next stage of work. I said we had to go over what I'd done, or how else would I improve? I knew where I'd lost the attention of the ASM, where he'd been bored, and Stephen helped me work out why. The run had taken 1 hour 37 minutes, so this was obviously a massive improvement. I am so over the top in the second half – shouting and screaming – that I said to Stephen that it sometimes occurs to me that the whole four weeks is a subtle piss-take. Maybe he is leading me towards a first preview at which I will be universally mocked. The whole event is being directed as a deliberate conspiracy against me. He laughed.

At the end of the short rehearsal after the run, he got up to go. I wish, just once, we could go off, have a drink, and wind down together. It's a valuable thing to do. Drinking in the bar after a run with Liam Neeson on *The Judas Kiss* was when we all began the process of making the show good. To be able to relax with an actor, and discuss the thing less publicly and less formally, is five times as useful as what's called 'giving notes'. The result was, I left, yet again, feeling shitty. No, that's putting it too high. I left unsatisfied, wanting the day's events to add up and to take shape. No shape was allowed because Stephen pissed off, as he always does, in a rush of bicycle bags and mobile phones. I can see that my friend Jonathan Kent sometimes takes the almoner's role to excess – talking to an actor at 2 a.m., and then maybe to the actor's girlfriend at 3 a.m. – but, on the other hand, the feeling that the director has time to give you is finally very enabling. Stephen is great while he's there. But how long is he there for?

Today will be the first run-through in front of people. We have invited ten or eleven, including Howard Davies. I remember something Camus said: 'Don't wait for the Last Judgment. It happens every day.'

21 August When I worked with the legendary Swiss actor Bruno Ganz on the film of *Strapless*, I had to put a fourth assistant on him, not just to get him to the set, but to stop him leaving once he'd arrived. After a take, Bruno would wander off down the road, or into a nearby wood. He was followed everywhere by walky-talkies. At the time I thought Bruno was odd but, my God, I now understand him.

Bruno-like, I did everything I could to avoid going to today's rehearsal. I passed time by going to the *Blue Room* rehearsal. Nicole Kidman had Japanese take-away from Nobu, so I stayed for lunch, delaying the moment when I would have to go to the Old Vic. Over lunch, Sam Mendes asked me why a well-known actress had backed out of Richard Eyre's film, *Mary Stuart*. Before I could answer, Nicole Kidman leapt in: 'Family! I bet she said family! She always says family!' This got us into an interesting discussion about the best reason to give for not doing something. Nicole was saying that 'family' is the best because no one can argue with it. Nicole recently tried 'I'm having a nervous breakdown' but it didn't work. I was thought ridiculously naïve for suggesting 'The script isn't right', because everyone said they will always come back to you with, 'Don't worry, we'll fix it.'

I said that when he ran the National Theatre, Richard had made it a rule not to talk anyone into anything they didn't want to do. The actor's only power is the power to say 'no'. You must take it to mean what it says. Richard had a horror of seduction. Sam agreed and said he followed the same policy. 'Either they want to do it or they don't.' The actors – Iain Glen and Nicole – took the opposite view. Sometimes you don't know what you want to do until you begin to do it.

All this was an elaborate delaying tactic for not going to my run-through, and we rehearsed the excuses I might give later to Stephen Daldry for not turning up at all. In fact, I had rather a good one for a while, since there were no taxis at the Oval. But unfortunately one came along, and I had to go and do my run-through to twelve people. The Nobu soy sauce turned out to have been a disastrous mistake because my mouth was dry throughout. I also regret the Listerine which I took in advance in order to make me feel less gummy in the mouth. Through most of Israel and a large part of Palestine I was thinking about when I was next allowed to drink. For some reason I didn't allow myself the little moment at the beginning either, where I settle and get used to the idea of doing the play. I leapt right in. A mistake.

I was so scared and trying so hard to respond to a note from

Stephen about speeding up that I got through the whole thing in a ridiculous 1 hour 27 minutes. Stephen said I rattled along like a madman, asking 'When is he ever going to slow up?' I had to be prompted once because I was so disheartened by one member of the 12-strong audience who sat with his head in his hands, as if exasperated by the banality of what I was saying. He gave me such a fright that I lost my way in the Sarah passage in the settlements, which is a bit I do badly these days anyway. 'He's hoarding, he's hoarding, he's hoarding,' said Stephen, in his favourite and illuminating metaphor. 'When is he going to spend?'

That said, the whole thing did go well. Or so it seemed. One of my old friends, the director Howard Davies, whom I had scarcely dared look at throughout, was complimentary at the end, and so was Patsy Rodenburg. Stephen got a broad thumbs up from all his friends, whom he had no time to quiz properly. Ian McNeil said it was more relaxed. It was at its best when it was like a dinner party. Patsy said that she could make me achieve the same effect and appear to work less hard. She said two-thirds of it came from the right place, but in one-third, my shoulders go up, my chest bellows back and forth, and my voice rises. She thinks she can eliminate this. One of the easiest people to play to was Marieke, Stephen's assistant from the Royal Court. By chance Marieke was a secretary when I first worked there in 1969, so the sight of her moves me anyway. Ian McNeil, of course, was bliss to play to, and so was a man with a lovely, sensitive face and dark eyes, who turned out to be Stephen's best friend.

I don't think audiences ever understand how important their contribution is. Obviously, it's crucial when, as in these run-throughs, I can see all their faces and body language throughout. In a theatre, spectators at least are able to enjoy the dark. But what is interesting to me is how unfakable intelligent understanding is. I only need to look at someone to be able to tell at once (1) whether I am really communicating to them or (2) whether they are simulating a reaction they don't really feel.

When everyone had left, it was as if Stephen had read yesterday's entry for this diary. To his great credit, he knew without my saying that he had to take me out for a drink and to give me the time I needed to wind down. We had forgotten to do something about Erez, the crossing point into Gaza, and he is beginning to think he needs to help me by illustrating the moment with a huge storm of brown dirt. He was generally friendly and easy-going in a way I have not known him before, ordering loads of beers and some disgusting pongy hors d'oeuvres. He said, 'Basically, it works. It works even if you do it the way you did it today. Anything we get from now on is cherries.'

The issue of my left hand is the deal-breaker. I kept it in my pocket throughout. Stephen had told me on no account to put it there. It was blind fear. My pocket was soaking wet by the end. It was my security blanket. Half way through, I thought I would rather die than take my left hand out of my pocket.

All the jokes worked, thank God, except the one about *The English Patient*, which will, says Stephen, with a less knowing audience. He then gave me a perfectly fair note. He said, 'You should trust me more. I have brilliant ideas, they are fucking brilliant, and you should commit to them more.' It was quite justified in the circumstances. I told him I did trust him. I could feel the production holding me up like a cradle – its shape is right. All the extra bits and pieces he wanted were dropped not because I didn't want to do them, but because I couldn't. I was too bloody scared. When I lay on the ground for the Dome of the Rock sequence, I could not get my second leg to lie flat. It was not wilful disobedience, but because fear gripped the soul. Hence also, my lack of good humour in the first thirty minutes. I was shaving corners throughout, smoothing my way across acute angles, because I was too nervous to go right round the track. But give me time and I will.

We then discussed why no one is booking for the show. I said I hadn't had a show which absolutely no one went to for about twenty-five years and I didn't really want it to be this one. I asked if the Royal Court ever did any publicity. He said that it spends one-third of what the Lyric, Hammersmith spends and much less than the Almeida. He has always had the philosophy 'Put the money on the stage'. Anne Mayer keeps telling Stephen that I am going to go nuts when only forty people come to the previews. I'll be fine at the first preview, she says, but after that, my patience will snap.

The *Evening Standard* has asked Stephen for his diary on 'What it's like directing David Hare'. It's the only feature they'll do. They said he didn't even have to write it, they'd write it for him. He asked how they would be able to do that. They said, 'Don't worry how. We'll just do it.' I told Stephen to bury his scruples, do it himself, and be vulgar. Make it sound glamorous. That's what they want. With no advance bookings, we are not in a position to be choosy.

We had been talking for an hour before Stephen mentioned that his friends were waiting for him in another bar, to give him detailed notes. I was very touched, but told him to go and join them. He says he has one friend he really trusts. He only asks him one question. 'Have we made twats of ourselves?' That is, after all, the only real question. And how, I ask, did he respond today? 'It's fine. We're not twats.'

23 August Encouraging phone message waiting for me over the weekend from Howard. I knew he'd enjoyed the storytelling very much, but he had also really understood the purpose of the whole piece – what it was about, and what its values were. He thought my acting was fine. He said something like 'On its own terms, fantastic.' Or did I make that up?

The Designated Mourner was on TV for the first time. To my eyes, it looked like a masterpiece. Harold Pinter rang me at 12.15 a.m. and said, 'I sat there thinking the man who wrote this is a genius.' And so he is. Of course, Wallace Shawn has influenced me. Maybe he's the only modern writer who has. It was Walter Benjamin who said people write books because they feel that the books which already exist are not satisfactory. I agree. But here I am acting in my own fiction and the only available model is Wally. He strips motive away to reveal us all as self-deluding and self-obsessed. He deconstructs the very idea of self. His view of the world is far harsher than mine. But he's the only writer I watch and feel we're playing the same game. We both try to show the strange, distorted routes ideas take as they drizzle through the porous stone of personality and self-interest. No one else seems even to recognize the territory, let alone occupy it.

Mike Nichols, on the other hand, is a model I must most certainly not follow, great though the temptation is. When we did *The Designated Mourner* in the Cottesloe Theatre, it was nightly packed with professional actors trying to figure Mike out. It was an absolute masterclass. Mike spoke every line as if it had just occurred to him, as if it were only *at that very moment* coming into his head. It was a knife-edge technique of total spontaneity, full of 'ums' and 'ers', and the suggestion of an almost existentialist freedom from the text – apparently to go where he chose, or make it up as he went along – which could only be achieved by someone with Mike's background in stand-up comedy, combined with his extraordinary intelligence. It was a devastating kind of brinkmanship – the line grabbed out of the air. As his friend Tom Stoppard said, you felt yourself terrified in the audience, convinced all the time that Mike was on the verge of spilling some intimate confidence which you would really rather not hear.

I once wrote a play about rock 'n' roll called *Teeth 'n' Smiles*. A member of the cast, Karl Howman, was a friend of Keith Moon, the notoriously drunken drummer for The Who. Karl kept trying to get Keith to come and see the play. One night Keith Moon drove down the Kings Road, crashed his Rolls-Royce into the side of the Royal Court, walked past an astonished stage manager on to the stage during the middle of the performance, shook hands with his friend and said, 'Hello, Karl.' The rest of the cast stood transfixed. The audience looked on, no doubt thinking that the latest character in the play looked extraordinarily like Keith Moon. When later asked why he walked on to the stage, Moon said, 'Well, Karl asked me to come and see him in the play. So I came and saw him.'

It was exactly that quality Mike Nichols had on stage. He appeared to be there by accident. I've never seen any other actor come close. But I have already learnt that if I attempt the same thing I look a total charlie. In me, the identical approach seems mannered. If I could understand *this* – why one technique suits one actor, and another another – I would be nearer to understanding the mystery of acting.

24 *August* Calm, serious day. We'd all had the weekend to think. Stephen's friends had given him an excellent note: it's wrong when

we are remotely aware of the director. Everything must look as if it comes from David and no one else.

By chance, watching Mike Nichols the previous night on TV I'd felt the same thing. When he got to the bit about the leaves growing outside the window in a voluptuous, sexual way, Nicole said, 'My God, he's a great actor.' I didn't bother to add 'And it was a great piece of direction.' The power of Mike's performance only grew with my apparent absence. Ditto Stephen's now.

I had a superb session with Natalie. Then Patsy arrived, giving me all the usual notes, but with her special authority. Don't force it, don't try to create energy. Don't work at being charming. You *are* charming. Why can you not believe it? Trust the story. Deliver the play, don't work at falsely animating it. Of course, I know all this stuff, but it's one thing to know it and another to be able to do it at the time. I *know* I can now be OK in a rehearsal room. I can also be OK ten days into the run, when I am relaxed. The only question is: how do I prepare myself mentally in a way which makes me OK when the stress is at its greatest?

I told Stephen and Patsy the story of my lecture in 1978 in Cambridge. This is when I broke with Marxist theatre. The lecture was angrily interrupted and denounced on all sides. I remember a street theatre artist, still in his clown's make-up, heckling 'Piscator did not die for this!' (In fact, Piscator died having done a certain amount of work on Broadway, but that sort of thing tends to get forgotten.) Afterwards, my novelist friend Reg Gadney said, 'You are so assured when you feel the audience is on your side, and you are so completely hopeless when you feel they are against you.' This is true. I can see that *Via Dolorosa*, like all acting, breaks down into two actions. Seducing the audience, and then ravishing it. I am fine when we get to the ravishing, it's the seducing I can't do. Or, rather, I can't do it unless I feel the basic act of warmth from the audience.

This confession was at the heart of a useful session, which was in a side room, because Stephen had had the abortive idea of putting a stage into the main rehearsal room. The boys carried the rostra up the stairs, Stephen took one look at them, and then asked them please to carry them back down again. This meant that, after the interruption, what was meant to be a private class with Patsy turned into a five-man session – in came the stage manager, in came the assistant director – and I froze. Our most valuable and intimate rehearsal so far – just Patsy, Stephen and me – turned into another public occasion. I don't have the basic self-confidence (or, unkindly, exhibitionism) which enjoys stripping yourself down in front of people you don't know. I feel free with Patsy and Stephen. Once others arrive, then I feel intruded upon.

However, we did get some work done, trying to make the opening more natural. Stephen and I worked methodically, with me feeling in command of the material. I made one major breakthrough, in the settlement passage, realizing that what I must emphasize is not the Israeli desire to occupy Jerusalem (which may or may not be a good thing) but the ambition of religious Jews to knock down Arab mosques and build the Third Temple (which is certifiably insane). This will then make sense of the passage half an hour later, where Albert Aghazarin attacks apocalyptic Judaism as nothing but a cover for military adventurism.

Stephen was doing a lot of backtracking – taking out things he had asked me to do. This is fine by me. It's the mark of a good director. Directors should stick ideas in like pit props to hold up the ceiling in the early days. They should then remove those props when the ceiling is being finished. Only stupid directors go on insisting on their early directions. Only stupid actors begin their sentences 'But it was you who told me to . . .'

I then had a calm session with Lesley, running through the lines. I went to the theatre to see the set, and found the whole front of house garlanded with posters for Sarah Kane's play, which is currently at the Ambassadors Theatre, and absolutely no mention of mine. As we haven't sold any seats, this seems to display a strange sense of priorities. Is anyone running the Royal Court? Inside the set looked great, sitting in exactly the right space in the theatre. Above it is a hideously ugly piece of black masking which Ian says is too expensive to change.

Then dinner with John Cleese, who said smiling was the hardest thing to do when you're nervous. 'Laughing is easy, and being serious is easy, but smiling is the killer . . .'

I didn't sleep very well because I have spent so much time in the last couple of days thinking about acting. I remember when we did *King Lear* at the National Theatre in 1986, we had some fairly rocky previews. Before the press night performance I rather crassly asked Anthony Hopkins to forget that he was playing a king, and instead to bring his own private pain and passion on to the stage. This is very far from being my normal style of direction, but because we seemed to be facing a problem of unevenness, it was kind of a counsel of despair. As it happened it worked triumphantly. But afterwards Tony was not at peace. 'Yes, David,' he said when I congratulated him, 'I know I've got the performance worked out for the nights when the juice is there. But what worries me is that I still don't have it for the nights when it isn't.'

This is the professional actor's greatest challenge. How do you juggle the mysterious balance between the felt and the faked? Some nights you feel it, some nights you don't. And when you can't manage the right mix of conviction and pretence, how big a phoney do you feel? In 1997 David Mamet published a typically forthright book called *True and False*, in which he argues that an actor's so-called 'feelings' don't, or shouldn't, come into it. An actor, he says, is no different from a carpenter. He is out there to do a job. He need feel no more anxiety or self-doubt about his work than any other artisan. He exists purely to serve the text. He should arrive, do it and leave. An actor wastes his time asking questions about his character's independent existence outside the scenes in which he appears, since a character is nothing more than a functionary in the overall play. To have 'feelings' about the degree to which you are or are not convinced by the person you're playing is a ridiculous form of self-indulgence. Say the lines audibly, says Mamet, and leave the audience to interpret them for you.

Mamet's book is a provocation. It's graffiti, scrawled in anger over the excesses of the kind of method acting which can often be unassimilated in American work. Personally, I hate that phrase American actors always use about 'making choices'. The word 'choice' implies a computer-universe, as if acting were a game of decisions. 'I liked your choices,' they say, or 'You made really brave choices,' meaning 'You failed.' But Mamet seems too pedagogic to bother to develop his argument. He simply repeats it many times over. Sometimes his impatience is refreshing. I greatly enjoyed his contempt for actors who insult their admirers by saying 'Oh I was terrible tonight'. However, he can also be quite misleading. If the truth were as practical as Mamet pretends, then acting would be a much easier business than it is. Wishing won't make it so.

As you read *True and False*, you can't help remembering that odd sing-song dullness, that deadness behind the eyes which sometimes affects actors who think they are doing what Mamet wants. They semaphore his lines, rapping them out in a curiously neutral tone which ultimately becomes tiring and undifferentiated. You can see the words on the page as they speak. You also can't help remembering that the most indelible Mamet performances – as from Al Pacino in *American Buffalo* or Jack Shepherd in *Glengarry Glen Ross* – have been given by actors who believe the exact opposite to what Mamet argues. Their method juiciness brings vital moisture to Mamet's clinical dryness.

This morning, I have prepared for the run-through by selecting a pair of jeans which make it very difficult for me to put my hands in my pockets. Nicole is coming, but I don't know who else.

25 *August* Much the best day so far. It had started in classic Royal Court fashion with my ringing the man responsible for the front of house. I said the display looked inappropriate since it advertised Sarah Kane's play at another theatre and didn't mention mine. The person in charge replied, 'Yes, I'm not very happy with it either.' I loved this answer. It didn't seem to occur to him that the difference between us was that it was within his power to do something about it. No, more than that: his *job* is doing something about it. I doubt if anything will happen.

Nicole arrived at the run-through with our dog, but I told her I couldn't act with Blanche in the room. (Since I once took Blanche to a run-through of *Ivanov* myself, I felt bitterly ashamed of my own past stupidity. She took one look at the estate manager in his gumboots creeping up on Ralph Fiennes and started growling. I had to lock her in the green room.) Blanche gone, I then did a much more relaxed run-through, feeling good, except during a couple of midway passages. It's annoying to have lost my feel for one of the play's most important sequences, where I walk with the settler Sarah and listen to her views on why the Jews have the right to be on Arab land. It used to be what I did best.

Afterwards, Nicole said, 'The strange thing is you're more at ease on the stage than when you are off it.' She said as soon as the play was over I started slouching and fussing again, but that when the play was on I looked completely in control. 'What did you think of my acting?' 'Well, you don't really do any acting, do you?' – a remark which Stephen received triumphantly, as the highest possible compliment, but which I felt rather less sure about. There were a couple of places where she felt that my gestures were not 'me'. She didn't like my dusting down my trousers after I'd rolled on the floor in Jerusalem – it looked forced – but otherwise she was pleased. She had cried. This time it was 1 hour 34 minutes, which is perfect.

Before we had started, Stephen told me that he'd talked to Howard Davies, who said the show's greatest pleasure was watching me playing all the characters. To my amazement, Nicole was not discomfited by these impersonations. On the contrary, she relished them, though she did say that in spite of all the vigour, the Palestinians remained more sympathetic than the Israelis. The settlers, Sarah and Danny, come across as such terrible people that it's hard to recover your views about the Israelis. Nicole said, 'It doesn't leave you feeling wonderful about being a Jew.'

The production team all went on together to the theatre for our first session on stage. I am so thrilled with the platform which Ian and Stephen have given me in the Duke of York's – a lovely floor of planks, right at the point of command, with an empty theatre echoing behind me – that I said to them both that the only danger is of over-confidence. You feel so powerful that it may lead you to all sorts of hideous behaviour. Put it another way: I wouldn't trust one or two of our more prominent actors on this platform. You'd have to scrape them off the ceiling at the end of the show.

Stephen was worried about my voice, which is showing signs of deterioration. By the time he had said this six times, I thanked him heartily for doing so much to build my confidence. We rang Patsy Rodenburg who said more water and no alcohol. This is not a prescription I can take seriously. The wine after the show is the thing I most look forward to. But I am resolved to become a real actor-creep and walk around with little bottles of water everywhere.

We worked for two hours in the theatre, sharpening my focus and coming up with a new routine for Jerusalem. I am now going to signal to a man in the flies and get him to hoist the model, not pretend to hoist it myself. He is going to be in full view of the audience. I am fine about this – I felt during today's run that the model of Jerusalem arrives in the nick of time. The audience is ready for something different. We are still not decided whether to offer a visual effect earlier to represent the 'unholy big brown storm of dirt' that is Gaza. Once more we are faced with the question: do we draw attention to the play's structure by clearly saying 'End of Act 1', or do we take the other strategy – the one we have largely preferred – of removing all structural signposts, so that the audience swims in the sea without seeing either shore?

Backstage, it was Royal Court culture at its most infuriatingly casual. My dressing room has no phone, so I traipsed downstairs. The stage doorkeeper said oh yes, they were thinking of maybe one day putting a payphone on the landing. The dressing room has no bed either. When I asked for the car home which I'm entitled to, Lesley said, 'Can you pay for it, and we'll refund you?' I said no, it was in my deal that I'd do the show for the Equity minimum, but that I would get a car to take me home. I'll get my agents on to the phone and the bed today, because it gets boring asking.

When I got home at 9.45, Nicole was ready to go to sleep. She said she was exhausted by the emotional effort of watching me act.

26 *August* Another terrific day. Very low-key. A few calm hours sorting out a series of practical problems:

(1) How to do Grossman
(2) How to emphasize lines about the Bible

(3) How to do Erez
(4) How to do Miriam
(5) How to play Sarah in the settlements
(6) How to do Jerusalem
(7) What to do with Aghazerin
(8) How to tighten the epilogue.

As we worked, each one went down like a domino. You come up with solutions to places where you feel false and you suddenly ask 'Why on earth have I been so stupid not to see the solution here?' Your own stupidity never ceases to amaze you. Stephen was worried about when exactly he was going to drop a nasty substance called Fuller's earth to represent the dust storm in Gaza. We searched for the right place. It's one of those things which in our hearts we both know will get cut. You don't want to admit defeat in advance.

We discussed what to do with heckling. I said I would go to the side of the stage, sit down, and refuse to engage with the heckler. Any kind of reply, however inspired, is a concession to the right of the audience to interrupt, and I don't believe they have that right. I am quite hard-line on this. It's the only part of Toryism I buy. There is such a thing as common restraint, and it's a mark of civilization to exercise it. It is only by convention that we don't shout 'Bollocks' at bad theatre. I certainly wanted to shout it at a recent West End hit, but I desisted. And it will destroy the mystery of the event if an actor has to step out of the text to deal with it. Stephen arranged that the house manager will appear and tell the heckler that he/she will be free to speak to the audience at the end of the show if he has things he wishes to say. We will allow anyone who feels passionately to stay on and address anyone who feels strongly enough to listen. This seems to me an ideal solution.

A discussion of freedom and ritual ended with me telling a favourite story about a play of Peter Handke's called *Insulting the Audience*. This was presented in London at the end of the sixties and was expected to be very shocking and outrageous. In performance, it turned out to be disappointingly thoughtful. About half an hour into Handke's low-key meditations, a member of the audience called out from the balcony in outrage: 'Hang on, I came here to be insulted!'

Rufus pointed out a piece in the *Guardian* about the Americans declaring that the Arabs are the people who will start the Third World War. This is exactly what an Arab in the play says the Americans believe of them. I said if you write anything truthful, then synchronicity happens of itself.

28 August I'm glad it's the end of the week. I was exceptionally tired yesterday because I went to the *Blue Room* run-through. They said of Spencer Tracy and Katharine Hepburn that he gave her sex and she gave him class. Today at least, Nicole Kidman gave Iain Glen sex, and he gave her wit. But by the time I had been through the emotional turmoil of seeing something I've worked so hard on for the first time, I really didn't fancy doing *Via Dolorosa* to an audience of eight in the rehearsal room. I also felt I'd already been through the hell of getting it in front of a rehearsal-room audience: why did I need to go through it again?

But something in the audience itself stirred me. Tony Bicât was bliss to play to, grinning broadly, as if he already understood the nature of the political argument, and was enjoying my take on it. There was a woman on my right who was also terrific. So was Vikki Heywood, the Court's manager. I did as Stephen asked and played longer on each person, taking whole passages of Benni Begin and Danny Weiss and holding them for long periods on one, single person. It was great. However, I was aware that I was getting a much more reserved reaction from the Court's new artistic director, Ian Rickson.

Rickson arrived late. This struck me as rather an odd thing for him to do since, one way or another, it was a fairly important occasion for the immediate future of his theatre. It was probably worth getting to on time. He was pretty straight-faced throughout the whole run, so I started playing long passages to him because I knew I wouldn't be thrown by anything which I could take to be a reaction. When it was over, he came over to me and made some anodyne remark. I said we were still working on bits. He said, 'Well, remember, less is more.' I said perhaps he'd better speak to Stephen Daldry, since Stephen was telling me the exact opposite. Why don't the two of them talk about it? He went away.

'*Less is more!*'

I told Stephen to make sure to talk to Ian so that, if we were about to hear the case against the show, we would at least know what it was. I always like to know early which window the snipers are going to fire from. Apart from anything, it's interesting. You have no duty to incorporate the objections to your work. I'm always conscious and appalled when lines of dialogue have been inserted defensively into an author's work to deal with so-called 'problems'. A character who is plainly unlikeable is suddenly described by another character as 'likeable', as if saying it would somehow make it so. But you're crazy, in the early days, not to listen to the reasons for people's dislike. However, when Stephen spoke to him later on the phone, Ian didn't seem particularly touched by the work either way. 'I think he should be a bit slower'. 'Where?' 'Oh, at the beginning. He does have to play an awful lot of people.' 'Do you think he should play the differences more or less?' 'Oh, more. Oh, and less as well.'

This kind of stuff isn't unusual from a certain kind of producer. They know something's wrong, but they're damned if they can tell you what. Sometimes you forget how useful the best of them can be. In fact, as the years have gone by, I've come to feel more and more that the producer is the key person in the theatre. If the producer's right, everything else follows. He or she, after all, appoints the director, and gives your play all the back-up and commitment it needs. Peter Hall will sit you down and tell you the five most urgent things to do before you open on Thursday. He will be right, too. Directing Howard Brenton's play *Weapons of Happiness* in 1976, I ignored Peter's advice because I was young and arrogant, and thought all producers wanted to do was interfere. I learnt my lesson when I reached Thursday without having done any of the five things he told me to. I knew what a fool I'd been.

The vital importance of producers was confirmed for me when we premièred *The Judas Kiss* in London earlier this year. It was the only play of mine which I have opened knowing that neither text nor production was anywhere near its potential. The director, Richard Eyre, and I were in the frightening position of knowing that we must take the play on to New York six weeks later. Naïve actors and directors say they prefer weak producers because they are then allowed to do what they want. They're wrong. When delicate changes have to be made in front of the public, the maturity and intelligence of the producer will be crucial. Richard and I found ourselves meeting nightly after the show to listen to the advice of Robert Fox and Scott Rudin. The four of us worked as a team. They attended the show as often as we did – i.e. most nights. Without their help, Richard and I would never have been able to make the improvements which shaped *The Judas Kiss* and saw it safely to New York.

Today, more serious, and to me more disturbing, was the reaction of our lighting designer Rick Fisher. Rick is somebody I like and whose talent I trust. To be honest, he looked bored. He put on dark glasses and once I saw him fall asleep. At the end he said it was good. I didn't feel he really liked it. In my defence I can say that all designers and lighting designers take forty winks whenever they can, because they are so badly paid that they all have to take on too much work. They are usually struggling to fit your show in between *Jenufa* in Genoa and *Falstaff* in Frankfurt. But I don't like seeing Rick sleeping on my watch.

Stephen was pleased I hadn't gone to pieces altogether, which is what he'd expected. He said if I could do it this well when I wasn't in the mood for it, then that was very good news. But I was aware of having overplayed, particularly in the bit where Pauline attacks Arafat's corruption in Gaza. We also have to solve the dip at Erez. The whole audience is with the show while I'm in Israel, then I see their spirits dip as I go into Gaza, and they think, Oh my God, now Palestine.

In the evening, to Bruckner and Abbado. The Berlin Philharmonic swayed together like the ocean in sunshine, and yet every note, every instrument was clear and distinct. Abbado was undemonstrative, but in control of the shape. For me, things were better than when

46

Karajan conducted and they seemed a bit like a military band. I never hear a great concert or see a great painting without feeling a primitive pang of jealousy. How effortlessly other art forms seem to communicate – how airily – compared with the moral, laboured net of words I have to throw.

The artistic ideal, put best by Valéry: 'To give the sensation without the boredom of its conveyance.'

30 August Friday was a terrifying day. I had breakfast with Sam Mendes and made a few quick changes to *The Blue Room*. Then at 1 o'clock I did my scheduled interview with Michael Billington. Michael has been the theatre critic of the *Guardian* since the year dot. It is the fate of my generation of playwrights not to have been reported by a critic whose experience of the world matches our own. The things that seem important to us have never had the same urgency for many of the older white males who write for the papers. We speak to journalists across a marked cultural divide. An architectural critic once said to me longingly 'I wish you were a building, and then I could review you.' Our liveliest contemporary, Peter Ansorge, got quickly bored with dramatic criticism and went off instead to become the sympathetic television producer of writers like Dennis Potter, Alan Bleasdale and Paula Milne. Likelier journalists, who might have shared a contemporary view of history, didn't choose to write about the theatre – for reasons too obvious to explain.

Forty years ago, Samuel Beckett was championed passionately by Harold Hobson in the *Sunday Times*. Hobson's Christian idea of human suffering chimed with Beckett's austere beauty. The result was a critic willing to go out on a limb. Much as he grew to resent it, John Osborne knew that Kenneth Tynan on the *Observer* had decisively advanced Osborne's reputation. No playwright since then has had the articulate support of a critic who sounded as if it mattered. As Hobson himself, mystified, wrote of his successors: 'nothing seems at stake for them.' The nearest any of us has had to an open ear – an ear attuned to life, in other words, rather than to show business – has been from Billington, and his friend Michael Coveney. Billington's pleasure in the medium of theatre is never in doubt. Edward Greenfield once divided critics into 'Yes' critics and 'No' critics, according to whether they went to the art they covered with the basic disposition to like it or dislike it. Billington is a 'Yes' critic. As often as not, he gets things thuddingly wrong. Sticks grow wrong ends just for Michael to pick them up. But, like Irving Wardle before him, he loves the basic transaction of theatre. He wants it to work.

The interview seemed fine, at least to begin with. Then I felt my concentration was wandering when I realized towards the end that I was having trouble understanding Michael's last couple of questions. I got alarmed, imagining he must think me an idiot. When he left I started trying to read the paper. Then the proofs of *The Blue Room* arrived. I set them down on the table but I could not understand a word. I began to sweat. It was as if the drink of coffee which Anne Mayer had given me was spiked. I was looking at little groups of words on the paper and trying unsuccessfully to link them in my head as sequential sense. But they refused to cohere. They were falling, like alphabet soup thrown over the side of a cliff.

Everything in my head was shifting and slipping. My brain felt as if it were slopping around in a pudding bowl on a tossing ship. By now I was in deep panic, and, as we know, panic itself adds to panic. I went to lie down on the floor. When Stephen arrived I tried to think of a subject to discuss. I knew I wanted to raise what Ian Rickson had said the previous day, and see if we could pick its bones to make any sense. But I was terrified to discover I couldn't remember what Ian had said. Less is more? More or less? Less is less?

I decided the best thing to do was to start a rehearsal with Stephen and pretend everything was normal. I was still lying on the mat. We began to try to solve a problem Tony Bicât had raised in a fax to me earlier this morning. There is a danger in the epilogue that my repeated use of the words 'Via Dolorosa' to describe my own journey home will lead hostile critics into accusing me of identifying myself with Christ. Tony knew that wasn't what I'd intended, but as he said, 'If you give the British critics any rope at all, they will hang you.'

My reasoning on this subject was not very high-powered but at least it was reasoning. I could see Stephen was relieved that my

48

brain was showing any guttering spark of activity. After fifteen minutes, I got up off the mat to see if I could remember some lines. Although I faltered and stumbled a bit, my memory began to come back and this awful blank-out passed off. I began to ascribe it to lack of sleep and the exhaustion of having come so far and faced already so many harrowing sessions.

We stopped at 4.30 and moved over to the theatre. I tried to take things easy. I was due to start a very low-key run-through at 6, but this was late starting and about two-thirds of the way through – to add to the day's problems – my voice gave out on me. I was clearing my throat a lot and taking extra sips of water all the time. We gave up at 8 and went to the pub, though Patsy has warned me that alcohol is bad for my voice. Stephen was very strong throughout the ordeal, saying he wasn't really worried, that he's always known there was a chance of my collapsing after all the tension of the week.

It was an odd event because, as usual, there was nowhere pleasant or quiet to have a drink in the centre of London. There never is. So we had to sit on the pavement in Shaftesbury Avenue – Stephen with his Guinness, me with a vat of warm white wine. Later, I went home and cooked myself a steak, then fell asleep at 10.15 p.m.

31 August Now it's Monday and I've spent a relaxing weekend in Paris. I loved the idea of leaving the country for a couple of days to prepare myself. We ate Chinese food and saw a couple of movies a day, though nothing very good. It's hard to find any film Nicole didn't see when she was a fashion student in Paris. Like me, she used to hop from one revival house to another. The other day I read a critic who said he had the basic qualification for writing about the cinema. Like a pilot, he'd done 'his 20,000 hours in the dark'. By this reckoning Nicole and I should both be up for advanced licences.

I slept well both nights, though I was more or less sleepwalking through Saturday. The main point was that I managed to sleep until 9.30, rather than the 5 a.m. which has been my style for the past week. I used my voice as little as possible, but this morning a large lump of phlegm was still lodged on my vocal chords, as I felt it had been ever since last Thursday. We got on the Eurostar back from

Paris, then as we passed Bexley, I was nervous for the first time. I had spent the weekend cheerfully free of nerves, but ten minutes outside London and wham!

I went to the rehearsal room where I was meant to run through with Stephen. We agreed to drop the rehearsal because it was pointless using my voice unless I had to. I knew I would get through all right on Thursday. My fear was that things would get worse as the week went on, so that by the time we reached Saturday I would be speechless. I wanted either to speak to Patsy Rodenburg now, or else to go to the throat doctor. Neither of us could remember his name. The National uses him all the time. We agreed that my memory is fine. The only thing that stops me remembering the lines is nerves. I *know* the text, and the next few days will, anyway, provide me with the chance to run it many times while Stephen does his technical work.

What I dread is what happened to Tony Hopkins on *King Lear* and *Antony and Cleopatra*. His voice developed a kind of rasp, which meant that the whole audience coughed when he spoke since they were subconsciously trying to clear his throat for him. This would be a disaster.

Patsy rang to tell me that milk, cheese, peppermint, dairy products, menthol, Listerine and throat-clearing were all bad for my voice. They all make more phlegm. The only good thing for my voice is steam. I wish she had told me this a week ago. There is the possibility that if things don't improve I will have a doctor give me a cortisone injection to clear the phlegm off my chords. The reason it is there is because my voice got tired and my throat constricted. Some actors don't like the cortisone because it induces mood swings. I don't want to have it before my first preview. I must have it tomorrow before the dress rehearsal when it won't matter.

It turns out I had the first night wrong. I thought we opened on Wednesday 9 September. This is wrong. *Phèdre* opens on that day. We open Tuesday 8 September. Only four previews, in other words.

2 September I got to the theatre and found a homeless man scribbling a message all over my photo display. He saw me looking and stopped and said, 'Ah, Mr Hare, I was leaving you a message to say

I think you should reset *One Flew Over the Cuckoo's Nest* in Britain. That would show the Americans, eh? Beat them at their own game. Isn't it a brilliant idea?' I was staring at him and realized he did look remarkably like Jack Nicholson. 'But here's the twist,' he said. 'The English version would be set in a gym!' He wanted to talk the idea over with me, but I wasn't sure I believed he'd really been leaving that particular message, because the only letter he'd managed to finish was a big S over my face, so I think I can guess what message he'd really had in mind.

I had no time to talk because first I had to head off to see the voice doctor in Harley Street. He told me I had strained my voice by shouting, and that the only solution was not to shout. He had apparently given the same advice to an actor who was playing King Lear. I simply had to come to an understanding with the director of how to achieve my effects without what he called 'vocal abuse'. He said, 'How does Marcel Marceau convey anger? Why can't you be angry the way he is?' I didn't find this terribly useful advice. I was also wondering how an actor playing King Lear could follow doctor's orders not to raise his voice. Whispering Lear, indeed. I am already beginning to find the things people say contradictory. Patsy said no dairy products. The doctor said dairy products were fine. Patsy said, 'Don't clear your throat.' The doctor said, 'Clear your throat but only in the approved manner.' He demonstrated, hawking and burping like a shaken Schweppes bottle.

This man had all the solicitousness of private practice. He had the manner, and the anecdotes. He is about to publish a book called *The Professional Voice*, which, he said rather airily, is going to be cheap so that professional actors can afford to buy it. He obviously thinks of them as living little better than lice. He put a long tube with a light down my nose and down my throat. 'You can't vomit as long as you keep breathing. Keep breathing!' he said, with the resignation of a man who is obviously used to people sicking up all over him. He said I had done my chords no permanent harm. He told me he believed that voice problems could often be down to indigestion. He prescribed a favourite brand of lozenges, while teaching me a trick of biting my tongue to produce saliva.

I had a quick lunch with the humorous Stephen Wood, who used to be head of publicity at the National Theatre during the period when, hardly by coincidence, it used to get nothing but good publicity. I then got into costume for the technical rehearsal, which began an hour late. Lesley brought me a steam machine, so I sat for a while with my head bowed into a sinister mask which fired steam at me. Out on stage I felt very happy at last to be given a chance to remember the text again, and worked away quietly at my own problems, learning to play the house, adjusting to the fact that I could no longer see the audience. The production team are a little alarming. Rick Fisher (lighting), Ian McNeil (design), Paul Arditti (sound) and Stephen have all worked together so often that they have a rapport which is both instinctive and disconcerting. Ian, in particular, gives the word 'loll' subtleties and shades that it has never possessed. He *lolls* in the stalls, his legs achieving an effortless 150-degree parting, managing to suggest a fathomless weariness with the processes of theatre combined, of course, with a mastery of its resources. He is that creature I recognize so well: the man who can see the arguments against his own work as soon as he creates it.

Rick, like Ian, is American. He is also, like Ian, a little on the bolshy side. On *The Designated Mourner* Rick was a complete gent, but with Stephen there is a caustic kind of badinage, which extends to his criticizing the production. At one point he attacked a move of mine, saying it looked completely phoney. These are three people who know each other very well. Stephen's manner is collegiate at the best of times. He asks everyone's opinion, and, when, at one stage, we get stuck with where to put the notorious 'effect' – the dust storm at Erez – he turns to whoever happens to be sitting in the stalls and asks their opinion. I suggest he would have been happiest in East Germany under the Communists where representative workers were invited from factories to express their views about the goings-on on stage. Stephen says he would have loved that.

I keep my lip buttoned, because they can see it and I can't. But the truth is, I begin to develop an instinct for a lighting cue during the course of the afternoon. When you are on stage the light seems soupy and general; you have no sense of its focus, because you are the thing it is focused upon. But its movement is reassuring, and quickly creates a sense-memory, where you can feel an individual line being carved into shape by the movement of the lamps around you. It's a lovely feeling when it's right. Rick is a great fan of side light, which is naturally sculptural. Actors generally hate side light because it means that when they look at each other the lights are shining right in their eyes. But as I never look sideways, I'm happy as a clam.

The stage looks fabulous. Rufus stood on it for me, and he seemed as handsome as Montgomery Clift. I said to Ian 'My God, if I can't hold their attention from that stage, then I shouldn't be doing this at all.' I also love the crew. All the electricians and the stage crew and the front-of-house and attendant people are tip-top. It is in this that the Royal Court culture shows its strength. Because everyone is a worker, so it is that the real workers are allowed real heft. They respond by being first class. Conditions backstage, however, are far from glamorous. A typical Royal Court touch, this. I have asked for a bed, but instead they have thrown down a mattress on to the floor of my dressing room which looks as if it's a reject from a particularly seedy production of *Entertaining Mr Sloane*, complete with sperm stains and rat holes in the foam rubber.

Also amusing is that people have to keep getting up to quieten auditions which are going on in various rooms near the auditorium for other Royal Court productions. I walked accidentally into a room where one actor was shouting at the other: 'I fuckin' bunked 'er up, I gave 'er a fuckin' goin' over, I gave 'er one right in the fuckin' eye', etc. It is terribly funny, the feeling that in all the cells round the main auditorium, bleak and heartless drama is being enacted in flights of fashionable incoherence, while in the main house, this ridiculous old knight of the realm flutes in the style of a long-gone age.

At the tea break, I went and watched Diana Rigg and Jonathan Kent drink champagne. Diana immediately gave me lots of advice. 'Oh, you've got quite the wrong steam machine' and 'Oh, you've got quite the wrong pastilles. I'll send you over a packet of the ones which really work.' I said to Jonathan I had turned into Total Actor.

I could talk about myself and my health obsessively for hours on end. Indeed, I can talk of nothing else. Diana stared at me in a way which was slightly discomfiting, and I didn't know what she was thinking. She kept saying I was terribly brave. 'Every writer should do it,' she said.

Jonathan was being a little more ambiguous, principally, I think because he gave up acting to become a director at the age of forty. He says now that he could never imagine going back to it. He claims to have no memory of any of his roles, though he says he was frequently unclothed. I remember him vaguely as a good-looking young man in early British costume crashing about on shingle in a David Rudkin play in Newcastle. I love the feeling of having these close collaborators – we did *Mother Courage* together – up the road in the next-door theatre. It is, as Jonathan said, how, when he was a child in South Africa, he imagined the British theatre would be: a community.

When we resumed, I began to feel quite ill, my voice going, and flushing with sweat when I drank hot tea. I thought, Oh, my God, I'm going to get 'flu. I mentioned this possibility to Stephen and he said, 'Don't worry. If we have to cancel the first couple of previews, we cancel.' My car, ordered for 10.30 p.m. arrived at 10.50. I went home, took two Night Nurses and fell asleep.

3 September Wednesday was a much better day. I woke up feeling that my voice was going to improve from now on. And so it proved. I had to do another photo for the *Guardian*, since they have decided they want colour. I had a quick rehearsal with Stephen where we worked on how I can achieve my effects without using volume. We then went into a protracted technical rehearsal. I could have predicted that, because the show has so few effects, they would take for ever. And, sure enough, it seemed to take hours to do Jerusalem and the ending of the play.

Stephen had wanted to rest me and get me home early, but I began to feel I must pull the threads together by doing a proper dress rehearsal at the proper time. It was nearly a full week since I had last done the play right through. Patsy Rodenburg turned up, marvelling at the acoustics, and saying I must, at all costs, take it easy at a dress rehearsal.

It did indeed start on time, and I learnt some lessons. (1) The start is far too fast – I must learn to ease my way into it, so that I let the audience in. (2) It is alienating when I laugh, because it seems as if I am enjoying the show more than the audience is. And (3) We still have not solved the problem of Erez. I felt I was pretty good in all the quiet places, but I was thrown because I couldn't do the big climaxes (protecting my voice, natch), and couldn't cope when the lighting cues were wrong. When I walked into darkness, I found it hard to keep going. I was also relieved when Stephen said he was going to cut the smoke which had greeted the arrival in Jerusalem. It's not just that I hated trying to act in smoke, but it seemed to me to tip the conventions of the evening into something else. All Stephen's beautiful effects are in some way supportive and austere. Once you start pumping smoke in, then you shift into another style – a full production, in fact – which is out of key with what we are attempting.

At the end, I found myself moved, and there were tears in my eyes – I suspect relief at getting through. Elyse Dodgson was teary because it's her baby, after all. Paul Arditti said, 'I know it's not cool to clap at dress rehearsals, but I felt you deserved it.' I said, 'I didn't hear any clapping.' He said, 'That's because there wasn't any.'

I'm always moved to see Elyse, and I'm glad it was she who sent me to the Middle East in the first place, on behalf of her International Department, which has a programme for developing playwrights in Israel and Palestine. The whole thing has a nice circularity, because I first met her in 1969 when she worked at the Combination Theatre which was up an alley just off the sea front in Brighton. The Combination was one of the most committed and inspirational of the theatres which sprang up at that time. In the refreshing style that was then current, the company argued passionately about what theatre was for, and about how theatres should be run. The result of their arguments was a company-devised show which was presented to the audience under my favourite theatre title of all time: *Don't Come*.

News from the outside world? Stephen did an interview with Jane

Edwardes from *Time Out*. He felt she was hostile – to him ('After all these years of not directing plays, is this all you can come up with?'); to me ('What's David Hare doing acting?'); and to the play ('After all, who's interested in Israel and Palestine?'). It was quite bracing to hear everything everyone has been thinking articulated quite so openly. Or perhaps it was devil's advocacy. Whatever, bookings are beginning to pick up, as we had hoped.

Went home, grilled lamp chops, threw caution to the wind, had two glasses of red wine (fuck it!), and waited for Nicole who came home from Edward Albee's new *Play About the Baby* raving about Frances de la Tour, whom she had never seen before. She, I think we may safely say, is an actor in a different league.

4 September

> Hysteria is concomitant with the arts of performance.
> Without it – for, after all, it is mainly a sign of high spirits as
> excess energy – nothing of much intensity can be achieved on
> stage.
>
> LINCOLN KIRSTEIN

First preview last night. Stephen was even more nervous than I was and when Jonathan Kent hugged Nicole in St Martin's Lane, he said her body was absolutely rigid. I did a superb two-hour session with Natalie, then a dress rehearsal with me marking in, barely raising my voice. Before the show, Patsy Rodenburg did a session with me, which relaxed me, but before I went out the intercom to the ASM broke, so that I didn't even know when to appear. What's worse, the whole audience went quiet as soon as they saw me, so the bit where I sit waiting on the stage became excruciatingly embarrassing because there was total silence for what seemed like an eternity till I spoke.

Once I got going, I felt friendliness from the audience and I at least appeared to be relaxed, though all the time I was fighting giddiness from the heat of the lights. In one part of my brain I was having the usual playwright's experience of a first preview, thinking, Oh, that bit didn't work or Oh, this turns out to interest them. They were very attentive. The Royal Court was never in any danger of overwhelming me with too many of them, and what was nice was they were non-theatrical, a regular mix of interested people. I was put off only by a couple of people making elaborate notes in front row. I didn't like those places where I was able to see them. Given that I can't contact them directly in the way I did in a rehearsal room I would prefer not to see them at all.

Afterwards, there was a great swell of relief, which merged into the drinking of a lot of champagne. I realized that there is a reason that Wally Shawn is the most approached person I have ever walked down a street with. After a one-man show people want to shake the hand of the person they now know. There was a whole crowd of people at the stage door, including a couple of men who had been soldiers in the British army during the Mandate period. Very moving. By the most striking coincidence, Susannah, who is one of the characters in the play, is on temporary leave in London. She happened to be walking past the theatre and thought: My God, it's David's play, and bought a ticket. She was thrilled with it and we laughed in the dressing room at the scene where Haider Abdel Shafi flirted with her.

Best of all, my university friend Humphrey Davies, whom I haven't seen for twenty-five years, turned up. He is a great Arabist, lived three years in Gaza, now lives in Cairo, has worked for the Ford Foundation and for Save the Children, and is generally one of the cleverest men I know. When I was at Cambridge he was my supervision partner on our English literature course. English bored him so much he took up Chinese in the afternoons because he said otherwise his brain would rot. After six weeks, he changed to Arabic, but kept up the Chinese as a hobby. It was being taught next to Humphrey which made me realize that I wasn't academic. I was out of my league. So it meant a huge amount when he told me that he thought my play was completely fair, and, what's more, real. 'You could smell Gaza,' he said. 'It felt true.'

This was the highest possible accolade, and so all the doubts and wrinkles of the evening vanished for me. Stephen was high as a kite and off to Old Compton Street to celebrate. I said I thought he despised Old Compton Street. Ian McNeil at once said, 'It's all we have. It's our Jerusalem. Gay men have waited two thousand years for the promised land, and all we come up with is Old Compton Street.'

Nicole kissed me a lot and wept, and we went up the Finchley Road to a small Japanese restaurant, where we ate sushi. Then went contentedly to bed.

5 September The day started well with Billington's article. The *Guardian* is notoriously staffed by misanthropic sub-editors who signal their contempt for their trade by thinking up the most negative headline they can find. In their world, everything is in doubt. If Billington says that Kevin Spacey is brilliant in *The Iceman Cometh* they still trail it as 'Can Kevin Cut It?' – regardless that the answer is plainly Yes. In this case, a blamelessly sensible article was headlined 'Why I Bent the Knee to Blair, by David Hare.' If you got past the headline, the piece itself was exemplary – judicious, informed and accurate. At the end of it, you had a fair idea of what kind of play *Via Dolorosa* was going to be.

However, if the first preview was reassuring, the second was correspondingly unsettling. There were two reasons. First, and much the more important, I felt giddy out there on the stage, on the point of fainting. The adrenalin started pumping for the first time when Eran attacks Israelis sitting by their swimming pools. The blood went to my head, and I felt very unsteady. I started losing lines, and fearing for myself, as if I were standing on the prow of a ship which was moving beneath my feet. Stephen noticed, and didn't know what was wrong. I thought perhaps it was because I hadn't eaten since 1.30 pm, and tonight I'm going to try a snack at 6.30 p.m.

The second unsettling factor was that whereas the first preview attracted real human beings, the second night found me in the dressing room with a whole load of professional people, whose reactions were rather more political. Or personal. (Or maybe the personal is the political.) Any room which contains Gita Sereny, Caryl Churchill, Richard Eyre, David Rose, Donna Grey, Judi Daish, Caro Newling and their attendant families is going to be a slightly uneasy place at the best of times. Richard and Caryl were particularly guarded, as you would expect. For them, the sight of me prancing about like a maniac is necessarily unsettling, and I began to think that maybe my unsteadiness on stage had come about because I sensed that Richard was in the house. But then, it turns out, so was Claus von Bülow. Perhaps I sensed him, too.

It was a hard evening for Richard because this is the first play of my last seven which he hasn't directed. It is clear to me that one of the reasons my collaboration with Stephen has worked thus far is that I don't really know him. I couldn't have tried to act with a friend like Richard or Howard Davies directing me. It would have been too embarrassing. But it was Richard who pointed out, when he first read *Via Dolorosa*, that I would have to begin by explaining why I was up on the stage in person. Unless I released the audience from their puzzlement – what on earth does David Hare think he's doing? – the event would never have a chance of taking off. The audience would worry about it all night. He was right. It was the smartest change we made.

Now, again, he had an excellent note. I should make my attitude to real actors clearer at the beginning, so that it's plain that I genuinely admire them. At the moment, there is a danger of my seeming to say that I can do it as well as them. Naturally, it's not what I think, but there's a danger that's how it comes across.

Much the best response was from Gita Sereny's daughter, who said, 'Frankly I did everything I could to avoid coming tonight. I felt that there was no possibility that an outsider could communicate the feelings of the subject. What the hell was David Hare doing interfering in the Middle East? But you won me over. I could see the way in which you put yourself into the material. And I'm going to go back and tell all the people who told me not to come that they were wrong.' Gita asked me how on earth I was going to keep it real for over thirty performances. I said I had no idea. I'm exhausted after two. Gita's husband said it was the best play he'd ever seen. I said, 'You've obviously seen very few plays.'

In fact, beyond the hothouse reaction of the profession, the audience was fine. They stayed with me, in spite of all the blunders I made from nerves. The opening needs to be re-conceived. My sitting on stage at the beginning doesn't work. The box office has picked up because of the big feature in the *Guardian*, and because Stephen went ahead and wrote the diary of our collaboration in the *Standard*.

We have been asked to go to Tel Aviv in December, and New York in March.

6 September Last night was much the best performance. I got my flight path right. A big pasta lunch, an afternoon in bed, a rehearsal of the lines I got wrong the day before, half a sandwich, a rest on the dressing room floor with my feet on a chair, as recommended by Patsy, and I was ready to go.

The entrance was much, much better. Instead of sitting in the chair at the side as the audience came in, I made a proper entrance to begin the show. By doing it, I at once pulled the house together. I obeyed Patsy's instruction, which was to take a huge breath, in and out, before I began. 'If they sense that you are not too nervous to breathe, then you will calm their own nerves,' she told me. 'You will feel your control spread through the house on the out breath.' I cannot truthfully explain why something which seemed so wrong and impossible three weeks ago now seems so inevitable, so right. Rehearsal is evolution. No wonder directors like André Gregory and Katie Mitchell dream of staying in rehearsal for ever.

From then on, there was the professional satisfaction of getting right the little bits I had got wrong the night before. Slipping correct lines into places on the right beat gave me a pleasure which sustained me. I had said to Neil, the box office manager, who saw the show on Friday, that I had been very nervous. Neil said, 'It didn't show at all. Except when you hurried on to the next line when we were trying to laugh. You should share our pleasure in the jokes.' This was a brilliant note – Stephen was preparing to say the same thing – and again, this liberated me in some way, and gave me precious time to breathe and think.

I was still giddy, but less so. One lighting cue went wrong and I was distracted by the sound of the flyman getting into position in a particularly quiet passage. But otherwise the show went like a dream, except for those poor people in the front row whom I showered with saliva. Stephen came into my dressing room screaming:

'We've got a show! We've got a show!' I said, 'Was it so terrible the first two nights?' Tonight's dressing room party was pleasant – Christopher Hampton, Roger and Liz Dancey, Harriet Walter and Peter Blythe, Nicole Kidman, Sam Mendes and Iain Glen, plus Sacha Wares who is the assistant on *The Blue Room*. I can see that the people for whom the show is most difficult are those who know me best. The closer you are to me, the harder it is to see the show clearly. Richard had phoned me in the morning saying that he had found the show very moving because of my 'hubris'. A strange choice of word.

I have already learnt that anyone who says to me, 'My God, you're so brave' means they didn't like the show. Just as I would find it peculiar to see Christopher or Richard act, so they find it odd to accept me on the stage. But Liz was happy, and so were the *Blue Room* brigade, whom I was thrilled to see. Iain Glen embraced me as if I were a fellow actor, which I found terribly moving.

Harriet Walter said to Stephen that the evening had disturbed her. 'How does he do it? David has a feeling of utter conviction which I can't get. I tried to get it in *Three Birds Alighting on a Field*, but, even then, I didn't convince people it was all felt and true in the way David did tonight.' Needless to say, this remark thrilled Stephen more than anything he had heard because this is the question which obsesses him intellectually: what is acting? I had said to him 'Is what Wally does acting?' To which he had replied 'In *Vanya* Wally gives one of the greatest performances I've ever seen. I scarcely care what you call it.'

I had run into Clare Coulter before the show. She's a Canadian actress who performs Wally's monologue *The Fever* all over the world. She was coming back to see *Via Dolorosa* for a second time, as a connoisseur of this kind of evening. She said she was confused by the separation – basic to the whole play – of stones and ideas. 'Surely stones *are* ideas?' An hour later I bumped into her again in the sandwich shop and she was contrite. 'I should never have said that. I feel so stupid for raising a doubt in an actor's mind two hours before the performance.' I assured her it hadn't troubled me. 'If I were only the actor, it might have.'

In the alley afterwards there were three Israelis who had waited patiently for me to come out. I find these encounters almost unbearably touching. The man had been at school with Shulamit Aloni. They said that when they come to London, they too walk on Hampstead Heath, just as I describe David Grossman doing. They gave me their card and asked me to look them up in Jerusalem. They also implored me to perform the show in Tel Aviv.

The mystery of who had been scribbling in the front row at the first preview was solved this morning by a profile in the *Independent on Sunday*, which transcribes a couple of my best jokes. It really annoys me – the right of people to give away all the best lines from a first preview. The profile tried to be bitchy – mostly, of course, about the knighthood – but the journalist's heart was not in it. There is going to be a lot of this stuff.

8 September I couldn't really be in a better position to open. If I fuck up now, it will all be my own fault. I read a sports journalist yesterday saying that people are either big-occasion players or they are not. Are they what Michael Atherton calls 'up for it'? Tonight we shall find out.

What pleased me was that the last preview seemed quite steady. I messed up more lines than usual, and the audience sensed it, but it didn't detract from a perfectly OK performance. It was £5 night, so the audience was more volatile and disparate than usual. But I enjoyed the fight. Nicole said they were the strangest group of people she had ever seen in a theatre. I thought at one point that the roof was leaking and the rain coming in, then I realized it was sweat from my brow. But, in some way that's hard to explain, I was putting out more physical effort without having to scour as deep as I had in the first three shows. I came off feeling: OK, if this is what it's like from now on, I can do this seven times a week and not die.

The question of how long I am to do it is a looming issue. Stephen thinks that we are going to sell out at the Royal Court, because the box office is taking bookings from people who have already seen it, and who want to come again, usually to bring friends. It's clear from word of mouth that even without the critics it is a popular hit, or rather what Max calls 'one of the three shows you have to see in

London'. It's astonishing how quickly this happens. Jonathan Kent was rather hurt that his parents, visiting from South Africa, put seeing *Via Dolorosa* ahead of seeing their son's production of *Phèdre*.

Stephen thinks I will be pressured to extend. I have no position on this yet. I want to get past the first night. I have decided I definitely don't want to go to New York, because the Jewish audience there will be so prejudiced against it that there will be no chance of it being listened to without a big and distracting fuss. But we are negotiating to get me to Tel Aviv. It is a delicate business deciding which theatre to go to. The Habimah wants us, but the general feeling is that it would send the wrong signal to perform there, because it is part of the official Festival for fifty years of Israel. It would be less of a statement to go to the one I know – the Cameri.

Wally came, and of course that was terribly important to me. He said, 'I am not going to tell you what Stephen Daldry has done for you, because it is not good for you to know how the play seems from the outside.' He's dead right. He thinks that Stephen had released an aspect of me which Wally knew was there and Nicole knew was there, and the outside world not at all. Mary Selway, who is one of the best casting directors in England, as well as being one of my oldest friends, was bantering about refusing to cast me. 'You must be joking,' she said, 'I'll do everything I can to prevent you becoming a boring actor.'

Lest I get sentimental about the scenes at the stage door, last night there were three students dressed in Japanese costume who had paid 10p to see the show and who stopped me to tell me that they were studying the form of comedy which precedes a Noh play. Standing there in their kit, they seemed to me totally insane. Even a people-politician like Bill Clinton would, I think, stop short of pressing the flesh with Village-of-the-Damned-type Norwegians dressed in Oriental pyjamas in a wet alley in St Martin's Lane.

9 September The opening was a slight anticlimax and, like all openings, slightly depressing. The audience were harder to play to than the previous ones, because they were asking what I was doing on the stage, rather than listening to a story about Israel and Palestine. Like all first nights, it started twenty minutes late – I think about 7.19, in fact. On the dot of 7 p.m., after a careful preparation and deliberate calm, I was absolutely ready to go. But by 7.19 I was a dish rag. Those twenty minutes were like lying on the floor with an articulated truck parked on your chest. It wasn't the entrance which killed me. It was the prolonged wait for the entrance.

When the comedian Stephen Fry threatened suicide after getting bad notices in a play, he left an ambiguous note, then disappeared. It later turned out he was in Bruges. This has become a running joke backstage. Whenever I have to wait more than five minutes to go on, I threaten everyone with my intention to make an immediate exit to Bruges. 'That Bruges plane is waiting,' I say. 'They're holding the last seat. Unless you put me on that stage in the next thirty seconds, I'm off to Bruges.' Last night, the Bruges joke was wearing distinctly thin.

When I did finally get out there, I was troubled for the first time by a man coughing. At very predictable moments critics' torches flared in the dark like fireflies. I would think: 'Oh, here comes a line they're going to want to write down.' I would throw it out, like fish to seals, and, sure enough, their little electric pens would gobble the line up. I had some fair success in the first half, achieving a few of the velvet silences I like (though fewer laughs than usual). Then at a certain point, I thought, Fuck you all!, and I made the evening terrifyingly serious. As Stephen said afterwards, 'Fuck you' is not a bad attitude with which to play large parts of this play.

I came off relieved that I hadn't bottled out, that I hadn't ballsed it up completely. When I once directed a play at the National Theatre, the wily Laurence Olivier came to an early preview. At the interval he said to me, 'Marvellous, marvellous! I smell success in the air!' Needless to say, I swelled with pride. He then named the leading man with whom he had himself acted many times. 'I've never seen him better. Never!' Then he added, 'Of course you'll find there's only one problem you're going to have with him.' I prepared myself for the killer blow, and, sure enough, it came: 'Can't do it on first nights!'

Truthfully, I have done it better. Sometimes when I get to the pivotal moment where Haider Abdel Shafi talks about 'the strife of the soul' I feel an intimacy with the audience which wasn't there last night. And that was my fault. Various good things happened afterwards. I had already received a fax from Richard, which pleased me because he was more generous on paper than he had been in person. But also, my children were not ashamed of me. They all said how nervous they had been, but after a few moments they had relaxed, and begun to feel they were in safe hands. It moves me so much, because the idea of watching your dad acting must be so peculiar. And, what's more, they are all three very good judges. I like their taste.

My regular producer, Robert Fox, had really enjoyed it. When I saw him, I wouldn't even let him open his mouth before I said, quite spontaneously, 'I've made two decisions – not to extend and not to go to New York.' I only later found out that Stephen had sent Robert over to me specially in order to tell me to extend and to go to New York. By some curious radar I pre-empted both entreaties. The most important reactions were from the Palestinian Representative who was truly delighted that here, at last, was something about his country, and from Eran Baniel, the Israeli theatre director who is a character in the play, and who was so kind to me when I was in Tel Aviv. He said it was, simply, the best thing he'd seen on the subject.

There followed a party at the Ambassadors Theatre which was crammed and sweaty. I was approached by the casting director who said to me, 'I came wanting to hate it, but I was won over.' This seemed to me an astonishing remark, and part of the good old Royal Court tradition of nobody there wanting the shows to do well. At moments like this, the Almeida seems such an attractive theatre, because its staff does manage to grasp the basic idea that it's best all round if the plays are a success, and that you should, ideally, choose a theatre whose work you are predisposed to like.

Ian Rickson was circumspect. 'You did it really well. I particularly liked the way you said one line about three pages in.' Peter Ansorge, who is the critic we lost, was the most amusing. Since he now makes television series, I asked him if he would employ me as an actor. 'Well, to play a Jew, yes.' Would he employ me to play a Palestinian? 'Oh, a Palestinian, perhaps.' Would he employ me to play anyone else? 'No, certainly not.' Otherwise the evening went by in a long parade of people, with me kissing everyone in sight, more or less indiscriminately. If I saw someone I kissed them. It seemed easiest.

We went on to The Ivy – the officers' mess of the British theatre – with my children and Nicole and Wally and the production team. Stephen was drunker than me, and kept saying, 'I like you. I like you. I really like you.' He told me straight men can't say that to other men, so that's why he was saying it. He said, 'The big question is what you are going to do next. This experience is going to change how you write.' I said I knew it would, but I did not yet have any idea how. In the book he has given me about Israel, he has written: *One show together and* WHAM! *Stephen Daldry is in your life for ever.*

I was a bit disturbed by him being drunk because, selfishly, I want him to be a father figure. Wally says you never want your director to be a slob like you. Even when you have fulfilled the role yourself – and therefore know that there is an element of pretence – you still need the director to serve a certain emotional function. Any fall from a standard of calm control is frightening. A drunk director is bad enough, but a depressed one, says Wally from bitter experience, is unforgivable.

This morning I searched out a quotation from Ingmar Bergman – who is perhaps a surprising person to say such a thing: 'It's part of a director's duty to be in a good mood at work. When I was young I didn't understand that at all, and took it all with me into my work-ing life, my hangovers and troubles with women, all my shortcom-ings and stupidities . . . Rehearsal [must] look like fun – we're joking and telling funny stories and so on – but the actors still must feel it's a matter of life and death. And when I say life and death, I actually mean just that.'

Nicole drove me home, and this morning we have woken up to very good reviews. Nicole has read them. I haven't. You wouldn't know they were good if you talked to Stephen who keeps saying 'They're fine', and promising he is going to write to Alastair Macaulay of the *Financial Times* because he has written the only bad one, attacking the production and saying it isn't theatre. I implore him not to. Nicole, however, is terribly moved by them, saying they have really got it. They are all commercial, and what's even better, they are over. They have all published overnight, so the bonus is that I don't have to worry again tomorrow.

Richard rang to congratulate me. It was particularly sweet of him, as I feel the critics are compensating for the horrible things some of them said about *The Judas Kiss*, which he directed. Critics always balance their review of a current work against the memory of whether they have overpraised or underpraised your previous one. My Almeida adaptation of *The Life of Galileo* was received like the second coming, when it was a bog-ordinary piece of Brechtian translation. The critics knew they'd underestimated my previous play, *The Absence of War*. Critics are always one behind.

Richard told me to enjoy my success. Oh God, I shall try.

10 September I thoroughly enjoyed the sixth performance. There was a different atmosphere when I walked out. They knew they were at a hit and were warmer towards me. I didn't have to work so hard and I could begin the process I have been longing to do, of experimenting a bit and being freer with it. I made the opening less coy; I cut a couple of joke expressions which didn't work and I generally worked through trying to clear up bits which I had never been happy with. A friend who had come for the second night running said she had relished the nerviness of the first night, but she could see that I was enjoying the second night better. Jenne Casarotto and her husband Giorgio came round. Jenne is the head of the agency which represents me, and she has a useful device for dealing with all the clients' work she has to see. She pretends that her tastes are very basic and unsophisticated. It isn't true, but I can see it gets her through what would otherwise be a lifetime of awkward conversations. I didn't feel the same enthusiasm from Jenne that I'd had from people the night before, but it didn't bother me. My whole being was directed towards the possibility that I could order a cab which arrived at 9.20. By 9.45 I was triumphantly lying on the bed with Nicole watching a TV documentary about Dennis Potter. It was all about sex. They somehow omitted to mention that the larger part of his early work was about politics.

This morning I said to Nicole that what pleased me most was that I had been allowed the freedom to experiment. I feared after *Skylight* and *Amy's View* that I would be trapped in an audience's expectation of a certain kind of bourgeois play. I wanted to pull my work back to Joint Stock, back to fact-based material, to freshen myself up with a dose of reality. I had the idea that the experiment would be very low-key, and it would somehow happen without too much attention. But after the previous plays, that is impossible. More pressure built up than I had anticipated. But we survived that pressure.

11 September Before the show, I went to a *Blue Room* technical rehearsal and had a last drink with Wally before he went off back to America. I drank three glasses of mineral water, which turned out to be a mistake. Once it's gone to your bladder it's too late to sweat it off. Wally said something very funny about the negativity of Royal Court culture. He had noticed that when you ring the National Theatre and ask for someone they say, 'Oh sure, I'll get them for you.' But when you ring the Royal Court, the switchboard says automatically, 'I don't think he's here.'

We got into a long discussion about acting, about which Wally would love to write a book. Wally seeks to get round some of the problems professional actors raise by getting non-professional actors like André Gregory or Mike Nichols to appear in his work. For the New York production of *The Designated Mourner* he has spurned a wealth of great American actresses and cast his own girl-friend, Debby, who is by trade a short-story writer. To him she has some essential quality which a regular actor cannot provide. She seems 'real'. Wally's first choice to take the third part was Arthur Miller, but Miller could not face the extreme slowness of the director's methods. (When André Gregory did *Vanya* on stage, it took him four years.) Even when Wally does use mainstream actors, he tends to favour eccentrics, like Woody Allen's first wife, Louise Lasser, or the actress who played the boy in *The Year of Living Dangerously*, Linda Hunt.

What is this thing called 'real'? What Wally means by it isn't the same as what Ken Loach means by 'real'. Loach's extraordinary talent is for mixing up people who've never acted with people who've acted a great deal, and making each look like the other. It's a myth about Loach to say he uses non-actors. He does sometimes. His proper genius is for smoothing out all stages of experience, and making them indistinguishable in the invented world.

Wally is deeply versed in conventional theatre acting. His early experience was at the great American productions of O'Neill and Ionesco. He was taken aback as a young man by seeing Ruth Gordon, who seemed to have some 'extra' quality – a mystical energy that communicates directly with the audience in a way that seems not entirely under the actor's control. Judi Dench, he says, has the same quality now.

The mention of these actors led me to tell a story about the time when, years ago, I was rung by a national critic who had reviewed *Plenty* in a regional theatre. He said that it was so good that he was breaking the rules of a lifetime and contacting an author to tell him to go and see his own play. I asked if the actress playing Susan was any good. He thought for a moment, and then replied 'Well, she isn't actually, but I think you see the play more clearly with a bad Susan Traherne.'

This remark is made more often than you can believe, especially among people who work in the theatre. Implicitly, the claim always is that great actors somehow stand between the audience and the work itself. This is why some directors go out of their way not to cast stars. When I first worked at the Royal Court Theatre, stars were disapproved of, because it was felt they appropriated the play's energy. They diverted it. Even in the sixties there was plenty of spectacular casting – Marianne Faithfull and Simone Signoret were brought to the ensemble-minded Royal Court while Juliette Binoche and Nicole Kidman were still playing with their rattles – but, in general, fame was distrusted. Clearly it's true that famous actors are not necessarily any good. But some actors are famous for the right reasons. For me, the chemistry great actors bring is more usually enrichment than obstruction. When I took the critic's advice and went to see *Plenty*, I could see it achieved a sort of earnest decency, almost like a staged reading. And, yes, you could say that my lines were clearly heard. But I still spent most of my time regretting that I wasn't watching Kate Nelligan.

To put it simply: *Plenty isn't* better without a great Susan. I'll be happy to see *Amy's View* played by a thousand actresses, but I'm not sure they'll thrill me in the same way as Judi Dench. Thanks to its one set and its three characters, *Skylight* has turned into what's called a warhorse – a play you can put on at any time with any number of different casts. But that won't stop my mind drifting back to Michael Gambon and Bill Nighy. In a way that is unselfish and inspiring, these actors throw light into corners of your play which surprise even you. Kevin Spacey gives you every line of *The Iceman Cometh* – but he also gives you something more, a feeling that the text is not just being spoken, but has melted right into the actor's being.

The kind of dull, modest account of a part I saw that night at the critic's suggestion really gets you nowhere. The popular myth is that British acting is unfailingly wonderful. I'm not sure. One of the most moving elements in the London production of *Amy's View* was a young actor called Christopher Staines who played his tiny scene at the end of the play to unfailing perfection, night after night. He made it like a small, polished stone. His acting displayed a resource and depth typical of the fringe and regional theatre, which are both, to this day, far better than the measly grant-givers have a right to expect. But lately, watching some of the laziness in our bigger houses, I've felt that the downside of a subsidized theatre is that it allows actors to lack ambition, as if 'quite good' were good enough.

Wally and I moved to discussing what acting is. Once I was eating dinner with the family. Blanche was sitting, begging at the side of table, putting on the most desperate expression because we weren't giving her any titbits. I said, 'Oh, Blanche, for goodness' sake stop acting. Nobody's impressed.' Lewis, who was then sixteen, said, 'Dad, she's not *acting*. Dogs can't *act*. She's showing you her real pain at the fact that you're eating and she's not.' I said that I didn't believe this. Blanche wasn't in that much distress. She knew perfectly well that I was finding it hard to take what distress she did feel seriously. Her intention was that by *exhibiting* distress she could persuade me that she was in real trouble – which only hunks of fresh meat could alleviate.

When I told this story, Wally sided with Lewis. Most people do. 'Lewis is right. Animals can't act. Acting is a function of self-consciousness. Therefore it is something only humans can do.' But I am left dissatisfied. What name do we give to the practice, common among animals and humans, of trying it on?

I went to the theatre. The seventh performance was very committed. My concentration was good. Stephen came and could see how the freedom to experiment in his absence had helped me. He gave excellent notes. There was a cougher in, so I put out a hand to say, 'Stop coughing, there's a good bit coming.' I overdid the passage about the Arabs starting the Third World War so much that I scared the audience. They decided I was a total lunatic and, after that, they never again laughed at my jokes until Shulamit Aloni. A note from Anthony Page says that Shulamit Aloni reminds him of the woman who was my much-loved agent for so many years, Peggy Ramsay. After this *aperçu*, it will be hard for me not in future to say 'Jews have always been victims . . . darling.' In order to get to the last thirty minutes of the first preview of *The Blue Room* I was smuggled out the back of the Garrick Theatre, so that I didn't have to bump into my own audience leaving the Duke of York's. Then I ran to the Donmar Warehouse in time to hear Nicole and Iain being cheered.

I had sent a fax this morning laying out some of my problems with the *Blue Room* production. In the rehearsal room, the run-through was very beautiful, when there was only the work of the two actors to look at. But at the dress rehearsal yesterday I had been alarmed to see that their work has been encased in a Brechtian production which seemed at odds with the text. No sooner do the actors manage to create a mood than it is swept away by pounding music for the scene changes and by harsh, modern lighting. The set, the lighting and the music are all too bleak for the words. Schnitzler's text is about cynicism and manipulation. But, in my version at least, it is also about yearning and romance. Sam, whose work with the actors is sensitive, has come up with a *mise-en-scène* which is more appropriate for a play by Büchner than for a play by me.

Sam was angry when he got my fax but, mercifully, he took notice. He's an equable fellow. Most people who direct have a very high metabolic rate. They're wiry and thin and tense. Their anger shows. Sam is a rare example of an endomorph director. His beat is quite slow, and his concentration is therefore exemplary. On this occasion, he has to remember that I did eleven drafts. It took me a very long time to find a difficult tone: world-weary, yes, clear-eyed, yes, but also full of the vulnerability of the search for love. I would not expect the designer and composer to find that tone immediately any more than I did. They can do their eleven drafts. Yesterday, they were only on Draft 3.

Earlier yesterday we had a meeting at my agents, Casarotto Ramsay, to discuss the following options: (1) Extend the play in London, (2) Take it to Tel Aviv and Ramallah, (3) Take it to New York, (4) Do the radio, (5) Make a film. Today the political situation on the West Bank has deteriorated, and we're all wondering whether Option 2 is even remotely practical. So the thing I would most like – to present *Via Dolorosa* in Palestine and Israel – looks less likely. A shame. But if I am to die for a cause, deadlock in the Middle East is not really a cause worth dying for.

12 September The life of an actor: from hysterical nervousness to open boredom in the space of four nights. It's unrewarding playing on Friday because Jews don't go to the theatre on the Sabbath. The house was only half full and the audience was only half alive. After Michael Gambon had played *A View From the Bridge* a hundred times, he asked me why I thought the audiences deteriorated in quality so sharply after about eighty performances. I said, 'Because there are only enough Jews and gays in London to give you eighty rewarding nights. After that, you have to play to the rest.'

13 September Curious day yesterday. For the first time I had to do two shows. This brings the number played up to ten, so I am one-third of the way through the run. At both shows, I walked out to an ovation. They have obviously read the reviews. At last I have the answer of how to play the opening: I respond to their applause. It makes things much simpler. I enjoyed the matinée, and so did my American producer Scott Rudin. He said that the subject of assimilation is one of the most topical in America, and implored me to do the play in New York. Because his partner is Arab, Scott had a fascinating afternoon. He said something true about Stephen. 'His gift is for taking apparently simple subject matter and managing to make it hover a few feet above the stage in some mysterious way that you can't understand.'

I then did what I thought was a good evening performance. But Nicole was listening on the tannoy in the dressing room and thought I was overacting. Jonathan Kent and Ian McDiarmid came round and we were back into the 'know-me-too-well-to-accept-it' mode. They hated it when I innocently told the story of Harriet Walter saying I had a conviction she didn't. I realized this was a stupid story to tell because they were longing to disagree. As guests in my dressing room they knew they couldn't.

This morning in the *Observer* Susannah Clapp accuses me of using too many gestures, but overall the reviews are, once more, said to be excellent. A piece in the *Guardian* by a Middle East expert was headed 'The critics loved it but does it really measure up?' Apparently the answer was 'yes'. I was relieved that *Phèdre* was equally well received, since the coincidence of having Jonathan's show next to us would have been unbearable if either of us had been preferred. But all is well. Jonathan rang and, in a shift I am already familiar with, was much warmer to me now the event has receded. Perhaps the problem is not with my friends' reaction, but with the intensity of my own self-doubt.

We now have to address the problem that the house is not full in spite of first-rate reviews and excellent word of mouth.

14 September The best thing about Sunday is that I don't have to drink any fucking water. I am so used to pouring gallons of mineral water down my throat that I have turned into a sort of human Romney Marsh, permanently boggy and saturated. It's the thing I like least about acting. The right to dehydrate is a basic human right. I exercised it to the full yesterday, drinking a glass of sherry before lunch so that I could doze freely at Stephen Spielberg's new film. It's hard to believe the man who made *Schindler's List* could make a film as ghastly and reactionary as *Saving Private Ryan*. Nicole said, 'Oh, it's because when he makes films about the Holocaust he's emotionally involved, but when it comes to the American campaign in Europe, he's faking it.' I wish I thought it were that simple.

We all do bad work, but none such distinctively terrible work as Spielberg. He piles on brimming ladles of treacle-thick emotion. Perhaps it's the inverse of his prodigious talent. Because he's better than other film-makers, he's also worse. If the well-known theory is correct that only second-rate artists are consistent, and that great artists like Dostoevsky and Wagner always produce long passages of the unbearable, then Spielberg (like Hitchcock) is about as great as they get. The more Tom Hanks tried to play heroic, the more brutal and stupid he looked. His putty-like face became pastier and pastier, conveying a message of insensitivity quite at odds with the uplifting lines he was given to say. Poor chap. Realism ain't real. But it disturbed me.

Talking to Stephen Frears, we agreed that five minutes of George Stevens' documentary footage of the Americans advancing through Europe in 1944, seen casually on television, moves you in a way *Saving Private Ryan* never can. The sight of a Frenchwoman embracing an American soldier makes you weep. Stephen Frears had seen the Spielberg film in the company of someone who landed on Omaha Beach at 7.10 that morning. As the old soldier began to describe it, Stephen cried in a way he never did at the film itself. All this proves *Via Dolorosa*'s contention about art. It is the facts that must illuminate the great subjects. In these areas artifice is often not just unhelpful, it too easily becomes positively obnoxious. As the play says, 'What is a painting of a starving man? What is a painting of a corpse?' It's Anne Frank's diary. Thank God it isn't Anne Frank's novel.

When I first went to Israel and Palestine, the idea was that I should write a play about the British Mandate. Elyse Dodgson also approached an Israeli and a Palestinian to do the same thing. But as soon as I went, I knew that my play would have to be modern. I was overwhelmed by the conviction that if I could explain to people what the area now feels like, and how little understood the true roots of the conflict are, then they would be as amazed as I had been. I had regarded myself as reasonably well-informed. But within a day of arrival I was brought up short. I began to feel that it was unhealthy that such a bitter dispute should only be understood by interested parties, and ignored or patronized by the rest of the world.

Alongside this revelation came the knowledge that I could never write so-called 'scenes' which would one day be played by British actors on a British stage. British-Jewish actors – who in no way resemble Israelis – would seem ridiculous if they tried to enact little dramas opposite, say, a couple of Arabs and the odd light-skinned Pakistani – the only people in London available to play Palestinians. It seemed impossible that it would achieve anything you could call 'authentic'. Or 'real'.

No, I decided the only way of my being true to my subject would be by rejecting enactment altogether, and drawing the material back where it belongs – in the eye and in the voice of the beholder. A hundred people have asked me: why did you decide to act? There is only one reply. Because, with this particular subject matter, the artistic logic was so compelling. Once I had decided to treat this part of the world, there seemed no other honest way to do it. How else could someone from an ignorant, neo-Christian background write clearly about the supreme issues of Jews and Arabs? In this case, you could only trust the witness if you could see who the witness was.

I was backed up in these decisions by reading George Steiner. In his autobiographical book, *Errata*, Steiner argues that the Jews are not cut out to be artists. Originally the play paraphrased his point of view, but the section had to be cut for length. 'The Jewish impulse is to know, not to invent. The world is there to be understood. It is a lifetime's work to try and interpret its complexity. Why fecklessly create new complexity? It is no coincidence that the great scientists and theorists are Jewish – Einstein, Freud, Marx. Yes, there are Jewish storytellers like Kafka, like Proust, but they are the exceptions. As in Talmudic study, the highest good is to work, to learn.' It was reading Steiner which confirmed that the appropriate approach to the subject matter was not to smother it in the sugar-ice of narrative convention.

I followed up these decisions with a period of research. As a writer I have met people for two minutes and then remembered them for the rest of my life. All writers are ambiguous about research. Henry James said that if he wanted to write a book about army life, he would need only to walk once past Chelsea Barracks to learn all he needed to know. According to your point of view, this remark either illuminates a great literary truth, or else it tells you why James's writing is sometimes unconvincing. Certainly nothing ever replaces the smack of first impact in a writer's exploration.

All my decisions seemed clear enough at the time, but at the end of the first week, I am more confused than ever about what I doing on the stage. Did people originally respond to a rawness and vulnerability in my performance which has gone? Is the show best when I am in control or when I lose control? When, at the matinée, I offered Scott what I call a 'contained' performance he didn't seem to feel he'd missed anything. And when I let rip, aren't I embarrassingly exposing my lack of technique? I really don't know the answer to these questions. Of course, I am more comfortable now we have reached the end of the week, and I am able to be more assured. But is the gain loss? In the Spielberg, technical brilliance destroys the material.

The French have an expression when someone fakes feeling. They say 'C'est du cinéma.' It's always said dismissively.

I look in the *Guardian* this morning and find there is no ad for *Via Dolorosa*. It seems unbelievable. Do they have any interest in publicizing this play at all? More extraordinary, they have put a huge ad for *The Weir* in the *Blue Room* programme. This is a play by Conor McPherson which is scheduled to follow us into the Court. But there is absolutely no mention of *Via Dolorosa*, in spite of the fact that I wrote both plays. Insane.

15 *September* Much better evening. It was Monday where the seats cost £5, so the house was full, and my performance seemed better. I took the two Palestinian artists George and Hussein right down, so that they were less mad, though they made their points forcibly. I

retained my own sanity, so that I didn't jump around the stage like a loony when I mentioned Hussein Barghouti's name. I also took Susannah Clapp's criticisms to heart, and flapped my hands around less. I understand how actors may become thrown by fixing on some stray critical remark. But in this case, I happen to think Clapp was right. Nicole came with my stepdaughter, Candice, who was over from Paris. Candice seemed very moved.

Nicole was pleased because the Palestinians were finally as lively and moving as the Israelis. It is so odd. Stephen and I had grown accustomed to not worrying about the Palestinians in the play because, at the beginning, everyone found them so attractive. We thought they would look after themselves. But they didn't. Now we've worked the two sides equally. Nicole said it was the best show she had seen yet. I felt so too.

Beforehand, we had a meeting with Stuart, the marketing manager, and Neil, the excellent box office manager, to discuss why we hadn't been full on Saturday night. Fortunately we'd had a terrific day at the box office after the Sunday reviews, so Neil was predicting that we'd do sell-out business fairly soon. I said the problem was that we all knew that in two weeks we'd be full. But the show was closing in three. Couldn't the advertising be more vulgar? At the moment, whenever I see an ad, which is, frankly, not very often, it is so discreet that you wouldn't know it was there. 'It is,' I said, 'as if the Royal Court feels no obligation to sell the seats.' Neil was outraged by this remark, which is fair enough. They claimed it isn't a lack of will to sell them. It's an argument about *how* to sell them. I suggested slipping the programme for *The Blue Room*.

My son Joe called round to see me before the show. He said, 'I know you hate being told the reviews, but the *News of the World* called you a bloody marvel.' I said I thought it would make great advertising copy – just the kind of vulgarity we want. I was always happy when we advertised *Paris by Night* under the strapline 'C'EST MAGNIFIQUE – *The Sun*.' Trish Montemuro, my old stage manager from the National Theatre whose theatrical taste and goodwill I have always respected, rang this morning to say how much the show had moved her. Since I had read her uneasiness in my dressing room on Saturday as dislike of the show, I felt sharply rebuked, and ashamed of my own over-sensitivity. How many times have I told actors to take no notice of how people behave in dressing rooms? God, how pathetically slow and stupid I am at learning my own lessons.

In fact, what is now noticeable is how few people come to my dressing room. Last week, I seemed to find myself holding huge parties, but as we settle down we are drawing a very un-showbiz crowd. When I go to *The Blue Room*, I bump into Sandra Bullock, and folk of that kidney. But *Via Dolorosa* is not the higher show business drug of choice. Our people are real people.

Stephen rang to say that a West End theatre owner had called to suggest we play the Piccadilly, alternating with a production of *Filumena*. Since this is a 1,200-seat theatre with a stage about forty feet wide and a notoriously chilly auditorium, I think not.

16 September Horrible day. I tried to live normally – submitting applications for planning permission for our new kitchen to Camden Council and getting a new passport, going to *Blue Room* rehearsals, doing interviews – and the result was that I was completely exhausted before the show. I went for a mineral water with Stephen at 6 p.m. He said our work will change nothing. The Royal Court will go back to doing Irish whimsy and 'isn't life awful?' plays as soon as *Via Dolorosa* closes. My kind of political work is not being put on as a statement about the Court's future intentions. Stephen says he himself was lucky enough to be the last generation who joined the Socialist Workers Party at Sheffield University. The result is that he is capable of asking the basic questions about a work of art. What is the point of its existence? What is it for? What is it saying? It astonishes me to this day how few people ask these questions.

Stephen, like me, had been to *Saving Private Ryan* and been angered and mystified, for the same reasons. What the fuck is it trying to say? I have always believed that the first character the playwright has to get right in a play is himself. *Racing Demon* didn't work until I realized I was a non-believer. I had started writing it as if my sympathies extended to sharing the vicars' view of life. But, in that great phrase of Anne Sexton's, 'Need is not quite belief'. As soon as I realized that, I had a play.

Stephen told me that he despaired after five years of running the Royal Court because he came to realize that few new writers feel the obligation to work out who *they* are in the equation. Somebody writes a play saying life is awful in Camberwell. You read it and you say 'Yes? And? So?' – and there is no answer. If you produce only this kind of play, you are reduced to the worst kind of tokenism, doing plays by gays and blacks and women and the poor, on the grounds that 'they ought to be heard'. But what does this mean, if the plays themselves have no analysis? To paraphrase Sexton, sympathy is not quite analysis. Andrea Dunbar, who wrote *The Arbour* and died at the tragically early age of thirty, was a terrific writer, not because she lived on a council estate. She was terrific because she had terrific things to say. You couldn't disentangle the power of her emotional convictions from the authenticity of the news she was bringing from the front line. The two were mixed up together. She was pitiless. Watching *Vanya* the other night in Louis Malle's sublime version, I realized how sloppy the lazy myth is that Chekhov's work is powered by compassion. On the contrary. He's the most judgmental writer who ever lived. *That's* his power.

Earlier, I had been interviewed by a highly intelligent young man from Cambridge University, Ajesh Pataly. He writes for *Varsity*. He asked me if it was Thatcher who made me fall silent in the early eighties. I said, 'Of course. History didn't take the turn we had expected, or advocated. So it took us all five years to work out what was going on, and to come up, thanks in good part to Howard Brenton, with the analysis which forms the basis of *Pravda*. Now,' I said, 'Marxist writers of all ages have been thrown for a similar loop by the fall of the Wall. That has knocked *them* back in the way Thatcher knocked me back. And they have been effectively silent for nearly ten years.

'But,' I said, 'these writers are too good to stay silent for ever. They will come back.'

As I prepared for the performance I remembered a quotation I love from Hemingway: 'We do not have great writers. Something happens to our good writers at a certain age. I can explain it but it is quite long and may bore you.'

Plainly, I was in a rotten mood for the show. Apart from anything I am terribly unhappy about *The Blue Room*. I had spent the afternoon at rehearsals of a show I have not seen. Every time Sam asked me a question about what works and what doesn't, I couldn't answer because I didn't know. At one point, shamefully, I lost my temper when he suggested a cut. It's entirely my fault, not his. It's the conflict of timing which is frustrating me.

I went out feeling terrible, got no reaction to my first funny line, listened to a few coughs, and got ready for a filthy night. I hadn't had a proper lunch, so the giddiness came back. A man in the front row didn't just cough, he racked and rattled the phlegm from his lungs, filling every tender silence with the expectorant hawks of a dying mammoth. At one point I once more resorted to gesturing towards him to hold him under while I worked. I reminded myself of how often I have told actors, 'Don't worry if it's a bad audience. Audiences are made up of individuals. For ten people out of the five hundred, it's going to be an important night in their life. Play for them.' I came off swearing to Simon, the ASM, that they were the worst bunch of motherfuckers I'd ever encountered. I walked back on to a solid wall of cheering, almost the best reception I ever had. Stephen told me it was the best show he'd seen. What do I know?

I went round to *The Blue Room*, which was having an even worse night. It's often the way. It was full of people in suits who don't go to the theatre, but who'd come to see Nicole Kidman. One of them sicked up in the foyer, and there was a rank smell of disinfectant everywhere. The show seemed torpid. Or was it the audience? In the dressing room afterwards an Australian woman was virtually masturbating over Nicole. 'You were wonderful, darling, you were marvellous,' she kept saying, availing herself of a shelf at a convenient height. Nicole turned sweetly and introduced her to me. 'This is the man who wrote it.' The Australian looked at me with naked contempt, and used the full, viperish, strangulated power of her accent – as Australians can – to spit out two words: 'Oh yeah?'

17 September I had a much easier day, eating pasta and lying in bed. It's taken me two weeks to realize I'm not very happy. When I went into this, I had no idea what a strain it would be. I had the idea that once the show began, my life would resume. I would write in the mornings, and after the show I would go off to restaurants and meet friends. It was a completely clichéd idea of a kind of velvet-jacketed existence, the show dispatched and evenings there to be enjoyed. Nothing could be further from the truth. I have, in fact, never eaten with anyone – I couldn't bear to – and the whole day is spent in anxiety and strain, working towards those 95 minutes which will either cheer me or throw me into despair. Throughout the day, it's impossible to think of anything else. Is all acting like this, or only one-man shows?

One of the reasons for my unhappiness is *The Blue Room*. I hate feeling that I am not doing my work properly. I know I will never relax into *Via Dolorosa* until my anxieties about my absence from rehearsals are resolved and *The Blue Room* opens to the press. But on the given calendar that means I shall only really begin to enjoy *Via Dolorosa* eleven days before it closes.

The result of spending the day in bed was that I had my best first hour ever. I then messed up Hussein and George by trying to rewrite it, a lighting cue failed and the last part was straggly. As it was the thirteenth performance, I was superstitiously relieved to get it over. I was home by 9.40 pm. Getting home early always makes me feel happy.

Again, a shower of letters and nobody in the dressing room. People want to think on paper, not to gush. So far, the acting profession is conspicuously slow to come and see me. A few have been in – Michael Pennington, Prunella Scales, Michael Medwin – but otherwise, they are notably absent. On the whole I don't like to know who's coming in advance. I don't want to see the show through their eyes.

A friend had rung me in the morning. At last I heard what is plainly the intelligent objection to the show – and clearly articulated. The friend thinks I have made a mistake by being so histrionic. It would be better if it were more like a conversation. The whole method of the writing is to aim for a stripped-down simplicity, to appear to take the artifice out of art. Why can the actor not do the same? Surely it should be performed quietly, almost casually. Let the facts speak for themselves.

One of the odd things about my line of work is that as soon as you achieve a particular way of doing anything, you can at once see the charms of doing its opposite. If you have any instincts at all, you feel the appeal of the counter-method. So this morning my friend's words struck a deep chord in me. But since we shall now never try the alternative way of doing the play, we shall never know which was right.

The waiter in the bar where I go to get my mineral water had seen the show on Saturday. He asked me what I was going to write next. I said I had no idea. He said, 'I can see it's hard for you. You're hardly going to go back to writing plays set in a room with people called Tim and Jim.' No, indeed.

18 September Much the most interesting dressing-room discussion. Nicole's friend Kathy Burkeman, who is also Jewish, also French, also from Nice, was there for the second time. She said I had grown in confidence since the third preview. Now I hit my points much harder. I asked her whether that was good or bad. Kathy thought a moment, then said she'd like it best if I was somewhere in between. 'After all, some of it's so powerful, it's better if you just say it, don't hit it.' I repeated my friend's objection, that it would be better if I didn't act. Jonathan Miller was at the other side of the dressing room, and said: 'But you didn't act. It was a conversation. That's why I loved it.'

The truth is, people are seeing different things. This morning a fax from Simon Callow: 'What you did this evening was a wonderful performance by someone who isn't an actor, all the more powerful because of a lack of the perhaps somewhat whorish skills which we old hands bring to the matter . . . The very fact of your standing before us unprotected by a shield of technique hits us with strange force . . .' I am bewildered by this, because I believe I have technique, but the art is to have hidden it. But am I fooling myself?

Tonight I am planning to take down the passage between George and Hussein Barghouti. Just as the use of smoke tipped Stephen's production over into something too stagy, so I feel that my shouting my way through George and Hussein is tipping me over into a kind of performance which is too conventional, too actorish. Overall, I plan to try to respond to Kathy's note by being less loud.

I am exhausted. I slept from 12 to 5.30, woke, tossed and turned, managed to stay in bed till 8.15. I dreamt that my parents' semi-detached had been knocked through and both houses converted into a lunatic asylum. Where our front room had been, twisted faces moaned out incomprehensible yawls of pain. (I am mindful of Henry James. 'Tell a dream, lose a reader.' I shall say no more.) This morning I am more tired than at any moment so far. After the show last night, I went to the end of *The Blue Room*. It was horrible to meet a whole lot of people who had seen something I hadn't. Tom Cruise, who is normally very friendly, seemed to me distinctly underwhelmed. He greeted me with his usual startling handshake – an iron vice gripping your lower arm – but I didn't think he was happy. Kevin Spacey was enigmatic. Though enigmatic is, of course, Kevin's preferred suit. It's the gear he idles in. My children had seen *The Blue Room* and I took them out to dinner. I asked Joe if he'd enjoyed it. 'Sure. But it's not *Via Dolorosa*, is it?'

All these judgments go in and churn round in my head uselessly. Once, I was having breakfast in a hotel in Budapest, sharing a table with Kazuo Ishiguro. He seemed a little grumpy in the morning. He was munching his Hungarian cereal when he said moodily 'These cornflakes aren't very good.' His spirited young wife threw her eyes to the ceiling, then looked at me. 'Living with a novelist! Judge, judge, judge!' Then she turned to him. 'Just eat your cornflakes and shut up.'

19 September Last night I reached a low point. Vikki Heywood, the delightful woman who administers the Royal Court, came to tell me that the business wasn't good enough to justify a transfer to another West End theatre. We are selling very well and very steadily – every day the same sum is taken to within an eerie 1 per cent – and yet we aren't establishing the kind of demand which would propel us into another theatre, even if such a theatre were available. We always sell 75 per cent of the seats but what we don't have is people to turn away. If we were to stay at the Royal Court, we could easily run for another six weeks, but in order to move, you need more than that.

I don't particularly need or want to do another four weeks, but it's a symbolic defeat all the same. We haven't broken out. Great reviews, very good word of mouth, everyone saying they'll come back with their aunty or their best friend and yet . . . finally, it's still a play about the Middle East by a man who isn't an actor. Something is wrong with the Royal Court that they can't sell all the seats for a show on this subject. I'm well aware that I've been spoilt by working with Judi Dench and Michael Gambon. The empty seats we have now are either a tribute to my acting or to the way the Court has pissed away its audience. It's annoying. I wrote a play in the 1970s called *Fanshen*, about the Chinese Revolution, and everyone felt in advance that it was going to be forbidding. But we still filled theatres. I love taking so-called untheatrical material and extending the range of things you can talk about. *A Map of the World* was about aid to the Third World. Here and in the US, it attracted perfectly reasonable audiences. The Royal Court has always had an honourable record of playing innovatory work to empty houses. But they seem now overly attached to that record.

All week Stephen and I have complained about the advertising. The Almeida had a great ad on Thursday in the *Guardian* – brilliant quotes, beautifully laid out and with real impact. This morning our ad is in. It's on the back page, there is a smudgy picture of me which you can't discern and a series of illegible quotes. Its laziness comes across as a form of arrogance, as if the Royal Court is announcing to the world, via its advertising, that they want to remain in the New Writing Ghetto and nowhere else. Their argument is that they don't like 'wasting' money on advertising. But they 'waste' money upstairs on management jobs which don't seem directly to serve the plays they put on.

I went on stage and realized why I was doing the play in the first place. I was expecting nothing because it is Friday when the Jews don't come. But the audience were superb, subtle, attentive and lively. I had read Kate Kellaway, whom I admire as a critic, in the *New Statesman*, saying that my gestures on the first night looked like appeals for help. I was much more circumspect. I brought down Hussein Barghouti and his points seemed more powerful, though the line about 'This is a typical Palestinian conflict' went for even less because, of course, the audience had seen less conflict. When I came off, I said to Simon, 'I really enjoyed that,' and he whooped with pleasure. 'I'd told you you'd enjoy it one day. I told you!' He's a nice man.

I went off to *The Blue Room*, where Sam immediately picked up on my mood. 'You look so much happier,' he said. Iain and Nicole both seemed very relaxed. The actor Simon Russell Beale told me how good the show was. I said I didn't know because I'd never seen it. Nicole Kidman interrupted 'You did see the dress rehearsal but we weren't much good.' I said, 'Not good? You were downright poor.' Nicole Kidman hit me and replied: 'Say it again. I love the way you say "poor".' 'Poor!' I said, cheerfully. 'You were piss-poor!'

20 September How startling it is when real life breaks into the dream. For two weeks I've been planning some tantalizing time off. Nicole and I had the idea of going to the seaside in the middle of the run. I'd dreamt of Aldeburgh and walking by the sea. I'd booked us into a hotel. But instead we were plunged into crisis. Nicole's best friend, Ilana, was taken into hospital. We spent most of our time at her bedside, or worrying with her family. The same night, Nicole's Aunt Visa, lying ill in a Paris hospital, reassured her daughter that she was feeling fine and told her to go off for dinner and not to worry. Visa then died peacefully in the two hours that her daughter was away. A hushed weekend of condolences, nurses, doctors and terror.

The past three performances have been purposeful, each one building on the other. Stephen came to the matinée and gave me some very good notes. I was desperate for direction, to give me something to work at while I was out there. He was on the nail, as always. He admitted that it was better with fewer gestures and that the Palestinian material, he said, had more emotional commitment now it was less loud. I said how interesting it was that it had taken two female critics – Clapp and Kellaway – to pick me up on my gestures. The male critics just think I'm a bloke, like them, and don't notice. It's the women who see me as a man, and remark my body language.

My sister saw the show and was confused. She said, 'It's hard for me because the person up there is you, yet isn't you.' She said, 'What's more I've just been to Jerusalem and had experiences like yours, but not quite the same. The whole performance is like, but not like. It's going to take me days to take it in.'

By the time I got to the evening performance, I was seriously tired and really getting through like a blind man in a darkened room. But I knew we finally had ignition. They drank up every word. When I came out for the curtain call, the front of the stalls all stood up and everyone followed. The first real standing ovation of my acting life. I'm afraid I cried, partly because I was so exhausted, and partly because of the feeling that, with a returns queue forming at last, we have begun to prevail over our problems.

People have been asking me whether I ever feel the release, the joy, that is meant to attend the work of an athlete or an actor. I haven't. Or rather, I think I'd have to act a lot better before I began to feel such a thing. Most great stage actors I've known hedge superstitiously against the dangers of disaster by refusing to indulge a feeling of success. I once ran into Michael Gambon on the night when he had the greatest triumph of his life as Galileo in Brecht's play. He looked as if he were returning from the dentist's. He sat gloomily, nursing his drink and muttering 'I'd fancy doing a nice little sit-com right now.' The good ones never arrive. They quietly repack their satchels and keep trudging. But this evening I admit I did experience the pleasure of progress – the feeling that by working hard over a long period, you can effect some qualitative change. No, I haven't known triumph. But tonight there was satisfaction.

Earlier, we ran once more round the advertising track. Stephen had seen the hopeless ad in the *Guardian*. 'You might as well go out into the street and give the money away to passers-by for all the impact it will have had.' Stephen says that the *Express* said that I was 'the best serious stand-up in London'. I asked why this was not on a banner across the theatre. Stephen said, 'They can't even spot a fucking quote, let alone use it.'

There is an oddness in Stephen's attitude to the Court which I have never dared bring up with him. He reminds me of Margaret Thatcher when she was Prime Minister. When anyone came to her with a complaint, she used to say 'I know, it's scandalous. Why doesn't the government do something about it?' Nobody liked to point out that she was head of the government. She behaved as if it had nothing to do with her. When I hear Stephen agreeing with me about the shortcomings of Royal Court culture, I do wonder whether he accepts any responsibility for it. He is, even now, called the executive director. He's not the artistic director, but he's close. His footwork is fancier than almost anyone's I know. One day he *is* the Royal Court. Next day he's not.

Alan Rickman came round with Rima and two friends. Again, I felt a bridge had been crossed. At last this show is beginning to attract first-rate actors who are not close personal friends. Rickman sometimes seems to be the V. S. Naipaul of acting – a man whose taste has become so exquisite that he can barely bring himself to do anything at all. Like Elizabeth David in later years, he plays with his risotto with his fork. It's a shame because, like Naipaul, like David, he's brilliant. He is going to do *Antony and Cleopatra*. I said, 'Isn't that the most difficult play ever written?' He said, 'It certainly is.' Bitterly, he quoted *Via Dolorosa*: 'It's half play, half poem.'

A letter from a 26-year-old Canadian moved me. He had been in the tickets queue and said to the woman beside him that he had never seen a play of mine. 'What should I expect from a David Hare play?' She replied 'Everything.'

I went on briefly to *The Blue Room* where Sam had had a migraine and gone home. This seemed to me a sign of confidence. Iain's wife Susannah Harker was there, seeming cheerful, and Tom Cruise, back for a second time, was in much better spirits, as if he'd now been able to take the show in. I chatted briefly to Atom Egoyan, whose films I like very much, and was introduced to John Woo. John Woo, eh? Oh, there's no second-guessing who's down the Donmar.

During the week I have read *The Madras House* by Harley Granville Barker, which the Almeida want me to direct. For a start, it's too close to *Heartbreak House* which I did last year. But beyond that, how can I go back to that kind of stuff?

22 *September* The worst thing about acting? That you have to do it again. Saturday night was so enlivening that I woke on Monday morning thinking: why do I have to do it again? What's the point? Why do I have to prove myself once more?

I think perhaps cussedness and depression are part of the process whereby I get myself ready to do it again. I'm foolish to act on them. But I sent Ian Rickson a letter, detailing all the fiascos and fuck-ups of marketing that left us with empty seats last week. He came round to see me at once. He was trying his best but he says things which illustrate a gap between us. For a start he said how sad it was we were talking about selling seats when he would like to be talking about art. I said, 'Ian, I don't find that sad at all. I love the idea that we sell the seats. And personally, at this moment, I don't really need to talk about art.' It's weird. I kept thinking that Joe Papp put on plays just as difficult and demanding as those Rickson is presenting, but you could still dial the letters J-O-E-P-A-P-P on the telephone and listen to a recording of the man himself singing to you about his forthcoming season.

Rickson admitted that it had all been terribly mis-handled, then said, 'You're doing very well. Mamet only plays to 55 per cent, and Sarah Kane to 17 per cent' – as if this were something to boast about. I didn't like to point out that Mamet is a superb playwright, but that *The Old Neighbourhood* was not taken to be one of his best works. Nor did I say that Sarah Kane is too young yet to have the following she deserves. He made the point that they did not have a huge budget for advertising. I said, 'Vital to use it well then'.

Ian hadn't seen the disastrous ad because he'd been in Berlin. He said *The Weir* was a commercial production. It was in some kind of super-category of its own at the Royal Court whereby it was allowed advertising and I wasn't. He could see that it was painful for me to be jammed between *Phèdre* and *The Weir* and given none of their resources. But then he shifted to a cultural argument. He said that whereas the National Theatre was an ocean liner, the Court was a pirate ship. 'We're a bunch of tricky fuckers.' I was bewildered by this line of argument. I explained that I had spent most of my life with tricky fuckers, and they had never bothered me. What did bother me was working for months on an important political subject and then knowing that it would disappear without people knowing of it – because nobody had the forethought to get the publicity organized. To take up the attitude of 'take it or leave it' is not tricky. It's silly.

In order to defend himself, Rickson had to go down an unwise route. He said the reviews hadn't been *that* good, that they made the play sound – his words – 'very interesting'. But, he said, they didn't say 'must see'. Suddenly, as he was talking, I remembered Lindsay Anderson laughing in a restaurant and saying 'If there was a button on the table and if, by pressing it, I could blow up the Royal Court Theatre in Sloane Square, then my finger would not hesitate for one second.' Listening to Ian talk, I resisted quoting Byron on Coleridge: 'I wish he would explain his explanation.'

I was not in great shape for the show. I was always one beat behind, searching for the line for that micro-second which can make the show exciting, but can also make it quite painful. It was £5 night, and I didn't think they were a great audience. I thought, Oh perhaps the young just don't know what this play is about. In a laughless auditorium some of my idealism about taking politics to the young became a little bruised. Frankly, I didn't think I was very good.

I usually try to screw my eyes up during the opening while the house lights are still on to avoid seeing anyone I know. By pure chance I caught sight of Michael Blakemore. I have always dreaded that recognizing someone in the audience is going to undermine me. Michael knew me when I was a young writer of twenty-six. He directed one of my first plays, *Knuckle*. I've always thought him eerily sardonic and perceptive. He's also an exceptionally good writer, as his novel about the theatre, *Last Season*, proves. The result was, I felt thoroughly phoney for the rest of the show.

There was a scrum in the dressing room. My French friends Yves Lefèvre and Sabine Haudepain had come. Yves said it was the easiest play for a non-English speaker that he'd ever seen. He *knew* what I was saying without understanding each word. Sabine thinks that I should play it in Paris. As far as I know, the last British playwright to play his own work in French in a Paris theatre was Noël Coward.

Gerry Schoenfeld was there. He runs the Shubert organization which controls seventeen theatres in New York. He offered to take me to Broadway. He said, 'I never liked one-man shows before, but this one has a story and is about something important.' I told him we had never considered Broadway because we had always imagined we would be picketed. American Jews would resent my speaking about the Middle East, and there would surely be a distracting row. But, to my surprise, Gerry assured me there would be no problem. He embraced me and whispered in my ear. 'Broadway now totally depends on you, David.' I don't think the producers of *The Lion King* and *The Phantom of the Opera* would believe this any more than I do.

Jack Kroll from *Newsweek* was also there. He'd caught the show by accident. 'I never knew this was on. I'd never heard of it.' His presence brought back the most shameful incident of my theatrical life. In 1989 I directed a production of my own play, *The Secret Rapture*, on Broadway. It closed in ten days, largely because of a vituperative review by Frank Rich, who wrote in the *New York Times* that my direction had destroyed my own play. He unaccountably failed to mention what he had said when he reviewed the play in London – that the play itself was, in his opinion, rather wonderful. I wrote him a letter, accusing him of being destructive and power-crazed. In support of my view, I cited a conversation with Jack, in which he had been very critical of Rich. He had spoken of Rich's compulsive need to display and exercise the power of *The Times* on all possible occasions.

Jack was only saying what everybody knew, but I had absolutely no right to quote a private confidence. I can only plead in mitigation that I was so crazy with grief about the play's demise that I got carried away. It's not a good enough excuse. What made the matter worse was that my producer, Joe Papp, was so fired up, both by my righteous prose and by the calculated partiality of Rich's review, that he released the text of my letter to the press without my permission. The result was that an incoming editor of *Variety* immediately sought to prove that he could rival some of that magazine's most famous headlines. He came up with the enduring front-page classic: RUFFLED HARE AIRS RICH BITCH. But for me personally, the release of the letter was a catastrophe. It meant that my abuse of a private conversation had been disastrously aggravated.

By an awful coincidence, Kroll's editors at *Newsweek* were at the time trying to downgrade what they called 'the back of the book'. They seized on the incident as an opportunity to try to get rid of Kroll, claiming it was unethical of him to have criticized another critic to a playwright. I was outraged. The incident was spiralling out of control. I faxed Katherine Graham, who owns *Newsweek*, saying that whoever was at fault it most certainly was not Jack. It would be scandalous if he lost his job because of an indiscretion which was not his. She never bothered to reply. Whenever I have since read that Graham is meant to be this noble defender of the freedom of the press, I have wanted to spit.

Anyway, thanks to Graham's non-intervention, the tribunal lingered on for some weeks. Jack kept his job. I was told that David Ansen, the *Newsweek* film critic, was so appalled by my behaviour that he said he would never review a film of mine again. I couldn't blame him. I thought he had a point. But behind the whole brouhaha which followed – and which climaxed in a gut-churning segment in *60 Minutes* – lay an element of fundamental human jealousy. Rich knew that Kroll was a far better man than he was. He knew Kroll was respected inside the profession in a way Rich never was. Kroll can be tough, but he is fair. No one has ever said that of Rich.

A few years later, the discredited Frank Rich accepted the inevitable and moved to another job on the paper. That, at least, was an honest decision. Like Cain, he is condemned to wander the op-ed pages for ever in the hopeless search for a subject. And, sadly, he is still writing articles trying to prove that he's a nice guy, really. As he said rather pathetically on *60 Minutes*, 'my children like me.' He has taken to defending his viciousness towards Joe Papp by claiming that Joe forgave him just before he died. It hardly needs me to point out that this is a despicable tactic: citing in your own defence a witness who is no longer around to confirm or deny. You can imagine Frank Rich's review of a play in which a forceful and admired producer sentimentally forgives his meanest critic on his deathbed. He would scorn it as saccharine and contrived. To retail the story stinks of bad conscience.

The underlying truth is that, at the start, Rich had two things going for him. He had a terrific critical gift, which he allowed to be corrupted by power. He abandoned the role of informing the public, and came only to enjoy the far headier pleasures of opening and closing shows. He lost touch with his readership. He wrote only for the profession. His prose came to be charged with the malign pleasure of the critic imagining the artist reading him. The second thing you could have said in Rich's defence was that he did at least once have the courage of his own unpleasantness. Lately, he's lost even that. Jack Kroll has been personally sweet and kind ever since, when he had full reason to cut me dead. That's the measure of the man.

23 September I hate the way death and illness move in waves. They have seasons. Mercifully, Ilana has opened her eyes after four days in a coma, but meanwhile our friend Eduardo Paolozzi has been taken to the Lister, unable to walk. They fear he needs an operation on his spine. The same tide then hit Stephen Daldry. The man who brought him up, and acted as his substitute father, died yesterday. So Stephen is off arranging the funeral for Friday. Suddenly, the drama around us seems unbearable.

Professionally, it was an interesting day. I went to talk to Kate Rowland about the radio version, and became quite scared at the prospect of how difficult it is going to be to re-conceive my performance for the new medium. It's more than just bringing it down. I also have to introduce an intimacy of thought – as if I were talking to a friend across a microphone.

I then went for a mineral water with Stephen Daldry and recounted my conversation with Ian Rickson. When I told him what Rickson had said ('The reviews weren't *that* good'), Stephen was astonished that I'd not lost my temper. I said there wasn't any point. First of all, the damage had already been done. The unsold seats were behind us – we're full now – and it was too late to do anything about it. And secondly, I have long ago arrived at a theory of artistic directorship. This runs as follows. An artistic director must present (say) ten shows a year. Out of the ten, the likelihood is that he/she will only care passionately about four. The rest complete the programme, but do not have the same personal investment. To the producer, they are makeweights. You cannot ask the producer to fake a reaction he/she doesn't feel. It's like demanding love. You can't ask for it. Love must be given voluntarily.

I had an excellent audience, who started out full of laughter and ended up much more sobered. It was the first night of *The Blue Room* at the Donmar, so Nicole Kidman had sent me six bottles of Château Pétrus to celebrate. Simon Relph, an oenophile film producer who happened to be at *Via Dolorosa* tonight, looked at the bottles in disbelief. He said he had once dropped a bottle of Pétrus but he had never drunk one, let alone six. Nicole gave Iain Glen a racing bike.

After my show, I went on to the party for *The Blue Room*, which was packed. All anybody asked me was how I felt about being satirized by Iain Glen. The first time I was asked the question, I pointed out that it was me who wrote the pompous dialogue for the self-glorying playwright who appears in *The Blue Room*, so perhaps there was an element of self-caricature. If Iain has augmented the satire with a lot of floppy suits and muttering, then so be it. But this answer pleased no one, so I stopped giving it. From then on I did a sort of Pollyanna-ish 'Gosh, is it meant to be me? That had never occurred to me.' People liked this answer much better.

This morning the reviews of *The Blue Room* are great for Iain and Nicole, and fine for the play, except in the *Guardian*. Billington says I have desecrated a masterpiece. It's hard to believe he's read the original or he'd know it's profoundly dodgy. Great idea for a play but, believe me, not a great play. Sam Mendes was upset but I don't give a toss. I said: 'We're always going to have this problem.

Because it's fast and funny people are going to think it's lightweight. We could put up a sign saying "Often this play comes across as slow, boring and repetitive. We apologize for not doing it that way this time." If it had seemed duller, then Billington would have acclaimed it as serious European culture.'

Charles Spencer got carried away in the *Telegraph*. He said the show had provided him with sexual images which would fuel his fantasies for the rest of his life. Odd, because when he was young Billington also used to write what you might call 'I-wouldn't-mind-giving-her-one' reviews. He regularly kept the wet sponge next to the critic's torch and notebook. He even called his collected criticism *One Night Stands*, perhaps in tribute to Pauline Kael's *I Lost It At the Movies*. But now he is an elder statesman he obviously thinks such excitability beneath him.

Only one thing could ever have endangered *The Blue Room*'s success, and that is if they had said that Nicole Kidman can't act on stage. But they haven't, and she can, so it's fine.

24 *September* Lively house. Perfectly normal performance until a terrible noise broke out on stage behind me as I went into Gaza. I had no idea what it was. Explosions? Falling masonry? Bombardment? I began to sweat, great lines of water pouring off my brow. Automatic pilot for Shafi, me not daring to look at Lesley to ask what was going on. I got to the bit where I shout about the Palestinians, and by the time I quietened down the noise had stopped. It was the worst six minutes I've had on stage.

It turned out that it was a firework display on the Thames which resonated in the empty fly tower. Only the first few rows of the house heard it. Nobody else in the auditorium would have known that I was battling. In fact, Ronald Pickup said he watched the entire show thinking 'When is the bastard going to sweat?'

Stephen was meant to come but he got held up in Liverpool. We have been wobbling about how we should proceed with the show, but finally we decided to ask my regular producer, Robert Fox, whether he would like to revive the play in London next year, and then move it to New York. In spite of Gerry Schoenfeld's surprising offer to put it on on Broadway, we both prefer the idea of down-town. It is a source of amazement that anyone is proposing to put such a serious political show in a commercial theatre in New York.

I always claim that theatre is a great barometer. It tells you what's really going on in society. In this case the message is clear. Israel–Palestine is no longer a no-go subject. Not only has the reception in England been a good deal less turbulent than we had predicted – we haven't once had the show disrupted by hecklers – but we are also finding that Americans who might previously have turned their backs on a non-Jew talking about Israel are positively welcoming the show and saying, 'We're ready for it.'

What do I put this down to? Netanyahu. It is his achievement – if you can call it that – to make even ardent Zionists doubt the direction Israel is now taking. Once, to be anti-Zionist left you in danger of being called anti-Semitic. But, even worse, any criticism of a particular Israeli government opened you to the same charge. Now, Netanyahu's behaviour is embarrassing to the high principles of secular Zionism. Netanyahu has so degraded public policy that Israelis no longer feel they have to be dogmatically protective of their own national government. Let it be criticized like any other. It is a mark of maturity. The play has so far ridden on the back of that feeling. On the other side, the play has benefited from a feeling expressed to me by one Palestinian: 'I don't mind what you say about my country. To hear the very word "Palestine" on a West End stage is a step forward in itself.'

In the papers today Ian McKellen is complaining about all-white London audiences. He says he saw not a single black face at *Oklahoma*. Does he not understand that the audience you attract has some relationship to the work you offer? Yes, of course *Oklahoma*, *Peter Pan* and *The Prime of Miss Jean Brodie* attract a boring audience. What the fuck would you expect? At *Via Dolorosa* you see every race on earth, and every age.

The coverage of *The Blue Room* got tackier. The *Evening Standard* had a piece saying bugger-the-plot-look-at-that-body. 'Thirty-one and no cellulite' seems to sum up the critical reaction to that particular piece of work.

25 September The twenty-first performance was absolutely standard. Slightly volatile house, and all went well until I reached the argument between Hussein Barghouti and George Ibrahim, the two Palestinians who argue about art. Yet another new way of playing this passage failed to pay off and I suddenly realized it was Thursday and I was physically very tired. I limped to the end. I have noticed I am sweating much more and my voice is giving out again.

John Mortimer, a long-time supporter, has denounced New Labour in the *Daily Telegraph*, so all day I was pursued by the *Mail on Sunday* who are looking to take bricks out of the dam of Tony Blair's support. Finally they doorstepped the theatre. Next week is the Labour Party Conference, so a few well-timed defections are just what they're looking for. Not that I'm a member. I had to send Simon, the ASM, out to tell them that I was far too busy acting to think about New Labour. The reporter in the alley told Simon that if I would come outside and betray Blair, the price was £5,000. 'More conventionally,' as they say in *The Judas Kiss*, 'it should be forty pieces of silver.'

The marketing manager, Stuart, came to see me before the show, bursting to agree with me about the awfulness of the marketing: 'The design of the ads has been absolutely terrible.' He was so vociferous against his own work that I found myself marginally defending it. 'Well at least we're sold out now', etc. It is pure *Alice in Wonderland* when the man in charge of publicity sits telling you how inadequate the publicity is.

In the afternoon I went to *The Blue Room*. Nicole had told me how improved Nicole Kidman was, but I was taken aback. She found a new power in the last few performances before the opening night. Now she commands the stage, and there is a variety and subtlety in her performance which is astonishing. I still have work to do. Scene 2 is awful. I have learnt that each scene works only if the audience understand its individual purpose. There must be a line in each which gives them the chance to respond: 'We know this situation.' In Scene 2, there is no such line.

Sam's production is still too mechanical in places, and not poetic enough. We need to make the last scene the liquefaction of the themes, not just one more bloody scene. But, apart from that, I was very pleased. The fact that the press has only reviewed Nicole's body and overlooked the play doesn't bother me.

26 *September* I walked to performance twenty-two. It was a warm autumn day and I thought it would be the last opportunity I would have to walk into town with the sun against my face. Regent's Park was ravishing, full of young lovers, everyone cheered by the sudden burst of good weather. I felt happy, and blessed. A good show followed. A huge number of people afterwards, including the novelist Reg Gadney and his wife, Fay Maschler. A bunch of lawyers, including Helena Kennedy and Katya and Anthony Lester. Nicole and I went on to a Chinese dinner with Anna Massey and Ouri Andreas, who were back for a second time. Ouri is a distinguished scientist who escaped from Russia and lived for four years in Israel. He loves England best. 'First, I lived where Communism was being built, then I lived where Zion was being built. The great thing about England is that nothing is being built. People just live. That's the greatest pleasure of them all. Just to be able to live.'

A card from Ian Holm said: 'Who needs Dench? You are a great actor.' But he said something serious, too. In his words, I 'didn't drop a stitch'. This has now become an obsession. I have never fumbled words and I have never dried. For three weeks on stage, I have talked a certain amount of rubbish, but it has always appeared as fluent rubbish. The ambition I now have is to get through the whole run without stumbling. This is making me more nervous as the end approaches, rather than less.

27 *September* The matinée was bad. I allowed myself to get annoyed by a cougher. I waited for her, I glared at her, I even directed pieces of the text at her, all to try and shut her up. When she started coughing during the Yad Vashem sequence, then I gave up. The result was, the show had no soul. But the evening was something different. For some reason, this is a great Saturday night show. You wouldn't expect it, since usually people want something lighter on the last night of the week. But they were fantastic, and I was free, finding bits

of text afresh and feeling very happy indeed. I heard the casting director Patsy Pollock laughing at Shulamit Aloni and was grateful I hadn't realized till that moment that she was there. I took the remains of my champagne bottle home with me and drank the lot.

A review this morning in my Sunday paper is sniffy about *The Blue Room*. The critic is pissed off that it has become such a talking point without his say-so, and the result is a mild backlash, aimed mostly at me. I am one of the many colleagues Nicole has accelerated past in the last ten days. Good luck to her. She deserves it. My attitude to the critics has changed. I used to write letters and have feuds. I only wrote a play every two years, and I was fearful critics would stop people coming. But since I started doing adaptations I have many more shows on, so I have learnt to expect an aimless wash of good and bad.

A fax from Eran Baniel asks me to tour to Tel Aviv, Haifa, Ramallah, Bethlehem and East and West Jerusalem. Oh God, I have got to get my head round this.

29 September Radio day. I started early with a big, ugly frog in my throat and it took me time to get going. By 3.30 pm we'd polished the whole thing off, thanks to Kate Rowland, who was an excellent teacher, and whose opinion I trusted completely. When I heard the bad bits back, I knew how awful I would have been without her and regretted that she hadn't pushed me even harder. Everything that I achieved by volume in the theatre had to be achieved by intimacy on the radio. The most difficult passage of all was Eran in the harbour saying 'Fuck the land.' It took an awful lot of takes, as did the beginning. It's an exhausting medium because wavering concentration comes across immediately. You have to learn to speak across the microphone, not to it.

I got to the theatre for a sleep. I found out from the Donmar's manager Caro Newling that the only bad *Blue Room* review was the one I had seen. The rest were excellent. The theatre was packed for *Via Dolorosa*, people falling out of the upper circle as though it were an over-stuffed jewel box. It was like those theatre paintings by Walter Sickert. Lesley thought the radio had affected me because

I did start very low-key, but they were such an inspiring audience it was impossible not to rise to them. The third great night in a row. Half the audience seemed to be in my dressing room afterwards. Crowds of happy Jews. What was most moving is that Nicole's cousin, the novelist Moris Farhi, who had been so critical of the original text ('It doesn't have the stature necessary for the subject') was bowled over. He had cried.

There was one dissenter, an actress who remained sour-faced and angry. When this actress used the formula 'I admired your bravery' then it was like time travel for me. I hadn't heard those words for so long that it took me back four weeks, and made me realize how long a journey I have been on. When I started, the first words of the play 'Partly I just want to see what it's like' used to be greeted with a laugh, because people were genuinely bewildered by my appearance on a stage. These words no longer get any reaction, because it now seems almost normal that I should be there.

The actress's hostility made me realize how tired I am, and self-pitying, as if layers of skin have been peeled off me, night after night and I have no resistance left in my body at all. I don't sleep well, or long, and I am in danger of dissolving in a puddle of tears. I have to get through to Saturday, then collapse. One benefit of doing the play may be that, as a writer, I had come to fear the audience so much that I was finding it impossible to sit through my own plays. Attendance at any more than necessary previews had become an ordeal. I was even blocking my ears at the end of each act, lest I accidentally hear anything anyone said. The only way of my being present throughout the entire span of a play of mine is to be on the stage, not in the auditorium. I hope I can rid myself of my terror. As the writer of *Via Dolorosa*, I will have attended every minute of every one of its performances. Very few playwrights can make this claim.

A message from my agent Tom Erhardt tells me that they want a meeting on Thursday to discuss the tour of the Middle East. I am very anxious and unhappy about this, and don't know what to do.

We drove back for sushi, Nicole very happy and her friend Elfi Navarre paying me the nicest compliment I have had so far. She was born in Austria and lives in France, so her English is not perfect. 'But even if I didn't know the word, I knew what the word meant, because it was placed so lucidly. Most serious work makes me feel stupid. But your work makes the audience feel intelligent.'

30 September A true red-letter day, because for the first time the audience laughed at the jokes about *The English Patient*. I have struggled now for four weeks, and finally found a way of doing it which produced gales of laughter. It made me realize that in some profound way I have never believed I am an actor. I always thought: This joke doesn't work. I never thought: I can make this joke work. But now I have. Once.

To my surprise, I made a mistake. I was put off by the flash of a torch very late in the show and I said Westerners expected the Museum of the Holocaust to end in 1948. I quickly corrected myself to 1945 but it was a lapse of concentration.

It's a shame Stephen hasn't been here to see any of these last four shows. The most intelligent people in London seem to gather together nightly at the Duke of York's. Stephen has gone to New York to find a theatre for us. Or so he says. He may have had some other reason. You can never be sure with Stephen. I explained to him once that he is a natural scientologist, because scientology teaches you to withhold information in order to seem powerful. 'Where are you sleeping tonight, Stephen?' 'I can't tell you.' 'Where will you be at lunchtime?' 'I am not at liberty to disclose', etc. You can't get Stephen on the phone and you can't get him to tell you what he's doing. It blemishes his mystique. He went to New York (he said) five days ago, and I haven't heard from him since.

The management haven't been near either. You think they might be curious to see why the theatre is full. Instead, André Bishop, the director of the Lincoln Center, came and offered me his 1,100-seat theatre for a run in New York. 'Spalding Gray's really good in there,' he said, rather surprisingly. Zoë Caldwell came with Robert Whitehead, whose productions of Miller and Williams make him the most revered and well-liked of American producers. He said, 'I turned to Zoë. "He's not a bad actor, you know."'

Last week, the fatwa against Salman Rushdie was lifted by the Iranian government, and this morning he gave his friends a telephone and fax number where we can reach him. I very much want him to see the show before it closes. Kate Rowland is still editing the radio version. She had hoped to finish by Tuesday lunchtime, but it is now Wednesday morning and she is nowhere near. I have become anxious that we had not been radical enough. She is still vexed by the opening. The minute she said this, I offered to redo it tomorrow if she thinks it necessary. It's going to be the only record of the performance and I want it to be right. In fact, you could say that I'm addicted. I enjoyed the radio so much that I would happily go in and do it all over again from scratch. Actors have told me that radio is much the most joyful of all media, and I now know why. You can work purely for yourself, as in a laboratory.

Nicole told me today she had been rung by a businessman friend called Peter Collins. She has known him for as long as she can remember. Seventeen years ago, he bought a house in Israel, and has been spending half the year there ever since. Now he has decided to leave. He said to Nicole, 'It took me seventeen years to realize what David explains in an hour and a half.'

1 October A weird thing. Before the show last night, Lesley suddenly looked at me and said, 'I've never really understood. Why *did* you do this?' Only one possible answer: 'Because I had to.' At the first morning of rehearsal of *The Designated Mourner*, Wally apologized to the actors that the play was nearly all monologue. 'I know actors like scenes where they talk to each other, rather than at the audience. I would love to have written such scenes, but, I'm sorry, I couldn't get the characters to do it. They only seemed to want to talk outwards.'

This answer chimed with one of my favourite artistic statements. Giacometti was asked in a documentary why his figures were all so thin. He replied: 'Yes, it's very odd that. Every time I sculpt, I start with the intention that this time they should be fatter. But then they make themselves thin.'

And that is my own response. I had no way of talking about these things save by talking about them myself. I would love to have written scenes, but no scenes were available to me. That's all you can say.

Luca Barbareschi, the director and star of the Italian production of *Skylight*, was waiting for me when I got to the theatre. With him was the actress Lucrezia Lante Della Rovere, who plays Kyra. They had previously acted together in David Mamet's *Oleanna*. This has been true all over the world: the actors who create *Skylight* have often done *Oleanna*. They said *Oleanna* made no sense in Italy because the concept of political correctness does not exist there. The actress said, 'You see, I like having my bottom pinched. It makes me feel men desire me, and I like that feeling.' I asked how it went. 'Well,' said Luca, 'when it got to the bit where I hit her, they all stood up and shouted "Kill the bitch".'

Stephen was back from New York, so, inevitably, the audience wasn't as good as it had been on the previous four nights. Oliver Ford-Davies had given me a note about not being convinced when I claimed that I went into Gaza knowing 'fuck all'. He said that if I knew nothing about Gaza, I bloody well shouldn't be going there on our behalf. He was right. I changed the line to say I knew 'almost nothing' and the change threw me, so that I cut the following paragraph. Beyond that, the audience were not very humorous, so instead I played it with the utmost seriousness. It works equally well but, my God, it's much more effort, and makes for a less differentiated evening. I like being free to switch tones. That element of variety goes when the jokes don't work.

A huge crowd in the dressing room. Emotional to see Vincent Malle, who recognized the play's genealogy, and so we got into a warm conversation about Wally. Memories of Vincent's brother, Louis, hung in the air, as ever. I'm not sure I've quite recovered from Louis Malle's terrible death. We flew over on a freezing cold day in December 1995 to the funeral at St-Sulpice to mourn a man whose company I miss more than any other. Paris was on strike as usual, and it was a struggle to get there. Inside the huge church Jacques-Yves Cousteau and Stephane Grappelli, both well into their eighties, looked so grief-stricken that I had to look away. There were tears pouring down Jeanne Moreau's face. I only knew Louis well for about three years, but as his wife Candice Bergen once said, 'There was no one whom you ever sat down to dinner with in more confident expectation of great conversation.'

Louis shared my fascination with techniques of storytelling. Once, we were meant to be working together on *Damage*, the film of Josephine Hart's novel. But I came into the restaurant for supper hugely dissatisfied with that morning's read-through of a play of mine called *Murmuring Judges*. 'It ought to bloody work,' I said, 'and it doesn't.' At once Louis asked me to tell him the story of the play. Together we sat for three hours, refining the narrative. Louis isolated every component of the story, and then put them all back together again in the right order. It was like watching a great car mechanic lay out the pieces of an engine on a clean white cloth before reassembling them. He did it for the sheer intellectual pleasure.

He wasn't a saint. We had written the synopsis of *Damage* together during some headbashing days when I was trying to take a holiday by myself on the beach at Ramatuelle. Louis had just turned up at my hotel and insisted I work. Every morning he would make me sit down under the vines and go back to the beginning of the story. He did it so many times that I thought I was going to go mad. 'Now, David, say once more, an MP comes home to his wife one evening, he comes into the house – what? that's through the front door, is it?' But while we worked, Louis rewarded me with stories about Brigitte Bardot and the Tour de France and Cousteau's bathyscaphe and the still-burning issue of collaboration. The French have made few honest films about the war. Louis made two of them – *Lacombe Lucien* and *Au revoir les enfants*.

Louis had a view on everything. He was shocked when I ate croissants or drank white wine, telling me all the time they'd kill me. He even taught me which red wine to drink with fish, to prolong my life. But it was Louis who died at sixty-three. 'He saved others. Himself he cannot save.'

Lindsay Duncan and Hilton McRae were also in the room. Nothing about this project moves me as much as being accepted as a performer by actors I admire, like Ian Holm and Alan Rickman and Lindsay. This morning I have resolved not to go the Middle East. I am letting Elyse down badly. She originated the project as part of her work in the area, so I feel guilty about this. But finally I don't want to lose the month of January, which will vanish if I do the Middle East and America. I want to be a writer again.

2 *October* I've always loved Patricia Highsmith's work because behind it lies the claim that, once you set your mind to it, any one human being can destroy any other. If I chose a name from the London telephone directory, it is my belief that I could, within six months, drive the elected person mad. It's that easy. There must be a measure of convention. We all agree to exercise the degree of self-control that stops us pushing each other off pavements in front of buses or trains. Out of good manners, we try to avoid committing suicide with the express intent of upsetting our families or punishing our ex-lovers for dumping us. It's a sort of discipline. We make the painful contract not to destroy each other.

Plays are equally easy to destroy. All you have to do is cough. Last night the first twenty minutes went fine, but as soon as I got to the settlements, the coughing began. I ducked and weaved around it. I stopped. I glared. I lowered my voice so that you wouldn't be able to hear me at all if you coughed. I came within an inch of stopping and asking the audience to make my work possible. Thank God I didn't. Shaking with anger, I began to emphasize every pro-Palestinian sentiment, and to bang home every anti-Israeli remark. I was electric during the passage 'We're all blind. We all see only what we want to. Don't we blank out the rest?' But it was too late. The show was sunk by then. There were no bravos. The play's soul wasn't there.

By a wonderful coincidence, Harold Pinter was. Wonderful, because he is the man who has most railed against coughing in the theatre. He instantly understood. 'It was aggressive,' he said. 'They weren't coughing because they were ill. They were out to wreck the show.' Harold said all the coughing came from one part of the house immediately in front of him. 'But you handled it like a pro,' he said, 'like a wonderful old pro.'

My whole life in the theatre has been marked by cards and letters from Harold, whom I have never once seen guard his position as the senior writer of the British theatre. He is the most generous and open-hearted of professional souls. I started to do my usual spiel about not really being an actor, and he grew impatient. 'Listen, listen, David! The thing is fucking marvellous. It's fucking marvellous.' I said that I owed a debt to Wally, and again, he shifted, interrupting me. 'I can see why you say that, but the thing we saw tonight is completely new. It's new and it's yours. There's nothing else like it. I want you to know' – Pinter pause – 'it's fucking marvellous!'

Something else came out of the horror. Lesley, the stage manager, came in to sympathize about the coughing, and Harold – who had never met her – started enthusing to her. Lesley looked at me and said, 'He's fantastic, isn't he?' In eight weeks she has never said a single qualitative word about the play. I found her pride in me in front of a playwright whom I admire very moving.

Earlier I had gone back to the radio studio, and redone my homework. We cleaned up a few passages, giving me a welcome chance to improve them. I then went to *The Blue Room*. Iain and Nicole were playing much better together, completely in the same genre and giving the same manner of performance. It's interesting. My friends don't much care for *The Blue Room*. Stephen Frears sent me a card saying he'd loved Nicole Kidman, but that his heart and head remained with *Via Dolorosa* from the night before. Richard Eyre rang me to say that you can't disguise the repetitiveness of the subject matter. For him, the play wasn't sexy. Why not? Because, he said, the actors were too clean. I have since tried to fathom the implications of this remark.

In fact almost nobody except my wife admits to being bowled over by the show. It's like *'Art'*. It's the biggest hit of the year, yet you never meet anyone who admits to having made it so. The West End producer Michael Codron once said of a play 'Oh nobody likes that play except the critics and the public.' His remark conveys the wry arrogance of the world I belong to, but I know what he meant.

While I've been working away on stage, and partly independent of anything I have contributed, *The Blue Room* has turned itself into a phenomenon. Nobody understands it, though I have developed some half-baked notion that it's to do with the loss of Diana.

The press wants Tom and Nicole – showbiz aristocracy – to replace the real aristocracy, who at the moment don't have anyone very interesting to offer. But my theory is as unknowing as everyone else's. Like all true freaks of popularity, *The Blue Room* infection can't really be explained.

People use the word 'hype'. Of course I resent it, because hype is what you do to something which isn't any good. *The Blue Room* has never been hyped. It does have a press agent, but I've never met her. On the contrary, it has successfully thrived on genuine word of mouth – people telling each other they've got to go. There's a certain amount of silliness attendant – Karl Lagerfeld saying he must come in specially from Paris for it, just because John Galliano did the week before – but, beyond that, there's a queue of people in the street, in all weathers, who want to see it because they've heard it's good. People come perhaps expecting a sassy sex revue and go away, some of them thoughtful about the ways in which we all use sex and romance to further our own ends. It has a real undertow, and it works.

I am obstinately fond of it. It's something the theatre never does successfully – to be charming and erotic and clever, all at the same time. Watching again, I felt a pang of professional remorse. How I wish I'd been around to see it through properly. I also suddenly felt that I had missed a big trick by not making the au pair a man. That way, the student could be bisexual and the cab driver could be in the closet. When I tried the idea out on Nicole Kidman, she was thrilled. She's always wanted to play a bloke. 'I'm tall and I'm thin. Let's do it.' I told her to ring Sam Mendes.

The problem is that the show is internationally publicized. Her success is not an arts story in the US, it's a news story. It would be impossible to make such a change quietly. At a baseball game in San Diego the other night a man called out to Tom Cruise: 'Where's your wife?' He answered, 'Doing a play in London.' The fan responded at once. 'Oh yeah. Is that the sexy one where she plays five parts?' Cruise grinned back. 'Yeah. That's the one.'

3 October It's now Saturday morning and I am writing this on the day we are due to close. I woke at 5.30 a.m., my body achingly insisting that I stay alert for the last lap. Yesterday Robert Fox, Stephen and I had a meeting to decide about New York. The Public Theater say they want me, but keep making difficulties. I can't face a management that thinks it's doing me a favour. This morning there is a fax from André Bishop wanting to produce it at the Lincoln Center – 'funny, sad, smart, *perfect* . . . your astonishing performance.' Robert thinks that if we present it commercially then all my usual producers will want to invest. This is a little gang of Americans who always mount my plays there. The only dissenter is Scott Rudin, who, he says, really believes that it is more appropriate to do it downtown in a 50-seat theatre.

Yesterday, I went off to the cinema to fill the gap before the penultimate performance, and saw another of this new British genre where people have no lives or thoughts beyond their romantic relationships. It was called *Sliding Doors*. How weird life would be if nothing counted for anything except our partners. Then I met with Elyse to tell her how little I wanted to go to the Middle East. Ian Rickson called by to thank me. 'Are you coming to the show tonight?' 'No.' 'Will you be there for the closing tomorrow?' 'Oh, babysitting problems.'

The subsequent show was a riot – a huge, appreciative house, and an overall sensation of swimming in velvet again. I was terribly happy out there. Tim Rice came round afterwards with a friend from Pakistan. Then I went to a fundraising dinner at the Garrick Club. I knocked back some glasses of champagne in quick succession. The diners all seemed extremely brainy and fabulously rich, ranged round at tables of beautiful linen and glass. The room gleamed with oils. Boy, was I drunk! I really don't think it was the quantity of alcohol, so much as the combination of an empty stomach, fatigue and the somewhat alien surroundings.

The plan was that Stephen should ask me questions, so that I could be spared from preparing a formal speech. I have no real memory of what I said. I will have to ask Stephen whether I was incoherent, but I do remember becoming extremely passionate. I discoursed for a while about the falsity of so much art, and railed against *Saving Private Ryan*. I heard murmuring at the other side of the room and asked a woman if she disagreed with me. She smiled back, ominously. 'It doesn't matter whether we agree with you or not. We want to hear what you think.'

Stephen asked me why I'd been with the Tories on election night in 1997. 'For the same reason that I was with Labour in 1992. Because I love tragedy. And because, as a writer, I am opportunistically drawn to losers.' He asked if I saw *Via Dolorosa* as a signal to the future. I said, 'No, it's a throwback to the past, to the great days of seventies theatre, when you went to a play and came out knowing more, having been enlightened.' He then asked if I saw this play being influential. I said, I feared not. 'Michael Codron said to me the other day that the entire British theatre is disappearing in a Celtic mist. I'd added, Celtic mist and post-modernist despair.' All we were offered was personal politics, which, boiled down, means no politics at all. For a British theatre to put on Irish plays is all too often not an artistic policy, but an abdication of policy. I spoke of the Talmudic tradition and said that I admired nothing so much in Jewish thought as the idea that knowledge itself is beautiful. Life may be awful, as weedy little plays insist, but the struggle to make it less awful is what marks us.

Or something like that. Is that what I said? Who knows? I remember some drunken phrase about too many theatres making policy from a 'diarrhoeic slop of personal politics and Oirishness.' I believe I quoted Raymond Chandler to the effect that pessimism and syntax are the opium of the middle classes. I did mercifully pull myself together to wind up with some remarks about how heroic it was to give money to the Court because it had presented the best work of serious writers like Athol Fugard, and cradled so many important British playwrights, except Harold Pinter. (When I worked at the Royal Court, I was told that after *The Birthday Party* closed so quickly, Harold Hobson demanded in the *Sunday Times* that the Court *must* now do Harold Pinter. Apocryphally, George Devine came in next day, threw down the paper, and said, 'I'm damned if I'll do what a theatre critic tells me.')

Waiting to drive me home, as he has every night, was Shakur, who is from Uganda. He got a scholarship to study medicine in Russia, learnt Russian and qualified as a doctor. He was told his qualifications were no use in Britain, so he has started all over again. He studies all day and drives a cab all night. He sleeps for three to four hours. By Saturday (I have experience of this) he's useless. He leaves only Monday aside to spend with his child and his wife who is a nurse at Greenwich hospital. He will one day return home to practise medicine in Uganda.

Let's write plays for Shakur.

4 *October* And so, last night it ended, very quickly. The morning brought an article by Simon Callow saying that I wasn't a very good actor ('I can imagine the text being better delivered') but the reality of my own pain makes it more impressive than anything an actor can do. The headline was GREAT PERFORMER WANTED: ACTORS NEED NOT APPLY. He said my departure at the end of the play was as moving as anything in Beckett: the writer, alone, facing the uncertainty of faithlessness. He also opined: 'Mike Yarwood he ain't.'

A fantastic postcard came from Julie Christie saying it was one of the three best plays she'd ever seen 'but you know my taste is very peculiar . . . those of us who love you are so proud of you'. An extraordinary matinée, perhaps the best audience I've ever had, and certainly the best matinée of a play of mine I've ever seen. They cheered like lunatics at the end, and there were knots of people at the stage door, all wanting to shake my hand. Then the evening enjoyable too, if not at quite the same pitch. I got tired and began to feel half way through that the pan-fried *foie gras* I'd had between the two shows was probably a mistake. A lovely group of people including Samantha Bond and Ian McNeil's family came to my dressing room, but I had to throw them out because I had the stage crew, lighting team, sound team and stage management due for a glass of champagne, as a way of saying thank you. Elyse brought in a tray of sweet pastries she had brought back earlier that day from Ramallah. I said that doing a one-man show is bloody hard work, and it's only been possible because everyone who works on the stage has been so continually supportive and friendly. Every night they have treated me with same courtesy and understanding. They're great.

Back from Paris, Nicole was too tired to join us for dinner. I went to Orso's with my American agent, Sam Cohn. Sam said the play was like a judgment from the Supreme Court – a piece of inspirational prose which definitively addresses a particular issue. He refused to discuss theatres in New York. 'How can you discuss what theatre to put scripture into?'

I am used to being patronized by my peers about *The Blue Room*, who all talk of it as if it were a meteorite which has landed from space. I get quite taken aback when I meet someone from the profession who genuinely loves it. But Sam was happy with that one, too, and so the evening went by in a pleasant haze of grilled chicken and red wine. Earlier Stephen had tried to make a speech to me, but we both knew it was the wrong night to do it. He had been pleased that I had not forced the last performance at all, that I had played it as if it were one more show like any other. I said that wasn't hard to do. It seemed natural, because I had known that it was not the last time I would do the play. 'Exactly,' he said. I said, 'It wasn't a closing, it was an opening.'

POSTSCRIPT: A legible ad for *Via Dolorosa* finally appeared in the *Sunday Times* on 4 October. It advertised a play which had closed the night before.

PART TWO

My Wife is George Bush

22 *February* 1999 I had been planning to re-start my diary en route to New York where it's been decided I am to present *Via Dolorosa* for a fourteen-week run, starting on 3 March. But yesterday something so terrible happened that I am responding in the only way I understand.

Sarah Kane killed herself. She was the young author of four plays. *Blasted* caused a terrific furore in 1995 at the Theatre Upstairs. *Cleansed* was at the Duke of York's in early 1998. And *Crave* was in the Theatre Upstairs just at the same time I was doing *Via Dolorosa*. She was twenty-seven. For a week now Stephen Daldry and I have been re-rehearsing in Islington for the five performances I shall give at the Almeida. These have been planned as a way of sharpening me up before we go to New York. As soon as I heard the news I reached for the phone and spoke to Stephen who had spent the weekend understandably shattered.

It was Stephen who first presented Sarah Kane's work at the Royal Court. It was he who protected her and defended her when that work unleashed a storm of synthetic protest as sanctimonious as anything Britain has seen since the première of *Saved*. Stephen said that Sarah suffered from manic depression. The lows could last up to eighteen months. She had felt herself going into a new cycle of depression and had been admitted into a hospital. On the first night there she was not able to face going down again into what she feared would be a long cycle.

By chance, yesterday was our first day on stage in the Almeida, and we tried gamely to get on with our work. Lesley, who is thankfully back with us for this brief London revival, had been the stage manager for two of Sarah's shows at the Royal Court. When Stephen broke the news to her she coloured, and nearly fell. 'Sarah wasn't equipped for life,' Lesley said, 'she didn't know what reality was.' Stephen's mobile phone kept going and we had to stop our rehearsals a few times for him to make memorial remarks to newspapers. At one point, he went off to do a live interview on the radio. He told the programme: 'They won't be lowering the lights on Shaftesbury Avenue, but they will be lowering them in the Deutschestheater in Berlin.'

I was working with two people who knew Sarah Kane well. Obviously, that was partly the reason why the event hit our little group so hard. But we knew it had a power beyond that. The suicide of this young playwright illustrated all too clearly the problems writers wrestle with all the time. Sarah Kane had been writing plays which were unashamedly bleak and excoriating, and for this the press had dismissed her as someone who must necessarily be in bad faith. They said she was out to shock. To my shame, I would have said that the young always feel that life is irredeemably awful and has no point.

We live in a period in which people do not stand by what they say. We slip around, redefining all the time. The characteristic intellectual pronouncements of our time are 'That's not exactly what I'm saying' or 'I don't think you've quite understood me.' Because art involves artifice, it always attracts the charge of pretence. By killing herself Sarah Kane had blown away that charge. It was shocking because she was young. As Stephen said, it was worse because she was a woman. There's such a history in this century of female literary suicide. But why exactly are we surprised when it turns out she meant what she said?

23 *February* This morning everyone is boiling Sarah Kane's bones to make soup. The newspapers are full of critics repositioning themselves, admitting they wronged Sarah Kane while she was alive. They rush to praise her now she's dead. Or else they use her for their own purposes. On LBC radio, as I drove in to work, they said: 'Sex and Violence Playwright Killed Herself In Her Own Flat.' The disrespect of that 'Sex and Violence' phrase seemed to me stunning.

I found myself staring at a remark by the great American essayist, Janet Malcolm. It's typically provocative: 'The truth does not make a good story; that's why we have art.'

When I got to the theatre everyone was having a purgative bitch about the media. Stephen had found *The Times*'s reporting of Sarah's death particularly inaccurate and spiteful. But he also, thank God, seemed to have got his spirits back, in spite of his anger at the usual broadsheet antics. Before the shock of Kane's death, we'd been rehearsing for a week and I'd never seen Stephen happier. But then, why shouldn't he have been? The work we'd been doing was extraordinarily interesting.

I knew from the start that a revival of *Via Dolorosa* would be judged on different terms. Richard Eyre had rung me before I'd started re-rehearsing and said, 'It's going to be difficult for you this time, because part of the power of the show was that it seemed so dangerous. It seemed charged because you didn't really know what you were doing. But now people are going to expect expertise.' I said I'd already worked that out for myself. I couldn't get away with 'Aw shucks, I'm not really an actor.' I said to Richard: 'This time I've got to go head to head with Kevin Spacey.'

To this ridiculous end, I put aside time early in January to see if I could remember the lines. Fascinatingly, they came back to me in the form I first learned them – before we made all our changes, in fact. Just as old people can recall their childhood but tend to forget their middle age, so I could remember all the text as I learnt it the very first time. But the rewrites and cuts that I had done in rehearsal were lost to me and hard to re-find. It is the first act of memory which cuts the deepest groove.

Later, other actors told me that I was lucky not to have had to learn anything in between. You can retain a whole play as long as you close the run knowing that you will one day open again. The mind, like a computer, simply retains the information and you download it comparatively easily. The problems start when you have closed believing you will never play the part again, or when you have had to learn another part in the meanwhile.

Once I had accessed the whole text – and it only really took a day – then Stephen and I had the luxury of profound reinterpretation. I had always been open to the charge that the play is, effectively, What I Did On My Holidays. From the very start Stephen has insisted that *Via Dolorosa* should not be a political account of a particularly fascinating subject. It must be a demonstration of how that subject overwhelms me and my own private beliefs. For months he said to me: 'It's not about Israel. It's about you.'

It is only by taking the play back into the garage and beginning to re-rehearse it have I been able to begin to effect this crucial shift of emphasis. It is only now that I have begun to have sufficient confidence in my own technique to let myself be moved by the subject matter – or indeed, on occasions, to *pretend* (for that's what it comes to) to let myself be moved by the subject matter. At the Royal Court I stopped short of doing what I would call 'faking' emotions for two reasons. First, because I imagined faking was dishonourable – a morally bad thing to do. (But what else is acting?) And secondly, I suspected that I didn't have the technique to get away with it, anyway.

But now, with the wind behind me, and with the confidence of knowing that the show, in some fundamental sense, *works*, I have set off on an extraordinary new course: I have begun to expose myself to the material and let it be seen to move and affect me in my own deepest being. Or – pretend it does.

This approach to the show is forcing changes which we both find exciting. After we ran through in the rehearsal room, Lesley said that I looked much more involved now, as if the visit to the Middle East had cost me something. Sometimes, she said, when I did it at the Royal Court, I looked detached. The result was that she used to think the show looked 'arrogant'. I didn't ask Lesley what she meant because, in my heart, I knew. The remark has stayed with me. But as Stephen and I fell over each other in our eagerness to re-examine every section of the play and to yield new insights, I kept thinking: If this is now so much better, how terrible it must have been when it first opened!

25 February Last night I did my first show of 1999, after a gap of just under five months. Samuel Beckett once confided to Peter Brook that for him a play was a ship sinking not far from the coast while the audience watches helplessly from the cliffs as the gesticulating passengers drown. Frankly, that's what it felt like last night.

I had been boasting, foolishly, for the last ten days that I wasn't feeling nervous this time, and that I could be completely relaxed on stage. I was humiliatingly wrong. Two hours before the show was due to start, I became rigid with fear, unable to take in the simplest direction. When I stepped out on to the stage I was like a drunken ice skater. In the Almeida the audience seemed much nearer than I expected and I didn't know whether I was too loud or too soft. I could also see them more clearly than at the Royal Court. I went through most of the show on auto-pilot but with a soft gear box. I thought I was far too fast, but afterwards Stephen told me, no, on the contrary, I was too slow. That's a measure of how hopelessly out of control I was. When I tried, as Stephen had asked, to be much more emotional, I felt that my efforts were reading as plain nervousness.

I learnt a series of lessons. First, I have had a fantasy that this time I would be able to do the show at less cost. Last year the whole of my day was taken up in nervous preparation. I had the idea this time I would be able to swan into the theatre and do the show. I was wrong. I can't. I am facing the prospect of a terrifying four months.

Second, the work is in transition, and I don't really know what I'm doing with each passage. Rehearsal is 100 per cent different from performance. The moment I got out there, it was if all the guide ropes which had steered me across the crevasse were gone. Wally always says that the only thing you can be sure of in life is that nothing feels the way you thought it was going to. That's the only thing I can tell a young actor. When you go out there, the heat, the adrenalin, the crazy tensions of the night smash through your plans like an axe through balsa wood. The great wind of an audience blows through, and nothing is what you thought it was going to be.

Third – and this is the only good news – however badly I did it there was a palpable sense of the audience wanting this play. The silences were so deep. I could tell there were fewer Jews in the audience than there had been at the Royal Court, so that certain lines did not receive the laughter of recognition. But this also meant that the Palestinian material cut much deeper. As the evening went on, you could feel the authentic sense of an audience travelling to the heart of real subject matter.

On BBC television on Sunday night, they showed the Tricycle Theatre's play about the Stephen Lawrence inquiry, *The Colour of Justice*. It proved everything I have always believed. Let real life in the door and you will create something as profound, as compelling and as unexpected as most of the plays which are brewed up inside a playwright's imagination. There has been no greater scandal in recent years than the murder of the eighteen-year-old Lawrence, and the subsequent failure of the police to pursue the case against the gang of white racist youths who are alleged to have killed him. The writer, Richard Norton-Taylor, had needed to do no more than organize and edit the long transcript of the judicial hearings. Set forth before you were all the nuances and intricacies of British racism with a clarity no other medium can achieve. No written article ever came close to creating a sense of the culture as vividly as this riveting two hours of drama.

People *want* this kind of work. You could feel it last night – to a point where Stephen and I sat afterwards in a restaurant discussing whether we should come back to the Almeida later. It seemed silly to be doing only five performances. People thirst for this kind of recognition of real life. Yet we go on offering them Noël fucking Coward and domestic gagfests. It makes me furious.

26 *February* Last night was much better, thank God. Or I thought it was. It turns out it was far too fast – I cut four minutes from the previous night. But at least I felt confident out there. An actor has to go out believing that what he has to tell the audience is worth saying. If he doesn't have that, then he's lost. I refused to let anyone visit my dressing room afterwards, because I felt better and, frankly, at this moment, I don't want to risk being told otherwise.

Stephen told me later that he'd said to Lesley, with eerie prescience, that if ever I was going to forget my lines it would be tonight. He was right. Quite a few times, I found myself hanging in the air without the slightest idea of what I was going to say next. It always happened after I'd just attempted some new piece of interpretation. Because the rhythm was unsettled, I then didn't know what followed. I rely for my performance on a drilled sense-memory, a kind of deep groove from which I can depart, but which is always there underneath for me to return to. These newly rehearsed passages – Miriam, in the settlements, for instance – do not yet have that groove and I wobble around alarmingly, like a vehicle out of control.

I woke up reciting the limerick by Maurice Hare (no relation).

There once was a man who said 'Damn!
It is borne in upon me I am
An engine that moves
In predestinate grooves
I'm not even a bus, I'm a tram.'

27 February Hectic day, having to run around because I'm leaving for America in a few days. A morning meeting with publishers in Bloomsbury, then lunch in Holland Park with Cate Blanchett and Jonathan Kent to talk about their imminent revival of my old play *Plenty*. And all the tubes running late. Central Line, Northern Line: no bloody difference. The result was, I arrived at the theatre completely frazzled and exhausted. I went out and did my best show. Who knows anything?

A beautiful note from a Member of the European Parliament who saw the show: 'All the passion has gone out of politics. We have to go to art for our passion now.'

28 February Last night there was an awful incident. Elyse Dodgson had asked me if she could bring twenty-five Palestinians to have a drink with me in the green room after the second Saturday show. I said I didn't think it was a good idea because I had to do two shows, at 6 p.m. and 9 p.m., and I was certain to be tired. Further, I said, I've made it a rule not to meet organized groups because it seems to me to dilute the event. The play is saying complicated things which take time to assimilate. People's feelings about the event may change a lot in the coming weeks – for good or bad. People have listened to me for an hour and a half. Surely now they should talk among themselves. But Elyse begged me, saying it would be very quick and purely social.

The only advantage of getting old is that you develop a skill for avoiding stupid situations. Last night I blew that advantage big-time. The Palestinians arrived. We gave them all champagne and tit-bits. One Palestinian, in his fifties, with an academic appearance, made his way over to me and said he'd found the play very disturbing. I said, undoubtedly it was disturbing. It described a very disturbing situation. He said he didn't mean that. What he had found disturbing was that the Israelis had been presented as real human beings – warm, complicated, rounded. Whereas the Palestinians were shown as flat, caricatured, and boring.

I thanked him for saying this and pointed out gently that perhaps this wasn't the moment to go into it. We were, after all, at a party, not a discussion group. But the man knew that everything had gone quiet. The Almeida green room is tiny and cramped at the best of times, but now it was like the Marx Brothers film where they see how many people they can get into a ship's cabin. My critic saw the opportunity for a confrontation and he wasn't going to pass it up. 'Because your own wife is Jewish, you extend a sympathy to the Israelis which you don't extend to us. You make Jews out to be real people. But you don't show us in the same way. You're biased.'

By now I was not in control. I was very quiet, but I was shaking with anger. I said it was offensive to me to accuse me of bad faith. I had spent a very long time writing the show and even more time preparing to perform it. He was the first person – Palestinian or not – ever to make this particular complaint. It was possible to criticize all sorts of elements in the show – and certainly to dispute what I was saying. But what you could not do was cast doubt on my fundamental fairness towards the Palestinians.

The man, however, was loving the situation. He'd brought the entire party to a standstill, and he was determined to exploit the situation to the full. There was that sort of crazy charged silence where you can tell everyone's brains are racing and nobody knows how to stop things getting wildly out of hand. The man went on and on, saying, 'It just isn't true. You like the Israelis. You come across as not liking us.'

At this point, we had a full-scale problem. There were about forty people in the green room, glasses in hand. A few tried to intervene.

One woman said, 'Well I'm Palestinian and I don't know what our friend here is talking about. It was a sympathetic portrayal of our people – it's the first one there's ever been.' The Palestinian Representative was shifting from foot to foot, putting his hand on my arm and saying, 'It's one man's opinion, David. It isn't anyone else's.'

The Palestinian Representative (he would be the Ambassador were Palestine a state) had brought his teenage daughter and her friends. They all had painted white faces and vividly dyed hair, so they could look like vampires. There followed an odd moment when the ruined party tried haltingly to resume. A man shaking with anger (me) was smiling and pretending to do small talk with a little group of female mini-Draculas.

The man who had made the scene came back to me more quietly, but he didn't apologize or back down. He said, 'It's my honest opinion.' I said, 'Honest, it's not. There's a fine line between being rude and being honest. You could see I was exhausted. You knew you were a guest at a party of which I was one of the hosts. If you felt so strongly you shouldn't have come backstage. Write to me. You knew you could bring the party to a halt. An honest opinion is one that is expressed in a way which gives your opponent an equal chance of answering. A rude opinion is expressed in a way which makes answering impossible.'

Things eventually passed off. Palestinians pressed to talk to me. Some tried nobly to compensate, while others expressed honest reservations about particular passages. This didn't bother me. When one man queried whether turds floated down the street in Gaza, it seemed to me a perfectly fair thing to ask, since it was coming from someone who had no desire to grandstand, or show off. He lived in Gaza City and he wanted to know.

Afterwards, I was upset because – as after all such occasions – I felt I had handled it badly, and contributed by my own behaviour to the spoiling of everyone's evening. The man had got me in that terrible double-bind where someone's very purpose is to make you feel angry with yourself for not being better at dealing with something which isn't your fault. If I hadn't risen to him, then things would not have got so bad. But here's the horror of the thing: I can't *not* rise.

My investment in the show leaves me hopelessly exposed. At the moment when I come off, you can no more tell me that my play is in bad faith than tell a wild dog please not to gnaw at that piece of dead sheep. I'm not yet, as it were, a professional actor.

The aim of a grandstander is to make everybody feel terrible – and, in that, they invariably succeed. The Representative was mortified because it had been his idea to invite everyone to meet me. Elyse was equally horrified because she had prevailed on me against my better judgment in the first place. And all the other guests looked like they wished the ground could swallow them up.

Nicole said two things. First, it was odd that it hadn't happened before, given the nature of the material. But second, it was odd that it had happened at the Almeida. The week has been curious and a little dismaying in that respect. I think of the Almeida as a sort of home, but if I am honest the audience this week has been less involved than at the Court. I spent the first half of this diary moaning about Royal Court culture. But their audience was superb. At the Almeida, I didn't get the same gasps or knowing laughter on individual lines. The audience at the Court was full of experts, a lot of them Israeli, whose involvement in the material was apparent in their response to every word. Much as I love the Almeida, their public has been more detached. It wasn't an evening of the heart. They were there to learn. I am slightly shocked to realize how apolitical this beautiful theatre is. Islington turns out to be a politics-free zone. Since Tony Blair's favourite restaurant, Granita, is three hundred yards away, perhaps I shouldn't be too surprised. It's a tribute to Tony.

Of course, as I am about to head to New York, I may look back on this period of cool-headed audiences with some considerable nostalgia.

2 *March* To America. And bliss it was, because the 8 a.m. American Airlines flight was almost empty. I recommend it. You can stretch out across the seats and be calm. I watched *There's Something About Mary*. In the States the film was received as being the end of civilization as we know it. But it didn't seem to me nearly as

offensive as, say, *When Harry Met Sally*. For a start, it isn't twee. And at least there are bits which make you laugh.

I tried to read a novel on the way over but, like many playwrights, I find novels a bit of a struggle unless they're in the top flight. For years I read mostly thrillers, because the English novel seems so inward-looking and constrained, a prisoner of its limited style. In my lifetime, the novel has rarely matched the range or depth of the performing or the visual arts. Too many novels seem unformed when compared with plays. You can throw in everything, including the kitchen sink.

It's interesting that the outstanding contemporary novelist in English, Philip Roth, became fascinated by the theatre when he lived in England. He particularly admired Steven Berkoff. Roth's late masterpieces have had an impressive dramatic line, which any playwright would recognize and kill for. Doris Lessing's best writing is informed with her love of plays. Gore Vidal believes that only film and television can teach the novelist 'the discipline of relevance'. It isn't chance that the some of the best British novelists – Salman Rushdie and Ian McEwan, for instance – developed most at the point when they said that they identified more with their contemporaries who were dramatists than they did with fellow-novelists. 'Every writer of fiction writes, in fact, for the stage,' said Charles Dickens. That's the reason Dickens' work is so much more popular than anyone else's. It's dramatic.

By contrast, Martin Amis remarked that writing plays must be easy, since they were 'only dialogue' and everyone knows that dialogue is the easiest bit to write in novels. I don't think Henry James would necessarily have agreed. James never recovered from hearing his play *Guy Domville* booed to extinction in 1895. Saul Bellow gave up the stage after the disaster of *The Last Analysis*. Graham Greene never found the same power in the theatre that he displayed so brilliantly in his novels. Having once seen a film with dialogue by Martin Amis, the kindest thing to be said is that Amis has a certain way to go before he's in any position to prove his case.

On arrival, I unpacked, then hurried to the Booth Theatre to find my old stage manager Karen Armstrong waiting for me. We're veterans, she and I. I liked Karen the first day she walked in as an assistant stage manager, when I was directing *A Map of the World* in 1985. She still has her beautiful mane of red hair and her incomparable solicitousness. But we haven't worked together for ten years – since I last directed on Broadway, in fact. It was lucky for me that the musical *On the Town* closed two weeks ago, so she's been freed up for this.

The set looked terrific. The Booth is, by common consent, the best dramatic house on Broadway, with its sober wood panelling and air of unforced intimacy. But it has one major drawback for our show. It has no door in its back wall through which I can enter. Everyone who saw the play in London remarked on the manner of my entrance and exit – it's the bit Simon Callow described so enthusiastically – so it has been necessary for Ian McNeil to build a whole fake back wall a few feet in front of the real one. In London we had a model of Jerusalem which came up from the excavated floor. Here in New York, the vision of Jerusalem will be revealed behind a moving piece in the fake wall. It will be a superb piece of trickery. Ian's beautiful pipework snakes across the empty stage and charges the whole stage with the romantic spirit of old Broadway.

The play is being presented here by the Lincoln Center, a nonprofit organization based uptown. When we first thought of coming to New York, we had been approached by about eight managements. But my regular producer, Robert Fox, said that he thought that it would be inappropriate to produce the show commercially. He's right. It isn't that kind of material. It would be wrong to be trying to make money out of this particular subject matter. The show has its own integrity. So also must the way in which it's presented.

As a result we searched downtown for a while for an off-off Broadway venue, but didn't come up with a suitable space. A whole lot of plans to play in temples or halls were considered. For a few weeks the air rang with that most dreaded of all vogue words: 'site-specific.' But the perfect place for the play – hey! – turned out to a theatre. And the theatre happened to be on Broadway. Robert came up with the idea that I should ask André Bishop and Bernie Gersten whether they would be willing to present me in a theatre not their own. We could benefit from their regular audience, who would cushion us against the harsh commercial reality of trying to present such an unusual show. Most important, their subvention would mean that we could offer the work at a lower price. Normally, you pay $60 for best stalls. For Lincoln Center subscribers, the price is $30.

I have worked twice before with André and Bernie. They mounted an excellent production of *Racing Demon* at the Lincoln Center, and then had Kevin Kline play the leading role in my adaptation of Chekhov's early play *Ivanov*. The two of them were waiting for me reassuringly at the side of the stage. André always looks a little lugubrious because he speaks slowly and thoughtfully at all times. But there's no mistaking his warmth towards the work he likes. I feel among friends.

On this second outing, I am to have an assistant. I can hardly wait. The point hardly needs labouring. At the Court I used to perform alone, facing a whole town council of underlings and auxiliaries, whereas one of the first things the Lincoln Center said to me was that, surely, I couldn't possibly hope to manage all by myself? How would I like it if they gave me someone to help? They had lined up three terrific choices, all over-qualified. The third intrigued me with a CV which said she was an expert in the migration of data. I plumped for her at once. I feel data has been migrating from me my whole life – life often seems to consist of little else – and if she can stop it, she's my ideal. Her name is Gabrielle Reznek. She starts today.

Then, disaster. Robert Fox rang to say that Nicole Kidman cannot finish the run of *The Blue Room* in New York. In December the play transferred here for a limited run. It is to close ten days before its intended final performance. Nicole has contracted a bronchial infection and damaged her vocal chords. On Thursday there was a gala to raise money for the Donmar. Her doctors advised Nicole not to do it, but she felt she could not let the Donmar down. Half way through her voice gave out. She started haemorrhaging in her throat. She has been told that if she works in the next few weeks she will get nodules on her throat and lose her voice completely. She is communicating by scribbling on a yellow pad.

I am devastated. It seems such a disappointing end to what has been an inspiring story. Nicole arrived in a rehearsal room in Kennington last July with only sketchy experience of how to act on stage. Since then, she has jumped every obstacle put in front of her. To see her fall at the last hurdle, and through no fault of her own, seems unbearably sad. It leaves you with a feeling of non-consummation.

The Blue Room has certainly been one of the odder events of my life. To the very end, the show kept its power. When one of its producers, Scott Rudin, saw it ten days ago, he said it was better than ever before. It confounded those people who had called it bitty, moving with a fluency and cohesion it had never had at the beginning. But the whole experience reminded me of something Degas said: 'There are some kinds of success which are indistinguishable from panic.'

The hysteria in New York never died down. Even in February when conventional wisdom told us that the snow would disperse the hundreds of fans, there were still the same crowds in the street waiting for Nicole. If it was sex that excited the English response, then here it was fame. People stood in the street because they thought they might catch a sight of a film actor, whether starring or visiting.

I must admit that, back in England, I've felt an intense rush of relief in the last month or two as I've watched the arc light pass off us and move on to *Shakespeare in Love*. Throughout the autumn the *Evening Standard* carried a picture of Nicole Kidman in her fishnet tights and miniskirt every day. Now the honour goes to the doelike Gwyneth Paltrow. In my memory, it was F. R. Leavis who described the publication of some poems by Edith Sitwell as 'an event more in the history of publicity than of literature'. Well, now it is the merry Elizabethans who can rise above jibes like that.

Some people found *The Blue Room*'s sexuality cold. For others, that was the whole point. For them, sex between strangers is uniquely exciting. I did everything I could to warm the play up, to stop it being mechanical. But the mechanical element is part of the point. There is a limit to what you can do without betraying the original work. In this way, show business is predestinately cruel. Richard Eyre told me that, before attempting a production of *Macbeth*, he made a list of every possible trap and error awaiting a director of that notoriously difficult work. He then proceeded to walk straight into every single one of them.

An element of evasion enters whenever a work is about sex. When I see revivals of *Look Back in Anger*, I'm always astonished that no one remarks that the play's true shock value and originality lies in its unusual focus on bed. (Why else, for goodness' sake, was Kenneth Tynan so drawn to it?) Before its première in 1956, the leading practitioners of British theatre were T. S. Eliot, whose attitude to bed, I think we may say, was somewhat to the right of mistrustful, and Noël Coward, who made no secret of thinking of bed as a place where you merely endanger your dignity and your sense of humour. Along comes John Osborne, childish or child-like according to your own point of view, but anyway with a D. H. Lawrence-like conviction that people can't be known, can't be understood except through the act of love. The character of Helena – the woman who affects to despise Jimmy Porter, but who longs to sleep with him – is there to tell you that nothing which is said outside bed matters. Nor does it for Jimmy. Rail and rationalize all you like, it's bed where the real business is done. My God, no wonder the play still takes the audience aback! No wonder Osborne's achievement is to this day resented.

Perhaps that's why I've been amused to see how much *The Blue Room* has rattled one or two of my colleagues. A fellow playwright got angry with me, as if it were my fault. 'It's because of the nudity. It's only because of the nudity. The day Iain Glen said, "Why don't we take our clothes off?" was the day *The Blue Room*'s fate was sealed.' He said it with terrific purpose, like a man trying to close a door in a high wind.

When I go into a video shop, I always think the saddest-looking films are the ones that have been over-publicized. In the long run, acclaim steals magic. It doesn't add to it. Meryl Streep, in the early days of her fame, told me she was once travelling on the subway and saw her own picture in a newspaper underneath her foot. Without even thinking who it was, she said to herself, 'Oh God, not her again.'

Because I am proud of *The Blue Room*, my last hope – given that it does seem to have closed for ever – is that my memory of it will not be tinged with that sadness.

I went home last night and moved into the loft I'm renting for the next three months. Before I went to sleep, I turned on the TV and watched Bob Dole, the Republican presidential candidate of 1996, talking about his problems with erectile dysfunction. He said, 'It takes courage to talk about these things. But courage is something I've never lacked.' Only in America. William Hague has been meeting American Republicans to pick up tips on how to make yourself more voter-friendly. We'll know young William is desperate for votes when he decides it's time to tell us about the failure of his erections.

3 March Yesterday we had our first day's rehearsal in the Booth. Predictably, last week's party-wrecker had planted the seeds of doubt in my mind, and I'd begun to ask myself whether there was any justice in his objections. In the second half of the play, the heart of the Palestinian case is presented by Haider Abdel Shafi, the patrician statesman in Gaza. Over the weekend, I decided that I was playing him too aristocratically, endowing him with a high-born manner which got in the way of what he was saying – that Palestine is in no shape to negotiate with Israel until it sorts out its internal problems of corruption. Shafi represents what I take to be the finest ideal of Islam – the belief that you must cleanse your own soul before you dare to attack other people's.

My own self-doubt was corroborated by a friend, Sabiha Rumani Malik. Sabiha had made her third trip to the play last week, and she recognized the original passage in the Koran which Shafi quotes. Mohammed returns from battle and says, 'We come back from the little strife and we return to the bigger strife. The strife of the soul.' Sabiha pointed out that the word in Arabic is *jihadi*, which doesn't really mean 'strife'. It implies 'crusade' as well. Shafi should not be a world-weary lounge lizard, but a man with a moral view, who sees life in terms of struggle *for* something – struggle *towards* something – not just struggle.

She's right. And her suggestion for correcting things is brilliant. She wants me to quote the original line in Arabic. The hope is that I will give the sentiment special authority by saying it in its true language. The idea of speaking Arabic on the Broadway stage excites me immoderately. The only drawback is that it's not the easiest group of syllables to learn: '*Raja na min al jihadi l-asgar ila l-jihadi l-akbar.*' Gabrielle is now getting a Lebanese friend to record them for me so that I don't make an utter prat of myself.

For the rest, we worked happily, not stretching ourselves too hard. As a group, the lighting designer, Rick, the designer, Ian, Stephen and I now have a sophisticated language between us, and a sense of common purpose, bonded by the memory of our own mistakes. I feared I'd offended Rick yesterday when I mentioned how many people said that they preferred his lighting at the Almeida to his original work. As the Almeida revival took him precisely two hours – he was busy doing another show – I was afraid he might think I was being rude. But Rick was smart enough to realize that it was a compliment. Once you capture the spirit of a work, you can create it more and more simply. The less sense of effort the better. Matisse said making a work of art should be like tying a perfect bow tie. You do it quickly, and if it doesn't work, you throw it in the laundry basket and tie another.

The odd man out among us is the newly joined local sound man who does not yet know how destructive any sense of show business is to this particular text. He has put a ridiculous series of floating microphones at the bottom of the stage to support my voice in the dodgier parts of the house. Their effect is making me sound like Liza Minnelli in full flight. They have the added disadvantage that they enhance my boots far more effectively than they enhance my words. You can hear my feet brilliantly, but nothing of what I'm saying.

4 *March* Yesterday was hideous. The worst day, in fact, since my early row with Stephen, and the most demoralizing. I didn't have to work until 3, but I noticed when I arrived that I was irritated with Stephen. He seemed to be wrapping me up in cotton wool, elaborately consulting me about everything to a point where – unfairly – I wanted to say: 'Look, it's your production. Please you do your work and I'll do mine.' I knew it was unjust, but his solicitousness

was making me feel that he must have come to think of me as an impossible prima donna who needs to be soothed all the time. But the problem with that approach is that it becomes a self-fulfilling prophecy. As soon as someone treats you that way, you start playing that role. It's horrible. Stephen was oppressively over-present, crowding me out, suffocating me. He suddenly seemed terribly large. His jeans, his boots and his pacamacs all seemed gargantuan. If he blew his nose once in my dressing room, he blew it fifty times. When I began to act, he would sit in the very front row, coughing a lot and usually jumping up to join me as soon as I began to speak. I wondered whether he'd prefer to be acting the show himself.

There is one director in England who is notorious for not letting an actor get out a single line before interrupting. 'If music be the –' and the actor doesn't even get to 'food' before this man's on his feet and saying, 'No, no, no, that's not how to say it.' It drives actors nuts. The director's art is to know when to be present and when to be absent. Stephen's behaviour today made me ashamed of all the times I've crowded actors out when I've been directing. We all do it.

So, plainly, I was antsy and looking for trouble. As always when you feel like that, trouble arrived. We began a run-through at 7 o'clock. I had got through four lines when I heard a door slamming below me and a security man shouting to another and then bursting into laughter. I stopped and said I couldn't very well act until we got some quiet. The deputy stage manager, Donna, went to deal with it and then we started again.

In the next hour, there was not a span of five minutes which was not interrupted by slamming doors, yelling and laughter. I battled through until we got to Haider Abdel Shafi, then I stopped and said that if I couldn't get silence, then it was impossible for me to go on. I said that famous actor's line, which I had never thought to hear myself say: 'I just can't work like this.'

The problem is that we have excavated the stage. Underneath it is not just the crew room and laundry room that you find in most theatres. No, this is the centre for the whole Shubert security operation – a sort of Broadway police station. To get to it, all these big guys have to walk directly underneath me – across the excavated area, in fact – in order to reach a space which serves as social centre, HQ and locker room. I hear everything they say.

We resumed after a break and carried on to the end of the play. I am now told that the Booth is notorious because it backs on to the far larger Shubert Theatre where loud musicals generally play. And, it's true, I could also hear the sound of *Chicago* reverberating through the walls. This didn't bother me because it's a *constant* sound – and, anyway, only I can hear it. It doesn't reach the audience. Nor can they hear the electric dimmers which provide another background noise behind me.

Obviously, I was in appalling spirits. If I can't trust that when I take a pause, it will be not be filled up by the sound of everyday life elsewhere, then I am finished. I throw a net of words across silence. No silence, no show. I was also aware that we had a major cultural problem. There is always a massive testosterone count in any Broadway theatre, as there is in a Hollywood film studio. They are places with primitive labour relations. They are crammed with big guys – real guys, macho guys – who walk around in blousons, trying to radiate the message that, although they work in the theatre, there's nothing nancy about them. 'Theatre?' they say. 'It's just like loading trucks.' On this occasion, it's not even the stage crew who are giving me trouble – on the contrary, they're impeccable – but instead it's a bunch of non-theatrical employees, who don't see why they shouldn't get on with their life while I get on with mine. There was a touch of aggression down there. 'Why should that pansy need silence for his work? We don't need silence for ours.' At one point I looked down to the pit as if to say, 'Please be quiet', and found a security woman staring back up at me, hands on hips, as if to say 'Why the fuck should I?'

At times like this you feel the frailty of the theatre, and its artificiality – how what we call life has to stop in order for us pampered creatures to flutter around in conditions of extreme unnaturalness. If the convention can't be controlled, then the illusion can't be created.

I went back to my dressing room. A few days ago it looked grim and depressing. But the wardrobe supervisor, who doubles as my dresser and whose name is Danny Paul, has transformed it with carpets and furniture, so that it now seems positively elegant. Stephen came up, and we opened a bottle of wine. He said, 'What are we asking for?' I said, 'We're asking for the headquarters of the Shubert security organization to be moved. It can go upstairs in the unoccupied dressing rooms for the length of the run.' Stephen looked at me in that slightly ambiguous, thoughtful way he has. We both know that the only person who can order the move is Gerry Schoenfeld, the head of the Shubert organization, who has housed all my Broadway work. The point about Gerry is that management consultants would describe his organization as vertically structured. Another way of putting it: he's the boss. I could feel Stephen quail for a moment.

Before he could load it on to me, I immediately said, 'Stephen, it's not my problem. It's up to you and Bernie Gersten. It will not be creative for me to spend tomorrow having a row with Gerry Schoenfeld. If I waste a day shouting and screaming then it will not finally help the performance I have to give on Friday night. At this point, it's your job to protect me.' Stephen agreed. 'Yes, yes, of course. You're right. You're right.' But he was still thoughtful.

A car came to pick me up. The driver asked me where I wanted to go. I said, 'Thompson Street.' He said he didn't know where it was. I said, 'Just head for SoHo.' He asked me which route he should take. I said, 'Look, I'm a visitor here. You've lived here longer than me . . .' He interrupted, proud. 'I've been a driver here for twenty-three years.' I said, 'Yes, well, if you've lived here twenty-three years, then surely you have some idea by now where SoHo is.' We travelled in humourless silence the rest of the way, both of us thinking what a pig I am.

5 March I had the morning off, so I went for a walk through the streets of SoHo, seeing how it had changed. New York always makes my feelings disorderly. I first came here in the terrible muggy summer of 1965. I was eighteen and the humidity was like soup. It was the first time I saw a man dying in the gutter – a man with the blackest skin I'd ever seen. By contrast, the huge stain across his back was a shocking bright scarlet. I had to sell vacuum cleaners, door to door. I didn't make much money, but at the time it cost only a dollar to hear Sonny Rollins at the Village Vanguard. For supper, we ate food which the supermarkets threw out at the end of the day. My schoolfriend Roger and I lived in a strange youth hostel which was suspiciously cheap on the Lower East Side. There turned out to be a good reason for its cheapness.

Thirteen years later, I arrived in New York with the aim of living here, as so many English people have before me – exhausted, like everyone else, with the class system and the lethargy of living in Britain. I thought 'America's different. America's democratic.' I stayed a year, living in SoHo, six blocks away from where I am now, and on the same street. It had dazzling views of Little Italy which, at night, seemed to be lit in the Technicolor gels of a film by Vincente Minnelli – ravishing ambers and warm, sensual terracottas. Two of my children were born uptown, fifteen minutes after the end of a hair-raising taxi ride through Manhattan traffic jams to St Luke's Hospital. Lewis and Darcy were given American passports and told they could choose to be American citizens at the age of twenty-one.

Throughout the eighties, I worked here in New York a lot, directing my own work, always for Joe Papp who made me lavishly welcome in his six-auditorium palace on Lafayette Street. It was a form of disgruntled exile, I suppose. But hating England isn't a good enough reason for living in America. My emotional life was centred here, grounded here, year after year. One night, I passed out in the Russian Tea Room and had to be taken in agony to the emergency room of a public city hospital. It was like a Sidney Lumet movie. The head nurse had a gun on his hip, just in case. I was made to wait two hours before I was seen, and in that time I managed to pass the kidney stone which it turned out was giving the trouble. They tell you that the pain from a kidney stone is the worst a human being can know. I've no standard of comparison.

A lot of actors and directors I knew said that they loved coming to New York because it was so much 'freer' and less 'inhibited' than home. Of course I knew what they meant. But because I was here rather more often than most of my colleagues and for much longer, the claim always made me a little suspicious. America may look freer, but the kind of freedom we all wanted we weren't going to get. You still spend every day with who you are.

Anyway, yesterday, around noon, it turned cold, suddenly, in the way only New York can. Once when I was here it dropped fifteen degrees in an hour. Another time, my friend Tim Rose Price literally fainted with the cold. He came through a swing door, the cold hit him, and he fell in Fifth Avenue at my feet. By lunchtime yesterday it had come on to snow. I went for lunch with Wally in the Noho Star round the corner. It used to be the kind of hippy place where waitresses slopped around in loafers and there were newspapers on the tables. Now, like everything else, it's gone upmarket. We had to stand in line for the pleasure of a burger and a tomato juice.

After lunch, I was nervous going to the theatre, because in spite of a couple of phone calls from Stephen I had no real idea whether they'd have sorted out the noise problem. But they had. The Shuberts had been accommodating. The meeting between theatre owners and our producers had started with raised voices and ended in handshakes. The result was that I did my dress rehearsal with only the occasional distraction from *Chicago* in the next-door theatre. When I got to the passage about the Holocaust Museum and the murder of six million Jews, I could clearly hear the sound of a band playing 'Give Them the Old Razzle Dazzle' through the wall.

I got a tickle in my throat from all the dust that's been disturbed, and had to splutter to a halt a couple of times. But otherwise the few people present were generally pleased. The play turns out to suit the Booth Theatre. When I wrote *Skylight*, which is centred on two characters and set in a single room, I remember Nicole asking which theatre we were going to do it in. I said Richard Eyre and I both favoured the Cottesloe because it was the most intimate auditorium at the National Theatre. Nicole was shocked. She said, 'The woman's bedsitter may be small, but the ideas are big. For big ideas, you need a big theatre. Ideas need space to breathe.'

Nicole was right. The play went on to Wyndham's in London – 800 seats – and then to the Royale in New York – 1,100 seats. It only got better. Last night, André and Bernie said *Via Dolorosa* had a new breadth. What they meant, of course, is that the stage had breadth – it's much the biggest of the three we've played in. And the play expanded to fill it.

6 March Last night I made my Broadway acting début – another sentence I never expected to write. In English theatres there is a call from the stage management of 'Beginners'. No one had reminded me that in America they say instead, 'Places, please'. I walked out hysterically nervous and was greeted by an audience who were relieved to find there were going to be jokes. So relieved were they that they became overly excited – then alarmed to realize that the evening was going to get serious. It was a tricky transition to get them to dig in to the darker material. I got past my new Arabic line without fluffing, and it sounded beautiful and startling in the dark. The sharpest difference from London was that when I got to the Holocaust Museum, there was not that respectful silence which I am used to. At the Court and the Almeida, nobody dared breathe when I said the word 'holocaust'. Here, they've been asked to mourn the six million so many times that they couldn't be bothered to go through the motions again. There were even a few coughs when I got to Himmler's letter about 'staying decent'. You can never predict any audience. To discover that the Nazi crimes don't evoke the same reverence as in Europe was quite a shock.

Afterwards, Stephen was delighted. He said to me: 'Has it occurred to you where we are? Tonight we opened on Broadway. Can you believe it?' Stephen recollected how we had started out with the idea that we would give six performances in the Theatre Upstairs – maybe not even six. We thought the material was so forbidding and esoteric that all we would attempt would be an experiment. But in the theatre, praise be to God, everything is possible.

Stephen said he felt the evening was cathartic. At the beginning he could feel the shock of the audience thinking: My God, this man is going to talk about a subject you don't usually hear talked about. A non-Jew is going to use the word 'Jew', not once, but a thousand times tonight. 'And,' he said, 'you could feel both their nervousness and then their sudden relaxation. They thought: Fuck it. Let him speak. They felt good that the subject was being aired.' Stephen was so over-stimulated that he then added, 'By the end if you'd told them that they must all go out and kill their first-born, David, they would have done it.'

Somebody said to me that the evening reminded them of my play about the Church of England, *Racing Demon*. I said that I had been astonished by that play's popularity, and had once remarked on it to the Dean of Westminster. He had replied, 'Oh I'm not surprised at all. People are always interested when you talk about the transcendent.' When I repeated this, Stephen added, 'Yes, they are, except when the Church of England talks about it.'

It turned out the theatre had been hideously cold. I don't know why. Everyone who came round to see me was blue-nosed and shaking. It wasn't emotion. As we walked across the street to dinner, Robert Fox said he wasn't sure about the vision of Jerusalem. He thought this kind of stage effect was not true to the spirit of the show. It looked expensive and overly literal. He had heard a couple of people on the way out, saying, 'What was all that about?' Robert's comment was curious because earlier in the day I'd asked Stephen whether he was happy with it. I never see the effect because I am on stage at the time and looking the other way.

In fact, the meal André and Bernie had laid on for us in a nearby Italian restaurant, although well intentioned, only had the effect of making me jumpy. Stephen kept getting up from his meal to take soundings. The box office and the press people have the same message. There is a buzz about us inside the theatre community and among intellectuals. But the general public don't know we exist.

Across the road, Patrick Marber is directing his play *Closer*, which will test the limits of Broadway's sexual tolerance in the same way that I am testing their religious tolerance. Robert joked that people walking out of *Closer* (having had enough of 'Thank you for your honesty. Now fuck off and die. You fucked-up slag.') will cross with people walking out of *Via Dolorosa*. Meanwhile Patrick is floating the idea that we should colonize the whole street by having Harold Pinter, me and him take over as the next cast of *'Art'*. I said he could count me out. I may at some level, however incompetently, have learnt to perform but only by myself. I still couldn't act *with* anyone. The idea of looking into another actor's eyes and saying, 'I love you' or 'I'm going to kill you' would still make me feel completely ridiculous. I've learnt chess. But doing it with someone else would be three-dimensional chess.

At the end of the evening, my dresser Danny was so pleased with the whole event that he kissed me and said, 'Goodnight, handsome.' This was the third new experience of the week.

7 March I woke up yesterday suicidal. I wasn't sure why – just feeling 'This is all wrong'. Then I had a Saturday matinée, which went really well – a much easier house to play than yesterday. I came back to my apartment to lie down for a sleep before the evening performance. I thought: That couldn't have gone better. So why do I want to kill myself?

I was lying there on my bed thinking: This whole thing's a mistake. We shouldn't be on Broadway at all. We don't belong here. We should be in a little space somewhere downtown, because there the audience would address itself to the subject matter, not to the event. I realized why I was so melancholy. The previous night's dinner was attended only by professionals. People talked to me only about whether the play was or wasn't going to 'work'. Back in England groups from the audience had formed at the stage door all engaged with what *Via Dolorosa* was saying, and wanting to debate it. Here I was suddenly a commodity. I was a Broadway 'show' which would be some sort of hit or miss. I hated it.

My first instinct had been not to come to New York but to tour the Middle East. I received some invitations which were tempting. But I insisted that if we went to Israel we would then be bound to present the play in the West Bank and Gaza. The question of which towns exactly I should play – East Jerusalem? West Jerusalem? Bethlehem? Ramallah? – became complicated and political. Elyse Dodgson's head had been spinning with possible itineraries. And there were fears for my personal safety. Salman Rushdie heard of my proposed trip and tipped the balance with a warning fax: 'Believe me,' he said, 'being a persecuted writer is not all it's cracked up to be.'

I came to feel that it was more important to tell people in the West about a situation of which they were ignorant than it was to present the play to audiences whose understanding would be far greater than my own. Once taken, it seemed the right decision. But in the last twenty-four hours, I have experienced agonizing new lows of self-doubt.

I think I am doubly upset because I do not have the usual popular reservations about Broadway. I've always loved it. My sense of being wanted as a playwright began when *Plenty* was presented here in 1983, and afforded a welcome it was given only grudgingly in London. I have known Broadway to be a place where political work is not just possible, but positively welcome. It is true that large numbers of intelligent people in New York have been alienated by midtown theatre because they think of it as spectacle only. Performance art, music and the ballet give them the nourishment they once sought from the theatre. But Manhattan is, after all, a world capital of the brain. Clever people live here. Once or twice a season, they will turn out again, as their parents did years ago for Williams and for Miller, but only after their friends have promised them that it's worth overcoming their habitual suspicion of what the word 'Broadway' is taken to mean.

Much of the important drama on Broadway in the last fifteen years has come from the left. Capitalism has been in one of its most spectacular fits of self-propaganda. But the plays which have prospered have often been those which, like *The Elephant Man* or *Angels in America*, were written, as it happens, by Marxists. It is precisely because I have such a high opinion of Broadway's flexibility that I was so disturbed by this feeling that I am now going to be judged by the wrong criteria. I don't have the lame excuse that 'politics don't work on Broadway'. To invoke that ridiculous word, so beloved of modern novelists, I'm *freighted* with the knowledge that they bloody well can.

However, the evening performance – my third in New York – changed all that. It was a good-sized house, and I could feel individual lines detonating in the audience, little hisses and groans. At a couple of points people applauded individual lines. I was reassured, because I could feel again the purpose of why, *why* I'm doing this. The woman in front of Patsy Rodenburg turned to her friend and said, 'Well, David Hare's lucky we've got free speech in this country.' Leaving the theatre, Stephen was pinned to the wall by a man, not angry, just insistent. 'Are you the director of this piece? Tell me, what is David Hare saying? Is Hare saying the Israelis treat the Palestinians in just the way the Nazis treated the Jews?' Stephen reassured him that I was not saying that – and I'm not. But, Jesus, thank God we're alive. We're in business again. Little groups of people stood outside the lobby for a long time after the show, arguing about what they'd just seen.

Some people walked out. That's fine. People were dissenting from what I was saying. But they were not dissenting from my right to say it. And, interestingly, the vision of Jerusalem as a stage effect worked tonight. Why? Because the audience and I earned it together. The emotional temperature was so much higher. The stage vision therefore took its place at the centre of the evening.

Irene Worth came round to the dressing room, and we drank the ice-cold bottle of good champagne she'd sent me. At last I was in the mood for it. Wally was back again. With his usual weird acuity, he said, 'How did you *know*? How did you know that it was possible to present this play at the Booth and find an audience who would engage with what you said?' I told him I didn't. 'And until two hours ago, I was desperate precisely because I believed I couldn't.'

Wally came with his lifetime companion, the short-story writer Deborah Eisenberg. She is in the middle of rehearsals for *The Designated Mourner*. She has known the director, André Gregory, for twenty-five years and always admired him. But she admired him all the more since she began working with him. I said, 'You never know anything about anyone until you do a day's work with them.'

I went on to have dinner with Sam Mendes, Iain Glen and Nicole Kidman. This was to say goodbye to *The Blue Room* before we head off in our separate directions. It was a relaxed reunion in an Italian restaurant, somewhere downtown. Iain had a new body, the result of working out in the approved American manner. He has a new-found air of gyms and weights and running machines. Nicole had given him the present of a suit which flattered his abs and his pecs. We were the last to leave.

When I described the depths of the depression I'm going through, Nicole and Iain instantly understood. Nicole said, 'You're going to feel like killing yourself for the next two weeks. Opening in New York is the worst experience in the world. But then playing in New York is the best.'

8 March It's Monday morning. The break is far too short. There is time only to have Sunday brunch with Howard Davies, who is here to direct *The Iceman Cometh*, to go to a movie and to attend a drink for the end of *The Blue Room* before it's time to get up and start work again. It's not enough.

A great American film-maker died. The *New York Times* honours the occasion by headlining him as a 'film-maker with a bleak vision'. In the second paragraph they point out that Stanley Kubrick never won an Academy Award. Who gives a fuck? He made *Paths of Glory* and *Dr Strangelove*. Rather more important than collecting a pot. This country is gong-obsessed. I watched the Screen Actors Guild Awards on TV last night in disbelief. Gwyneth Paltrow is presumably a reasonably articulate woman when ordering her limo or asking if she can have her alfalfa sprout salad gluten-free. But give her an award and she can't put six consequent words in grammatical order. Nothing so stereotypes actors as stupid. Both Paltrow and Calista Flockhart gibbered and shuddered at the microphone as if auditioning for the ravishment scenes in *The Exorcist*.

Before I left for America, I talked to Cate Blanchett, who is nobody's fool. She is currently enduring a circuit of gong shows on behalf of the film *Elizabeth*. She said to me: 'It's funny. There are more and more awards for acting at the very moment when there's less and less acting going on.'

What she meant is that nobody really acts any more. The great names of Hollywood are brands. They're labels. They turn up and do what they're expected to do, what they've done a thousand times before. They give the audience their identity, their imprimatur, their presence. But they don't *act*.

9 March There are pieces today about the play in *Time* and *Newsweek*. One is by Jack Kroll, the other by a young journalist who seemed charming when we met in London. I didn't read them because I knew they would confuse me. Besides, I was in the grip of another terrible gloom, brought on by the shortness of the break and the need to go in at 3 p.m. to do two hours' rehearsal. The unions insist on a two-hour break for the crew between 5 p.m. and 7 p.m. They won't consider lifting it. I had to work for two hours, then hang around aimlessly in mid-town for three.

We had work to do. The most important section of the whole play is the epilogue in which I return to Britain after my trip to the Middle East. It is the passage which implies the meaning of the title, and leaves me facing my own, personal Via Dolorosa. As I look back on individual memories, I contrast the vitality of Israel and Palestine with the comatose familiarity of Britain. I take us back to the question posed at the beginning of the play: must our lives in the West necessarily be shallower than those of people for whom the stakes are so much higher? It is this contrast which has become a problem. In the US the audience doesn't know the world I'm talking about. The word 'Hampstead' doesn't give them the image it gives the British. The words 'Fitzjohns Avenue', which spoke volumes in London – often getting a groan of recognition – give the Americans no image at all.

I have had to come up with my own description of Hampstead-ness, and not leave the audience to imagine it. To do this, I wrote a line with which I am dangerously in love. 'Leafy street after leafy street, with sleeping houses, sleeping bodies, sleeping hearts.' Only when I've said it ten times do I realize I have been influenced by reading an essay comparing a Sylvia Plath poem:

My boy, it's your last resort
Will you marry it, marry it, marry it

with a similar Anne Sexton couplet:

Or the prince you ate yesterday
Who was wise, wise, wise.

Stephen was pressing in on me again, but by now I welcomed it. We were both keenly aware that we have only five more chances to experiment before we lock off the show at the moment the critics begin to arrive. Because of all the changes, I wobbled around a lot during the show, but the result was creative in the right way. Suddenly, and without forethought, the assassination of Rabin moved to the centre of the evening. This is the mysterious thing about plays. They can acquire a different emotional meaning according to only the subtlest changes of emphasis. Even the author finds himself saying, 'Oh, *that's* the real subject of my play.' Last night, without my having planned it, every reference to Rabin was picked out in bright letters. The play became a lament for the loss of his decency. You could feel the audience move to his memory. When I came off, I said, 'I like this. I like this feeling we honour Rabin.'

My irritation with Stephen is over. It was, as they say, part of the process. There is always a stage where the director annoys you – or annoys me, anyway. In my experience, there are two kinds of directors, and sometimes I get confused because I'm never quite sure which Stephen is. I call the two types editors and interventionists. Crudely, interventionists possess a vision of the work towards which they are, at all times, working. The show is already conceived before they begin, and they have an idea of the production which they need the actors to help them achieve. They have, in short, a Platonic show in their heads. Editors, to the contrary, work pragmatically, looking all the time at what they are offered, refining it constantly, and then exercising their taste to help the actor give of their best.

Editors tend to stay in the stalls; interventionists get up on stage. The editor is someone who stays *in front of the actors*, sitting there on behalf of the audience and telling the actors what the effect of their performance is on an averagely intelligent and sensitive person. An editor then helps actors to direct that effect more powerfully. The interventionist works *behind* the actors, pushing them towards an artistic ideal whose effect even he probably does not yet know.

The atmosphere at the rehearsals of these two creatures can be very different. Interventionists tend to talk a lot and they are not frightened by conflict. They don't get upset when actors chafe at their rigidity, because they believe in their right to impose their vision. Bad interventionists are unbearable, because the rehearsal easily becomes about them and their blessed obsessions, rather than the play they are meant to be doing. The worst of them also believe that conflict is 'creative' and therefore desirable. This is a needless pain in the neck.

Editors talk much less. They're shepherds. They believe in pleasantness, in nurturing, in providing a support system of confidence and solidarity which will enable actors to do their best work. Bad editors let too many things go by, always allowing things on the grounds they're part of 'the search' or 'the process'. They keep saying, 'Oh, it's a stage we have to go through.' The worst editors say, 'Marvellous, darling' to everything, and end up with a show which is a lot less pleasant than the rehearsals.

The editor is the audience's representative; the interventionist the artist's. The editor judges; the interventionist invents.

Neither kind of director is necessarily superior to the other. Fellini was a great director, and the ultimate interventionist. *La Strada* is as good as any European film of the period. It belongs, in retrospect, to those three contemporary works – the others being *Mother Courage* and *Waiting for Godot* – which all find their power in the idea of waiting around. It's a big mid-century theme. *La Strada* and *Mother Courage* even share the image of the cart, though Fellini motorizes it. He'd started as a cartoonist, so the picture was already drawn in his head. He would film close-ups of an actor's individual gestures without even deigning to tell the actor which scene he was planning to use them in.

Louis Malle, by contrast, was also a great director, and the ultimate editor. He wanted to show you how interesting the world was, not how interesting *he* was. He would take some phenomenon – like, say, Atlantic City in decline, or an already-existing stage production of *Uncle Vanya* – and bring his clear eyes and his sharp intelligence to bear on it. He let the actors present him with some-thing and then he refined it, with blinding taste.

Of the English directors I know best, Howard Davies is very def-initely an interventionist, Richard Eyre an editor. Yet both can achieve outstanding results by their opposite approaches.

10 *March* Yesterday was my worst day. We had no rehearsals, so I didn't get to the theatre till 6. The half hour while an actor gets ready is meant to be sacrosanct. I have my own little procedures which are identical every night. But tonight Stephen was standing outside my dressing room ten minutes before the show began, doing deals with his agent – a man I've never met – and roaring loudly with laughter. It pissed me off. The audience were slow and lifeless. I worked extremely hard, then tripped at the curtain call. I looked like a lemon. Afterwards, Stephen was unforgiving. He didn't pause before criticizing the bits he didn't think were as good as usual. I told him to stuff it till tomorrow because I'd done my best and didn't need to be taken to pieces right now. He asked if I knew that the show had run three minutes longer than the night before?

I walked to have dinner with Sam Cohn. Foolishly I said I thought I was much better than in London. 'Well, London was great because you were so raw. I'll never forget how exposed you were.' This remark worried me, so I asked Sam if he thought I should work to get that quality back. He looked at me as if I were ten times stupider than he had ever imagined. 'It's a meaningless question. The play works entirely according to what you are feeling. That is what the audience experience. It is completely pointless to wonder if you can get back what you felt in London. You can only work from what you feel now.' I felt an idiot for having asked something so crass. And then Sam added, 'And don't take notes from people telling you it's three minutes longer. That's laughable direction.'

Sometimes I fall victim to this terrible feeling that my show falls between all possible stools – that it never seems to settle into one thing. When I am low, this whole exploit seems like a mad pursuit of the impossible – trying to fake an actor's skills when I don't have them, trying to strip art from art. As I walked across 7th Avenue with Sam, I remembered William Goldman's story in his book about Broadway, *The Season*. A customer came out of Judy Garland's one-woman show and said to his companion, 'But is it theatre?' The companion replied, 'It had better be, because it sure as hell ain't singing.'

Jane Gelfman, Sam's companion, had skipped the play but was waiting in the restaurant. The meal was a disaster. I got into some riff about how disgusting it was that Joe di Maggio, the baseball player who died on Sunday, should be so much more honoured than Stanley Kubrick. Jane started saying that di Maggio was an American hero, and that as a foreigner I couldn't hope to understand. I asked, wasn't Kubrick an American hero too? Jane didn't seem to think Kubrick was American. I told her he was born in fucking Brooklyn, for Christ's sake.

It was one of those crazy conversations which I enjoy writing but hate being part of. I was white hot with anger as I raged against Clinton for speaking in memory of di Maggio and ignoring Kubrick. That, I said, was the end of Clinton, as far as I was concerned. Sam looked at me, not fooled. Psychologists call it projection, I think. It's not Clinton I'm furious with. It's me.

11 *March* I had two shows yesterday, including my first Wednesday matinée, and thank God I got back on track. I did the afternoon show, went to the cinema in Times Square ('What film do you want to go to?' they asked. I said, 'Anything that starts at 4 o'clock.'), then came back and started all over again. There was an alarmingly small audience tonight, but the show was going better than it ever had. After twenty minutes I thought: My God, today is the day I could actually do the whole show right. But when I got into Gaza, I realized I didn't have enough physical energy to keep the line completely tight until the end. Never mind. All my life I have told actors that my work is like a musical score. You must learn it, every single note of it, before you can earn the right to jazz it. If you try to jazz it before you've mastered it, you will make a fool of yourself. I have always used a phrase which has a nasty German ring to it. Beyond Discipline, Freedom. For the first time in six months, I

had a little taste of what freedom might one day be like.

I came off, drank half a bottle of wine, came back to my loft, and watched *Inspector Morse*. There are quite a few British shows on Broadway in the current season – among them Patrick Marber's play *Closer*, the Almeida production of *The Iceman Cometh*, and my own *Amy's View*. I was told that one middle-aged Jewish woman came out of *Via Dolorosa* tonight saying, 'The Brits come over here and tell us how to write plays. They tell us how to direct plays. And now they're trying to tell us how to be Jews.'

Waiting for me at home was some news from Australia. A member of the Melbourne audience has complained about my play *The Judas Kiss* to the police. The vice squad have been twice to see the show, which is about Oscar Wilde, and have now threatened to close it down. There have been huge amounts of attendant publicity, and jeering articles asking why the Melbourne vice squad has to see something twice to know whether it's obscene or not. Needless to say, the few remaining seats have now been sold.

12 *March* The way plays open here is completely different. In England there is one official first night to which the press come en masse. Friends and supporters also attend, and the whole thing is over in one highly charged evening. But in New York, the ordeal is gruesomely protracted. There are several, or many, press nights, with the actors usually ignorant of which critics are coming to which performance. Then, at the end of the press previews, there is also an opening night, which becomes something of a formality, since it is watched only by guests and admirers. For that reason, the opening night almost invariably goes well – or at least it goes well until that moment at the subsequent party when you are summoned upstairs by the press agents and producers to have the sense of the reviews conveyed to you.

As I write, it is Friday morning and I am facing the following schedule:

Friday evening	Press Performance
Saturday matinée	Press Performance

Saturday evening	Press Performance
Monday evening	Gala for Lincoln Center
Tuesday evening	Press Performance
Wednesday matinée	Press Performance
Wednesday evening	Gala for Royal Court Theatre
Thursday evening	Opening Night

Because of this succession of what someone neatly described as 'eight pressure performances', both Stephen and I had hoped for a quiet show last night. In the dressing room he said, 'Take it very gently. Keep it down. Save yourself for the big performances that are coming. On no account let yourself give out too much energy.'

Doomed advice. As soon I walked on I knew I was facing the most volatile and unruly house I've ever had. The air was charged with powerful feelings and resentments. Groans, boos, whispered remarks and wild laughter filled the auditorium, rippling back in waves and then grumbling along as an accompaniment to whole paragraphs. It was electric. When I got to the line about the religious Jews using the Bible as a contemporary operations manual, then there was passionate and shocking applause from one section of the house. To counter that, there was applause from an opposing faction when Danny described the Six Day War as 'the greatest victory in Jewish history'.

I was skeetering about, losing lines and tumbling over simple passages because I could feel the audience scanning my every line to discern my bias. When I came to the moment when I say of the settlers that there is nothing wrong with the philosophy This is How We Want To Live, so long as you don't attach the lethal dangler This is How We Want to Live, So Fuck You, my heart was in my mouth. I felt there was a real chance of the whole thing getting out of hand.

However, I got through somehow. Stephen came backstage, pouring with sweat, saying that was the most uncomfortable ninety minutes of his theatregoing life. He thought I'd managed to quieten them, and I guess I did. They were silent by the end. But the effort was as if I'd spent the time lion taming, not acting.

I was meant to go serenely into the coming ordeal, but this morning I'm still shaking.

13 March Hollywood screenwriters have a perfect expression: I'm better on paper than I am in the room. I woke up feeling exactly that. The pressure of the coming week found me as nervous as I have ever been in my life. I had a brief lunch with my son Joe, who is over here for a week, and then tried to sleep. I lay in bed all afternoon and watched *Interlude* on TV. Douglas Sirk is always said to be the most romantic of directors, but there seems to be no irony intended when June Allyson tearfully rejects art, Europe and romance in the shape of Rossano Brazzi in favour of small-town boredom in the shape of some American dropkick whom I'd never seen before. It didn't seem very romantic to me.

I got to the theatre in a state of high terror. It wasn't just me. Everyone was in a peculiar state. It's this awful thing of not knowing. You have no way of telling whether one critic is in, or one hundred. Danny said reassuringly that in all his years as a dresser he had never met a single actor who was immune from nerves. He asked about Judi Dench. I told him that when we were previewing *Amy's View* at the National Theatre, we had been forced to do a corporate gala. Collectively the audience comprised the most godforsaken prospect any of us had ever beheld. Judi took them by the scruff of the neck and forced them to pay attention. I asked her afterwards if she hadn't been nervous. She said, 'Of course I was nervous. But then I thought: I haven't worked forty years in the theatre to be intimidated by people like you.' I said to Danny, 'It's only Judi Dench who can get away with that.'

Anyway, I was shaking as I walked on, and the giddiness returned. I have not felt I was tottering since I got to New York, in spite of the fact that the stage itself is more raked than it was in London. I kept getting little rushes of blood to the head. I had to keep rebalancing my feet. A man interrupted quite early, but in a way which seemed friendly. He wanted to join in Eran Baniel's condemnation of the religious right. But, thank God, his whoop of enthusiasm didn't scare me or the rest of the audience. In fact it rather bonded us all.

When the show was over Stephen told me that a whole bunch of front-line critics had indeed been in tonight. I couldn't have been happier. I would have been crushed if I'd put that much effort into a show and then found that it wasn't going to be written about. Stephen felt they'd seen the show at its best, and so did I. If they don't like it, it won't be because the actor let the playwright down. That's all I care about.

Stephen said: 'You now have two versions of the show. One where you start very relaxed, and one where you start very edgy. Tonight was the edgy version, and that isn't a bad thing.' I laughed and said I now have no memory of how on earth, only four days ago, I was able to play the relaxed version. It now seems inconceivable. What was I on? Nembutal?

We had a bottle of champagne. When I got home I had take-away chicken and fries. It was one of those very rare, luxurious moments when, briefly, the pervasive cloud of anxiety which has become my life lifted. I seized the moment and was happy.

14 *March* The two Saturday performances could not have been more different. The matinée audience was small and barely reacted at all. Afterwards, I went to a movie in Times Square. The film showing this week had Michelle Pfeiffer mislaying her four-year-old at her High School reunion. It was hard to concentrate because I was thinking: Something's wrong. They're telling me all the time that it's going so well. But why is nobody coming? The Lincoln Center subscribers were meant to provide us with a cushion of audience for the early performances. But, perversely, they have all chosen to book for later in the run. The result is we are papering the house with non-paying audiences. The ultimate humiliation? Somebody who was given a complimentary ticket was trying to sell it for money outside the theatre last night. Thus the saying: You can't give them away. It's an empty sop to my pride that he succeeded. I'm facing the classic question: If my play's so good, why is it empty?

The evening was packed and went like a bomb. They were the best American audience I've had and I established a great rapport with them, playing them as if I were a Catskills comedian. Unfortunately, only one critic was in. The others missed a great night. It's always the same. When I visit my plays the actors always say, 'You should have been here last night.' It'll be the title of my autobiography.

A whole lot of people stood up at the end. In fact, rather to my embarrassment, the whole theatre would have stood if I hadn't rushed off the stage at the earliest opportunity. I knew I was cutting things short. Everyone backstage asked me what on earth I was doing? Why didn't I stay to enjoy the applause? I told them I had to sacrifice the standing ovation because I was late for the Lennox Lewis/Evander Holyfield fight at Madison Square Garden.

Gabrielle told me I wouldn't be able to get a cab, so we jogged together down to 34th Street. I'd never been to a boxing match before, and I went on the grounds that you should do everything once. We were very near the ring, and we had the Russian mafia in front of us. One guy had a cigarette burnhole in his cheek and to turn it into a design feature, he had put a diamond stud in his cheekbone. On our other side, across the aisle, was the celebrity pen, in which Rupert Murdoch was mingling with Jack Nicholson and Michael Douglas. Boys, boys, boys. I can never think of Rupert Murdoch, or read his papers, without remembering Fassbinder's masterpiece *The Marriage of Maria Braun* and the moment when Hanna Schygulla asks the capitalist: 'Why are your ideas about people so much duller than you are?'

The only one the crowd was interested in was Keith Richard, who received a massive roar of approval. His girlfriend appeared to be there to help him stand up. He is incredibly cool still, with razor blades and bulldog clips hanging from his greying hair. There were 21,000 people in all.

There was a fight before Lennox Lewis even got into the ring. A huge man in a green suit, very stoned, fell on top of me, then crashed along the row to try to land a punch on the boxer as he walked into the hall. We were close enough to be able to see the full power of these men. When Evander Holyfield was in my eyeline and heading straight towards Lennox Lewis, I could feel my stomach churn involuntarily. It was exciting, in an awful sort of way. When the punches landed, I found myself recoiling in terror.

You could tell the result was going to be fixed the minute the celebrities were hustled away from the ring before the announce-ment. It was clear that the security people had warned them not to be around for the verdict, in case any ringside fights broke out. It doesn't do media chieftains any good to be in full view at the scene of the crime. Lewis had so clearly won that when the fight was judged to be a draw – with the obvious financial prospect of another money-spinning re-match – the crowd didn't even turn ugly. They groaned in disbelief. This morning, the *New York Times* calls the fight a fiasco.

I walked away, like many others, I'm sure, with the feeling of having been completely fucked over. They get you stirred up, and then they swindle you. There were no cabs anywhere, so I had to walk another thirty blocks to get home at 1.30 a.m. There will be endless post-mortems in the press and everyone will say that it's a scandal. But, at the end of the day, they've taken your money and they've cheated you. It made me like theatre much more. Incompetent? Often. Openly dishonest? No.

16 March

> *All happiness is a masterpiece: the slightest mistake throws it off, the slightest hesitation corrupts it, the slightest heaviness mars it, the slightest foolishness makes it dull.*

MARGUERITE YOURCENAR

Monday was horrible. I picked up *Variety* on the way to the theatre. In England managements are secretive about how many seats they are selling. In this country you have to publish the figures. We are playing to 43 per cent. Only *You're a Good Man, Charlie Brown* is doing worse than us. I'm seriously disturbed. André Bishop came into the dressing room, and I asked him what was going wrong. He said, 'Nothing's wrong. We always knew this play would be a hard sell. The word of mouth is fantastic. The same people come back the next morning to book to see it again.' I said, 'We're going to be the only show in New York to play for three months to the same two thousand people.'

He reminded me that things had been the same in London. The subject sounds medicinal. I said I was feeling that things were different from London. There, my doubts had necessarily been about the play itself. Now we were confident in the play. We were just wondering whether we'd done the right thing in bringing it to Broadway. My nightmare was that we would get good reviews, and yet still not find an audience.

There are three good reasons which will keep most people from going to *Via Dolorosa*:

(1) It's about Israel and Palestine
(2) There's only one person in it
(3) He isn't even an actor.

I've already worked out that it isn't going to be enough to read something good about the play in the paper. You are actually going to have to meet someone who orders you to overcome your preconceptions and go.

There followed a fundraising gala night for the Lincoln Center, which confirmed my worst fears. Gala nights are dismaying at the best of times. Last night, from the beginning, I could feel the house split between the three hundred rich bastards in the stalls who were sitting in stony silence, and the two hundred real people in the balcony who had paid normal prices. Upstairs: rapt fascination. Downstairs: moneyed indifference.

Because I was so angry with the audience, I fell into the trap of working too hard. I must have seemed insane. I remember shouting the words 'We're all blind. We all see only what we want to' with a violence which was probably very disturbing to watch. But the words seemed urgently relevant at the time. It was very hard work, and the applause seemed grudging.

However, as always, Bernie came to my dressing room to tell me the whole thing had gone wonderfully. By the standards of Lincoln Center galas, it was a positive triumph. This unreality is driving me nuts. Everyone tells me all the time that everything couldn't be going better. But I don't *feel* it.

I took Joe and Candice with me to the dinner, which was held at the Hudson Theatre. Appropriately, this is where Isadora Duncan danced for the last time. She was booed off the stage for pro-Russian sentiments. I sent Isadora a little prayer of fellow feeling as we walked into a sort of glorified supper club. These occasions always recall the scene in the film *Mephisto* where Klaus Maria Brandauer has dinner with a pack of Nazis after he has played Faust. They resolutely refuse to introduce him by his real name, simply calling him over, one to another, under his character's name; 'Have you met Faust? Hey, Faust, come over here.' At a National Theatre benefit for *Amadeus*, Simon Callow told me the scene was eerily re-enacted by a lot of upper-class Englishmen. 'Gosh, look, it's Mozart! Hello, Mozart!'

The meal had a mystifyingly Greek flavour. Stephen made a charming speech, but the unreality remained. I couldn't help remembering Maurice Baring's authoritative pronouncement: 'If you would know what the Lord God thinks of money you would have only to look at those to whom he gives it.' I haven't yet got used to the fact that in the higher echelons of American society, when people speak, only their mouths move. The face itself stays rigid, like a stocking mask. If the assembled men and women could donate to the Lincoln Center only half of what they spend on reconstructive surgery and liposuction, then theatre in Manhattan would be revitalized at a stroke. I grabbed at Brian Murray, whose face has reassuringly natural contours. Brian gave a heart-breaking performance as Harry in the New York production of *Racing Demon*. I clung to his arm for dear life, not letting go, because he was the only one there who knew what I was going through. Brian's played galas.

On the way out, I met Spalding Gray. I was touched by his coming to see the play, because he is, after all, the godfather of the monologue. It was *Swimming to Cambodia*, his account of the making of the film *The Killing Fields*, which gave the genre an invigorating new lease of life in 1986. Since then, he has been the form's acknowledged master. It was kind of him to come and see what I was up to.

Gray was very shocked that I was giving eight performances a week. I have somehow always accepted that I would do this. Given that we still have to build an audience, I didn't feel I could ask the management to let me do less. 'You're crazy. How is that possible?

How on earth will your voice hold up?' I asked him how many performances a week he gave. 'Two,' he said. He likes to play on a Monday night at the main 1,100 seat theatre at the Lincoln Center, while the regular show there is taking its day off. What was the most he ever gave in a week? 'Five.'

I asked him if he had a problem with concentration. I said that I'd found tonight particularly difficult. My mind had wandered a few times to a conversation I'd had with Nicole about first-night tickets. At one point I'd found myself thinking about laundry. Spalding Gray looked at me: 'But that's great. You can do it and you're not even thinking about it. What's wrong with that? You're becoming a professional.'

17 March Scott Rudin's an intelligent man. He had a ticket for the gala. He took one look at the audience and thought: I'm not going to sit with that lot. He changed his ticket and sat upstairs. He said everyone in the balcony was sitting forward, lapping up every word. It was Scott who was originally against the play going to Broadway. 'You know what? I was wrong.'

He said the first cheering things I've heard in days. 'You're acting it better, the storytelling's clearer. The danger was that by becoming a better performer the play would lose its passion. But it's still just as passionate – but clearer as well. When you got to the word "Gatwick", I thought "I can't bear it, it's almost over."' He'd wanted it to be longer.

Last night's press performance started with the heating going berserk, so that for the first ten minutes all I could hear was loud industrial clanging. A woman in the front row spent the next twenty minutes folding and refolding her coat. Then she embarked on a prolonged exploration inside her handbag. That also lasted twenty minutes. She was less than five feet away from me. Does it never occur to people?

Unknown to me, Sigal was there. Sigal was my official companion in Israel. She took me round on my first visit. She had brought a friend with her. He said how curious it was that when he met Sigal he was able to say, 'But I know you already. I've seen a play about

154

you.' Sigal thought that I had not been tough enough on the Israelis. 'You should be much harder on us. Much, much harder.'

I would love to have discussed it, but Nicole had arrived at JFK. I hurried downtown to meet her in a Japanese restaurant where we ate exquisite sushi. Cyril Connolly once said the true index of a man's character is the health of his wife. I have always been suspicious of this saying, for the obvious reason that my wife looks wonderful. We could have stayed up all night but Stephen had ordered me to get to bed early, because I have two shows today. The man is even in my marriage.

18 March Tonight we open. I had to do two shows yesterday. Stephen told me not to bother at the matinée, to try and do it effort-free. They turned on microphones so that I wouldn't have to project my voice. I found myself so relaxed that I spent most of the show standing in what I call Actor's Number One. This is the physical position where you stand upright with your hands hanging loosely at your side, thumbs pointing down the seams of your trousers. It is a profoundly unnatural posture and yet it is the one which nearly all professional actors use as their base from which to launch all other gestures. When I started acting, I couldn't do it at all. It made me feel like an ape. Now I find it curiously comforting. I spent half the show in it. I came off without sweat having broken from my brow.

I went off at tea-time to talk to Vicki Mortimer, who designed my production of *Heartbreak House* in 1997. I want to direct *The Sea-gull* at some point, because Penelope Wilton wants to play Arkadina, and because, for some reason, it's become my favourite play in the world – my comfort play, the one I read to make myself feel better. We spent a happy hour discussing how to display its closeness to *Ivanov*, the stunning young play which I adapted for the Almeida a few years ago. I love Chekhov when he's young and passionate. I react less personally to his later, know-all persona. Vicki is the ideal designer to strip the play of its floppy hats, while my hope would be to aim my guns at the swanning about which often passes for Chekhov acting in England.

I went back and did the evening performance, putting a lot into it.

Once more, the balcony were educating the stalls, teaching their richer brethren by the speed and intelligence of their reaction what the play was about. It seemed a good show to me.

Where are we this morning? What, in my heart, do I expect? Booking has picked up since Monday, and the house manager of the Plymouth Theatre, just down the road, came up to me in the street last night and said: 'It's the best thing on Broadway. And it's not just me who thinks so.' You shouldn't put your faith in remarks like this. The people who think it's the worst thing on Broadway don't come up to you.

When I wrote *The Absence of War*, about the Labour Party, I was privileged to follow Neil Kinnock around as he led the 1992 campaign. It was the saddest electoral loss of modern times. I certainly thought it the most moving, because I admired Kinnock and thought him a decent man. There was something touching about him. Weeks after he lost I asked him, 'Did you, in your heart, believe you were going to win?' He replied, 'You believe both things. You believe them at the same time. You believe you're going to win, and you believe you're going to lose. And you hold both views with equal conviction.'

So it is this morning.

19 March People tell me what an extraordinary thing it is to have four plays on Broadway in the space of just over twelve months. But they seem not to consider the downside: four Broadway openings.

They always say that moving house and a bereavement are among the two most stressful experiences a human being can know. I would put four Broadway openings somewhere close to whiplash from four car crashes for its general impact on your health and well-being.

Mine was the least glitzy opening in Broadway history. Normally the streets are lined with limos, the police patrol the crowds and TV crews fight each other to film famous people going in. But earlier in the day all the celebrities in New York had phoned each other with a nuclear warning that the *Via Dolorosa* opening was red-starred Place On No Account To Be Seen Dead At. Just by sitting in the stalls at the Booth Theatre, any person who has ever been recognized in the street would automatically contract rabies. The contrast with *The Blue Room* could hardly have been more shocking.

By chance, an advertising hoarding had also blown down in Times Square, so that the whole area had been shut down to traffic for hours anyway. Even if a rogue limo driver had steered in the direction of my theatre, he couldn't have discharged his precious load on to my street. As Ian McNeil remarked wittily: 'David Hare Opens. Broadway Closes.'

I got to the theatre early and went through the happy process of opening and giving presents. Danny had been ridiculously generous, and Gabrielle gave me a beautiful mug. I gave everyone *Love Is Where It Falls*, Simon Callow's memoir of Peggy Ramsay. The book describes the love affair between them when she was 70, and when Simon was 30 and gay. Peggy was the person who most helped me when my early plays needed to be established. So I murmured a dedication of the night's performance to the greatest play agent in living memory, and blessed her, as I always do, for everything she gave me.

The performance started a regulation fifteen minutes late. The audience was friendly, as you would expect, though I was quite surprised to hear grumbling pockets of religious hostility within the house. I'd assumed this would be the one night when nobody would dissent openly. The play was going along quite reasonably until I reached the last encounter of the play. It's the scene with the ex-Minister of Culture Shulamit Aloni, who rages against Netanyahu and against the loss of Israel's integrity. Suddenly I found myself overwhelmed with genuine emotion. It was partly because I knew Sigal Cohen was in the audience, and that she had been with me on the unforgettable day in Tel Aviv which I was describing. I began to think how strange it was that, eighteen months later, she was now sitting watching me in a theatre in New York. Shulamit Aloni, in all her crazy sadness, seemed unbearably present and I began to cry.

I lost a line or two. I now thought: what am I doing? I'm meant to be acting in a play, and here I am weeping, and not even remembering to get on with it. It was one of the weirdest moments I've ever known. At the end, the whole house would have stood up if I'd let them, but I was filled with a mixture of exhaustion and disgust at the rituals of show business. The standing ovation is such an automatic and degraded phenomenon of New York theatre that I spontaneously decided that I was damned if I was going to go through it. Pure arrogance, I suppose. I scuttled off the stage as fast as I could and started pouring alcohol down my throat. Nicole was rightly critical of me. 'If we have enjoyed you, then all we can give you in return is our applause. I saw you put your hand up to say "That's enough." It's not up to you to decide. We all felt cheated of our right to give you something back.'

The only defence I could offer was that I don't know a single artist (painters are the worst) who does not have an immensely complicated love-hate relationship with how people react to his or her work. Praise is salt water. Drink it and you become thirsty.

Howard Davies was first back to see me. He was rigid with emotion. There is no way of disguising the feelings of the people for whom the play has been a real experience. Howard had not seen it since the first public run-through in the rehearsal room six months ago. Like me, he'd been crying. The tears were still on his cheeks. The memory of Howard's genuine response stayed with me through everything that followed.

'Everything', of course, being chiefly the party. Opening night parties are notorious for their fickle nature, but they have been changed by the fact that what is called 'the review' no longer appears at 10.30 p.m. Modern technology is meant to have speeded the production of newspapers, but for some reason you can no longer pick up a copy of the *New York Times* on the night itself. To read what their critic, Ben Brantley, has to say about your play, you have to start cruising the Internet. You're unlikely to find anything until well past midnight.

In the old days, the life of the party depended on the review. After *The Secret Rapture*, I watched people vanish as if a piece of soap had been dropped in a bubble bath. Gerry Schoenfeld was standing across the emptying space, looking like an undertaker with indigestion. As I moved across to him, he intoned, with terrifying gravity, 'David, it is not a good review.' I think I'd worked that out for myself. There was no one left in the room.

In the *New York Observer* yesterday there was a gloating article saying that the *New York Times* no longer wields the power it once did. That astonishingly wealthy local newspaper, which happily lists sports events for free, takes millions of dollars a year from theatrical advertising. It is, in fact, the only newspaper in the world so rich that its editor has the right, without consultation, to bump any advertisement from its pages should he consider a breaking story sufficiently important to merit taking the space. Over the years, while happily accumulating all this cash from advertising, the paper has consciously built and protected its right to slaughter the cash-cow which ensures its own prosperity. But now, says the *Observer*, musicals are regularly prospering without the approval of a critic who, by his position rather than his personal authority, could once open and close shows at will. The unhealthy and demoralizing influence of the single newspaper has been broken.

Much as one would like to believe it, this article is wishful thinking. For those of us still trying to put on serious plays – particularly without stars – the validation of the current critic is still essential. The Lincoln Center is peculiarly dependent. If you have Nicole Kidman or Liam Neeson in your cast, you can walk straight across the flaming coals without getting your feet burnt. But if I'm the cast, you can't. Nicole Kidman once sweetly remarked to me during *The Blue Room* previews: 'The pressure's bad enough without having to worry about whether we're going to sell tickets.' She was free to be ingenuous because the whole run was sold out as a result of the good word from London. But last night, as I headed across to Sardi's for the buffet dinner, I knew I was going to an ordeal which would have no definite outcome.

Maybe because the axe was not hanging directly over it, the party turned out to be highly enjoyable, as relaxed as these affairs ever can be. Warmth from all my friends and colleagues began to spread across the room and infuse the whole occasion. The most touching reactions were from fellow playwrights. Alfred Uhry had been sitting next to Tina Howe. When I got to the line where I say that for some years now, my subject as a playwright has been faith, Uhry turned in panic to Tina and said: 'Oh my God, I have no idea what *my* subject is.' John Guare had been very taken with the whole enterprise, and he admitted to powerful jealousy. 'Why didn't I do that first?' he said. I suggested a whole season of playwrights' monologues. Everyone seemed up for it.

My son Joe had two friends with him who had both lost their fathers early in life. For them, the whole occasion had been about fatherhood. The girls told Joe how lucky he was to have a father. Watching me on the stage with Joe in the audience made them realize how much they had missed. This reaction moved me more than anything all evening.

A succession of people, most of whom I didn't know, lined up to shake my hand. People always use the word 'insincere' about American effusiveness. I don't know why. I always find their enthusiasm gratifying and, what's more, perfectly sincere. They certainly mean it when they say it. It's just you can't always depend on them to remember what they felt the next day.

ME: That was a wonderful film we saw yesterday, wasn't it?
AMERICAN: What film?

I think this the most attractive thing about America. You cross out and move on. When I worked in his theatre I used to have terrible rows with Joe Papp which appeared to bring our relationship to a screaming halt. Next day I'd go in to the theatre with a heavy heart. But Joe would greet me cheerily and carry on as if nothing had happened. I knew it would be the height of bad manners to mention that the previous day we'd sworn at each other. You never had to spread salt to purify the battlefield. Surely this policy of a clean slate each morning is better than the English way where you don't even have the row, but still bear the grudge for twenty years? There is a downside. Kissinger one day destroys Cambodia, then next day is accepted as a TV-style statesman. But if Americans can't always recall yesterday's enthusiasms, then it seems a small price to pay for the fact that they don't nurture yesterday's grievances.

Things were slowing down by 11.30, but we still didn't have any reviews. Stephen said he would call me as soon as he got something off the Internet. I went home with Nicole and, for the first time in

New York, fell fast asleep without knowing the critical verdict. I woke, hung over, at 4.30 a.m. and crawled to the answering machine, where I heard a noisy message from Stephen, which sounded as if it had been recorded in a bar in the meat market. It said, 'We're fine. The *Times* is fine. We're over that hurdle. We're fine.'

I know Stephen pretty well by now. Nothing in the press ever pleases him. We both like to quote Wally Shawn's favourite saying that if you wake up in the morning and find that the newspaper has not changed its name from the *Daily Telegraph* to the *Daily Shawn*, you feel a shudder of disappointment. And if the critic says anything remotely kindly, you feel an equal degree of astonishment.

I could tell from Stephen's tone on the machine that he hadn't really liked what he'd read. This morning, I couldn't face reading the reviews. I threw my eyes briefly over the *Times* to get the gist. It was excellent, but it was not what they call 'a money review'. My attempts to act gauche and clumsy at the beginning of the play had proved to be so successful that the critic appeared to think that I was indeed a gauche and clumsy actor. Such, indeed, are the perils of acting. It's acting, Ben. I'm acting.

However, there was really nothing to complain about. You couldn't ask for better. The press agent, Philip Rinaldi, has now rung to say all the others are equally good, and we already have indications that there is more good news next week. These are the first across-the-board approving reviews the Lincoln Center has had in years. But I knew from the way Philip was speaking that he is worried whether all these serious appreciations of my play are going to sell a single ticket.

I'm feeling absolutely terrible, as low as at any moment since we started this process. It's partly physiological. I'm exhausted, and last night I drank a great deal of red wine. I feel wasted.

Nicole wants, reasonably, to know why I can take no pleasure in the response. It's simple. Of all the things I most resent about critics, it is the fact that they have taken away any satisfaction I might have got from what they write. My early work was established in the teeth of their opposition. For years I wrote plays which the critics rejected but which the audience enjoyed. If I had credited what critics had to say, I would have given up years ago. I did not believe them when they damned me, so how can I now trust them on those occasions when they don't? When I see other playwrights grinning from ear to ear at their notices, I envy them. Proust says: 'What is so touching about the happiness of others is that one believes in it.'

20 *March* There was a lovely sense last night of the real business beginning. When I got to the theatre, everyone was in great spirits from reading the reviews. Business is still bad. When Bernie and André came to see me, I said that I didn't want the house papered. I would rather play to small audiences who genuinely wanted to see it than to full houses of people who didn't really want to be there. I asked them to stop printing corporate ads where all three Lincoln Center productions are grouped together. My play must try to stand alone on Broadway. I raised the question of whether I was going to be able to continue giving eight performances a week. Eric Bogosian, another well-known New York monologuist, gives seven, max.

The house was indeed small and quite quiet. I was filled with a deep sense of satisfaction. I realized that I didn't give a damn whether we filled up or not. Here I am, at the Booth Theatre, telling people about Israel and Palestine, *and they are listening.* Who cares whether it is or isn't going to be a commercial success?

By chance, Richard Eyre had sent me a Margaret Atwood poem about the humiliations of being an artist. Atwood compares her heart to a shucked oyster which is flipped out of its natural spot 'like a sea anemone coughing a pebble'. It is then put on ice to be shown to the world. Observers proceed to criticize the organ, as if it were no more than a bivalve. Instant gourmets stand round, saying the heart is too salty, or not salty enough. The artist, meanwhile, is left heartless.

Some people sell their blood. You sell your heart.
It was either that or the soul.

The odd thing is that I found this poem totally inappropriate. It doesn't speak to how I now feel. Atwood is describing a feeling I have known well as a writer and a director. Curiously, it is not what acting feels like. I have gone through that stage. I no longer feel that my heart is on display. What's more, I have discovered acting's most powerful privilege. Every night you get the chance to do better. Yes, as a writer you often become jumpy and wasted because day after day you hack at the same block without ever feeling you progress. And you resent every slight, real or imagined, done to your play. But to acting there is a religious dimension. You go out each night and try to redeem yourself.

Realizing this made me ashamed of the times that I have drawn actors' attention to the fact that few people are coming to a particular play. The actor has always looked at me hurt, bewildered by the scale of my discontent. I realize now that actors are far less upset by small houses than I am, because they at least can get on with their work. Reminding them of your own impotent dissatisfaction is bad manners. It also has helped me understand film actors who always say that their entire interest is in the shooting of the film. They are as near as dammit indifferent to the end product. 'If the film's any good,' they say, 'that's a bonus.' The writer or director worries about the film itself and its reception. But for actors – lucky people – the pleasure is in the process. John Barrymore called the actor 'the garbage man of the arts'. But it isn't the whole story.

Wally says, quite rightly, that I should be grateful for anyone at all who comes to this show. Just by coming, they join a self-selectingly brave group. Anyone who books for *Via Dolorosa* probably fits into one of two categories. Either they are people who never go to Broadway but have decided this sounds different and they will risk it, or they are people who always go to Broadway, but have decided that they will overcome their anxiety that this sounds so unlike the usual Broadway fare. Both groups, he says, are worthy of respect for their adventurousness.

Tonight, as I worked, I felt heady and liberated. Or at least I did until I realized I was ill. I started sweating, I felt dehydrated and my throat was sore. Oh my God, I thought, it's 'flu. As I got to the big passages when Pauline explains the betrayal of the intifada, I realized I couldn't breathe in without choking. I made my way to the end, keeping power in reserve. At the curtain call, a man in the front row called out to me. 'Hey Dave!' I looked down at him. He said: 'Keep writing plays. They're great.' I said, 'Thank you.' He added, 'I liked *The Blue Room* too.'

I came off and took advice. Karen and Danny have both worked on musicals, so they are well used to divas struggling through eight shows a week. They began telling stories of singers who communicate with each other entirely by writing notes. They then handed on all the folkloric advice. I must gargle with warm salt water. I must drink something called Throat Coat. I must never answer my telephone, but always leave the machine on. Another helpful person presents me with fenugreek tea, by which both they and their mother swear.

I was due to have dinner with Nicole at a fashionable restaurant, but instead I took a big bag of Chinese take-out back downtown and went fearfully to sleep as early as I could.

21 *March* Oh God, am I ill! It's classic. Patsy Rodenburg says she deals with more cases of vocal collapse directly after the first night than at any other time. My voice has completely gone. It's a husk.

I marked my way quietly through the matinée, then went to the cinema with Joe. At the evening performance, I didn't feel too bad until I got to Gaza and realized I had nothing left. My voice wouldn't do what I wanted. Only certain parts of my range were left, so I became like a junkie searching desperately for a vein I could use. As soon as I hit on a working register, then I stayed in it for as long as I could. I considered cutting the whole passage between George Ibrahim and Hussein Barghouti altogether, but decided it would terrify Karen, so I battled on. As the big set piece of Shulamit Aloni approached, I was groaning inwardly, and my distress became obvious to the audience. The reception was generous, but you couldn't have missed the fact I was in pain.

I went to dinner at Bernie Gersten's, then came home to bed. This morning (Sunday) is the day off. I am on what's called 'vocal rest'. I shall not speak at all. I pass notes to Nicole and she answers the phone.

The highlight of yesterday night's performances was a scarcely credible dressing room visit. Gabrielle came in and said, 'Kurt Vonnegut is here to see you.' She might as well have said: 'Nelson Mandela's waiting for you' or 'Have you got time to meet Marilyn Monroe?' I nearly fainted. Gabrielle's jaw was slack with disbelief. I was so overwhelmed that I started joking around, saying, 'How do you know it's Kurt Vonnegut? Ask for his ID. What if he's an impostor? I don't believe Kurt Vonnegut really exists.'

Unfortunately, unknown to me, Vonnegut was only a few feet away in the corridor, so he may have overheard my so-called comic reaction. We weren't sure. He turned out to be a slowly spoken man. He was with his wife, the photographer, Jill Krementz. We had a slightly strained encounter, probably because of my awe at meeting him. As proof of my embarrassment, I have to report I found myself praising the novels of Philip Roth. Tactful, or what?

I love these meetings. Most of them no longer throw me at all. Let 'em all come in, as far as I'm concerned. At the Royal Court, I cared what people thought. Now, I am so committed to the value of what I'm doing – or maybe I *have* to be committed in order to do it – that it all washes over me. Nobody upsets me. On the way out of the evening performance I signed a programme for Dr Ruth Westheimer, the eminent sexologist, and was introduced to her equally charming family and friends. We stood round in the street for a few minutes, chatting cheerfully about Israel. If the added value of acting is that you get to meet people like Dr Ruth, then it's a bonus.

22 *March* Not being allowed to speak is very good for me. It means I listen. I went to Chinese lunch with Nicole and Howard Davies. Nicole drew Howard out on the question of what a director does. Howard says many actors speak badly when they speak about acting because they imagine it to be self-expression. When Howard works he is searching for the actor's instinctive gift, which is to access certain emotions which only the best actors can intuit. The better the actor, the more complex the range of feelings they can reach. Howard then sees his job as helping to persuade the actor to find a way of replicating these discoveries.

Plainly, Howard is not what's called a 'nurturing' director. With his view of the job, he can't be. Against himself, he tells the story that when Maggie Smith considered working with him, she was reported to have said, 'But Howard's not one of those directors who takes care of you.' Howard's been able to sidestep all the questions from people who ask him what Kevin Spacey is like by saying, truthfully, he has no idea. An angry Welshman himself, Howard leaves the room at the end of rehearsal, and rarely sees actors outside their working day. Currently, he spends his evenings learning to paint. He doesn't do drawing. He's a colourist. Howard has directed some of the best productions of my lifetime: *The Iceman Cometh*, of course, but also a blistering *Who's Afraid of Virginia Woolf?* He is one of the few directors around who can *stage*. He knows how to use space and bodies to create images. He's in the dying tradition of Tyrone Guthrie and John Dexter, and of the supreme stager, Michael Bennett. When Howard did my play *The Secret Rapture*, he found colours in it I didn't know were there. He pitched the play at a higher emotional level than I had expected, and it only benefited. But it would be a brave actor who called Howard for comfort at two o'clock in the morning.

I have a new gargle. I've given up warm salt water and substituted equal parts of apple cider vinegar, honey and hot water. Superb. It really works. Nicole is off for four weeks. We spent our last evening together finding out if Judi Dench and Cate Blanchett would win any more awards. The Oscars are like pornography. Enticing in prospect, then boring as hell. When we turned off after three hours they still hadn't reached Best Actress. Geena Davis asked Helen Hunt about winning an Academy Award. 'Did you have the same experience I did, that when they called your name you went, like, out of body?' Good question.

This morning, Nicole has left for the airport. I croaked goodbye, then suddenly felt terribly lost and lonely at the prospect of ninety-four more performances, all by myself.

23 *March* And tomorrow I will lose Stephen. He's also going back to England. So last night I grabbed at him, like a child at its mother. My voice had returned to some degree, but I said we were going to

have to find a new way of doing the show which didn't stretch me vocally. I could no longer go on giving the second half of the show such size. This is where my limitations of technique were really going to show. I needed Stephen's help to re-conceive the evening for less voice.

After a lot of gargling and spitting and chewing, I went out and did a very low-key performance, slightly assisted by microphones. I opened my mouth and the most unbelievable non-sound came out of it, a sort of wavering parrot screech, which shocked the hell out of me. I was so frightened that all my gestures got out of sync, and for five minutes I was in an alarming state of desuetude. But slowly I began to trust that my voice would do what I wanted. I was always suppressing a cough, but the out breath at least did deliver something like my intended inflection. When I walked out at the end for the curtain call I got one of the warmest receptions I've ever had. I came off and said to Stephen 'I don't understand it. That performance had none of the usual heft and yet the audience didn't know the difference. They loved it.'

Stephen was at his most brilliant and clear. 'They loved it for three reasons. First, you didn't take it down nearly as much as you think you did. It was still very emotional. Second, the fact that you didn't use pure volume meant instead that you explored meaning and inflection within individual phrases which you usually shout your way through. And third, you performed the basic act of theatre, which is what Jacques Lecoq calls the *joue*.'

I asked Stephen what the *joue* is. 'It's the idea which is basic to Lecoq's teaching of theatre. The audience takes delight in you playing, in both senses of the word. You play with the meanings, but you also play with them. Tonight, you let the audience in. You took it slowly enough for them not to feel – which they sometimes do when you act – that you're barging your way through the text, slightly contemptuous of whether they need to follow it or not. Instead, you played. You let them into your playing. And most important of all, you convinced them that you were having fun in the act of re-inventing the text on the stage at that very minute. They believed, fundamentally, that you were finding it tonight specially for them, and in a manner in which you had never previously performed it. And they were right.'

Didn't it lack sheer power? 'It did. For my taste. But what you put in its place – spontaneity – is just as important. We mustn't lose sight of that.'

I have been off alcohol for a while because of my voice, but I celebrated getting through such a difficult show with a glass or two of wine. Today there has finally been a bad review. It has come from the *New Yorker*'s critic, John Lahr. No one can quite make out what he's trying to say. One producer took it to be a good review until someone was heartless enough to translate it into decent English. People say the piece stinks of the personalized, inarticulate bitterness which is Lahr's hallmark. The American playwright who knows Lahr best said to Stephen: 'If John wants to write like a cab driver, let him.' We discussed whether it would affect business. Everyone says not. Professionally, Lahr is thought of as a bit of a joke. The overall verdict is fifteen critics in favour, two against. Meanwhile, John Simon has written so glowingly in *New York* magazine that Stephen blushed when he read it.

I have had two great letters. One was from Kate Nelligan who, for me, will always be the person who spoke my lines with most sense of their underlying rhythm. When she played Susan Traherne in *Plenty*, both in London in 1978 and in New York four years later, she sprang the dialogue along so that it sounded like a spontaneous poetry of the heart. Kate wrote how rewarding it had been for her to hear me speak my own lines. She loved the experiment of taking them at a speed which most actors would regard as reckless.

The other letter was from Kurt Vonnegut. It was, of course, beautifully written. He quoted one anecdote of his own which goes to the heart of things. 'The architect Philip Johnson once said to me moments before I gave a lecture: "Don't worry. They won't be listening to what you're saying. They'll be deciding whether or not you're an honest man."'

24 *March* Judi Dench blew into town. Believe it or not, she hasn't been to New York since the late fifties. At the time she was being

courted by Gerry Mulligan. She loved it but she never came back. Now she's here for rehearsals of *Amy's View* which opens in twelve days' time. She's just won an Oscar for eight minutes' work on film, and I've never seen her looking better. In the play, she plays Esme Allen, a genteel actress whose career is on the skids. Her daughter, Amy, is played by Samantha Bond. It was a luxury to spend an afternoon watching other people work. As Richard Eyre directed them in the crucial scene in the third act where Esme attempts to be reconciled with her daughter I realized how first-rate actors always anticipate you. Samantha or Judi have you catching at your throat because the emotion arrives when you're least expecting it. They throw you off balance in a way that precisely mirrors the unsteadiness of the characters themselves.

Amy's View is a four-act play. The four-act structure is one which the modern theatre has abandoned, although it's the form Chekhov, Ibsen and O'Neill all frequently favoured, and one which gives a superb subtlety to the feeling of time passing. Mastery of the form involves controlling not just what happens in each act, but also the sense of what happens between them. I had to redraft constantly. I came to believe that the form has been abandoned because it is fiercely difficult to write a play with four principal actions. All my problems were with the second act, which did not seem to be advancing the plot. Try as I might, I was not able to make the second movement anything more than a re-statement of the first. I was in such despair that I went to see *The Cherry Orchard* in order to see how an expert handled structure. I was astonished to find that I followed exactly the same pattern that he had:

FIRST ACT: We're going to have to sell the cherry orchard
SECOND ACT: We're *really* going to have to sell the cherry orchard
THIRD ACT: We're selling the cherry orchard
FOURTH ACT: We've sold the cherry orchard

It made me feel a little better about my own story which went:

FIRST ACT: Mother resents her daughter's love for new boyfriend

SECOND ACT: Mother *really* resents her daughter's love for once-new boyfriend, etc.

Seeing Chekhov's play reassured me that within a four-act structure, the second may be used purely to deepen the characters' dilemma, not necessarily to advance it. But I was never at peace with my work. Here in New York we have an actor called Tate Donovan playing Dominic, the ambitious boyfriend. I liked him as soon as he began to act. I began to feel that he will find texture and variation in the second act which will give it new tone. My first rule of playwriting is that scenes must be rivers, not lakes. They must go somewhere. My second act does flow, but in the same direction as the first.

We all got in the elevator to go and have a drink. When we stopped at another floor, a woman stared at Judi and said, 'Congratulations.' Judi thanked her and asked if she were getting in. 'I couldn't.' We left the woman on the sixth floor because she was too overwhelmed to travel down with us. You can't beat fame in America. Judi later entered a restaurant where everyone stood up and applauded. She's obviously got used to playing queens, because she waved with one hand and murmured, 'You're too kind.'

People say actors are boring, but given that they are forced, by the nature of their work, to think about themselves all day it's a triumph to me that they are able to think about anything else at all. My whole day was about myself and my rebellious throat. Would I be able to speak tonight? I drank pints of water, gargled with the apple-cider vinegar, stuck my face in my personal steamer, chewed lozenges, did physical exercises, and still managed to come totally unstuck.

I did the first fifteen minutes thinking what good shape my voice was in, then found it excruciating to go on into the passage where Danny describes the importance of Hebron. I coughed and choked, then went to the side of the stage to have a glass of water. I continued for a couple of minutes, then had to admit defeat again. I took on more water, apologized to the audience, and ignominiously continued. It was as if my throat were being twisted by a hand in a red-hot glove.

The audience went very quiet. They don't like to see performers in trouble. The thread of the story was broken, but I was very touched by how they struggled to recover it. I could feel them concentrating like mad, trying not to be distracted by what had happened. After ten minutes, they were back with me. At the curtain call I tried to express my gratitude to them for their kindness.

There was nothing I could have done. Karen, the stage manager, says the worst thing about her job is that actors call her at home to discuss their symptoms. 'Well, you see, I woke up feeling a bit gassy, and then by lunch I was seriously nauseous.' They then ask her whether they should do the show tonight or not. Karen says she always tells them she has no idea because she's not a bloody doctor.

The only remedy I haven't tried for my present predicament is Judi's recommendation. She believes in a raw egg swallowed just before bed. But Danny and Karen warned me that you can't eat raw egg in this country because of the dangers of salmonella. The alternative some people use is semen. Apparently, it's just as good as egg. I mean, I'll do anything to become an actor, but don't I have to draw the line somewhere? Just how badly do I want to be a star?

This morning I have already done Natalie's exercises, taken a Turkish bath, drunk six glasses of water, taken Vitamin C and zinc lozenges and now I am off for ten minutes' gargling. Yes, I'm a bore. But how else do I deliver?

25 *March* At the matinée yesterday I started coughing in exactly the same place as the night before – when Danny describes Israel as the insurance policy for the whole Jewish people. I got a glass of water and carried on more fluently this time, so I didn't lose the audience. But, at the end, I urgently asked for Patsy Rodenburg, who by great good luck happens to be in town, so that we could analyse what I was doing wrong.

Michael Gambon has often told me that if an audience is restless the trick is to become quieter, not louder. He says it's a mistake to try and dominate them. Always draw them in.

This is one of these dangerous pieces of advice which are great for your Championship players, but a little riskier for your Saturday hacker. But working with Patsy increased my dynamic range. She taught me how to use a potent, charged quietness instead of the volume I've always relied on.

The result was a sensational Wednesday evening, one of my best. I did get a tickle in the passage where Pauline describes the disillusionment of Palestinian youth, but I mastered it. The performance had more variety than I've ever had. When I got to the moment where Albert Aghazerin complains that Arabs are not allowed to visit Jerusalem, I was suddenly fired up with a righteous indignation which was completely genuine.

In *Plenty*, Kate Nelligan would weep every night when she came to the speech describing men dying naked in Dachau. Julie Covington, who was on stage with her at the time, asked her how she managed to cry every night. Did she think of her mother's death? Or the death of someone else close to her? What trick did she use? Kate said, 'I'll tell you what I do. Every night I think about men dying, dying naked in Dachau. And then I weep.'

Last night, the same thing happened to me. I said that Arabs couldn't get visas from the Israelis to exercise their right to visit Jerusalem. I suddenly found myself thinking: Fuck! *Why* won't the Israelis give Arabs visas to visit Jerusalem? It's a fucking scandal! and I rapped out the lines, straight from the heart, and into the heart of the house. I could feel the whole theatre swell with outrage. A man was loudly saying, 'Yes, YES!' at the end of individual sentences.

The popularity of golf is explained by the fact that, however poor the player, he or she can occasionally hit a good shot. It's a sport for optimists. You are spurred on, deluded even, by periodically playing above your true ability. For me, acting is like golf. The pleasure of a couple of professional shots obliterates the memory of my hundred poorer ones.

(I have to say, golf is a sport I find hard to take seriously. Once more, the downside of a life pissed away in the movie house. I have never recovered from my schoolboy sighting of Marcello Mastroianni trying unsuccessfully to make love to Jeanne Moreau in a bunker at the end of *La Notte*. Antonioni's decision to ask two of the most attractive people in Europe to lie down in the sand and grind hips somewhere off the fourteenth fairway has always seemed to me the moment when the pretensions of the European art cinema go right off the end of the weirdometer.)

Getting my voice back was like getting my show back. I began to enjoy it again. In fact everyone notices that my voice has changed considerably since I started acting. It's deeper and has more timbre. At the end of the London run, Harriet Walter was surprised to meet me in the street. 'Oh, you've got one of those sexy actors' voices,' she said. She then looked embarrassed and added tactfully, 'Not that it wasn't sexy before, of course.'

There was a great ad in the paper this morning and business has been better today. News is also spreading on to the street. I am stopped quite a lot now by people who want to talk about it. As I was getting soup between shows, a man came in specially when he saw me and said, 'I want to thank you for reminding me that the theatre is a place where we go to learn.' I thanked him. The two young girls serving soup had stopped work and were staring in pleasure. 'Oh that was lovely,' they said. I agreed. 'It was, wasn't it?'

I had dinner with Richard Eyre at a Greek restaurant where they grill fresh fish very simply, then fillet every single dollar from your wallet with exceptional finesse. It's like watching a medical operation. At the end they leave you without a single cent. The man driving me home was a Jew, who, like many others, had been forced to flee Iran. He went to live in Israel. 'It's chaos. I didn't like it. There are no rules. Anything goes. I like it here because there are rules.' He asked me if I was the man who does *Via Dolorosa*. I said I was. 'I want to see that show. That's the show I want to see. I drove three people home from it, and I listened to what they were saying. They were very happy. They were very, very satisfied.' I said I was pleased to hear it. And I was. Perhaps most of all because tonight I was very satisfied myself.

26 *March* Disaster. I couldn't believe it. On Wednesday I felt that we had turned the corner. The audience was great and the word of mouth was building. Last night, there was a much smaller house and they didn't respond at all. When I reached Yad Vashem, the Museum of the Holocaust, a woman coughed loudly all through my

description of the murder of six million Jews. Not just loudly – violently, destructively. Was she from the Holocaust Denial Society? I flashed her some filthy looks. It was wrong of me, but I was furious. Judi Dench says that audiences take on the character of one single member. It's true. The people who wanted to enjoy the show were slowly cowed by those who didn't. At the end there was none of the usual enthusiasm, just tepid applause. I got to meet Celeste Holm, who was waiting to speak to me, but that was about all that could be said for the evening.

Oh damn and fuck show business and all its ways.

Theatre art is the most elusive art of all and acting its most accidental factor.

WILLIAM REDFIELD

27 March The question of when Judi Dench is going to come and see *Via Dolorosa* is giving the other actors in *Amy's View* a lot of amusement. When Tate Donovan and Richard Eyre announced that they were going to come, Judi looked distinctly sheepish and said, 'I'm not coming tonight, David. I think I'll save it.'

This joke goes back a long way. Judi and I have been 'saving' each other's work for years. It could be said that we've somehow managed to 'save' each other's entire output. It all goes back to when we made *Saigon*, our first film together. I wrote it, Stephen Frears directed it, and we made it in Bangkok. One day Judi asked me casually if I had seen something she did at the Royal Shakespeare Company. I replied, 'Oh, I never go to that awful Royal Shakespeare bollocks. I can't stand it.' Judi looked at me, full of reproach. 'That is very wrong of you, David. The RSC is a wonderful theatre company. You should always try to see its work.' I exploded in disbelief, knowing she no more believed it than I did. 'Oh yeah?' I said, 'And tell me, when exactly did you last see a play of mine?'

We both roared with laugher. I think Judi has since managed to see *Racing Demon*, but only because two of her best friends were acting in it. I saw Judi in Rodney Ackland's play, *Absolute Hell*, in which she transformed herself. In *Mrs Brown* she was incomparable.

But otherwise, our respect for each other is based on a profound mutual ignorance. I bet she never comes.

Richard and Tate got a very good show, or so I thought. The house was lively and I could put the memory of Thursday night out of the way. I was in excellent spirits when I headed downtown for dinner with Wally at the Union Square Café.

In the past years I have sought to defend theatre at a time when the medium has been out of fashion. My view as a working playwright has always been perfectly summed up by Willem de Kooning's parallel remark about art: 'Painting is dead, they tell me, but it's never concerned me.' However, as someone who has found the challenge of the theatre so profound, I have tried to understand why it attracts such hostility. For years, Murdoch's in-house intellectuals have sustained an attack against the theatre as the prime symbol of their belief that art is an establishment conspiracy – an attempt to foist highfalutin' rubbish on a gullible public. They share the conviction of the book burners in Ray Bradbury's classic *Farenheit 451* that 'anyone who reads Aristotle's *Ethics* must think themselves a cut above other people.' In England, social Thatcherism is disgraced. But cultural Thatcherism thrives.

For that reason I had been fascinated to read Wally's interview with the one of the senior American poets, Mark Strand, in a recent issue of the *Paris Review*. In the theatre, we feel embarrassed about the fact that we are marginalized. From the sixties, when I first started writing and directing plays, I have taken part in arguments about how to attract larger audiences from a different social spread. Theatre workers are convinced more people *ought* to be coming. We feel it must be our fault – a failure of our art, and of our commitment – when they don't.

By contrast, Strand's interview made it clear to me that American poets see their own marginalization as a positive opportunity. They are so completely outside the mainstream American culture of entertainment and celebrity that they are able not to worry about it at all. As Pauline Kael once said, 'Yes, I've noticed the British are very keen on American popular culture. Perhaps that's because they haven't had as much of it as Americans have.'

Strand is unapologetic about the fact that poetry is difficult, and involves huge effort on the part of the reader. He does not expect everyone to like it, or indeed to make that effort. The expectation that he will always speak to few people and that he will always be overlooked gives him a perverse kind of strength. Strand is seeking to add to the body of something called 'poetry', not to proselytize for new admirers of that body.

Wally is a fan of the people he reverently calls 'the poets'. 'Oh, the poets are wonderful,' he says. 'I love the poets.' He is fascinated by their confidence, but at a loss really to explain it. Wally points out that he also attends modern music events and finds the atmosphere completely different. At a concert of contemporary music, everyone is thinking the same thing. The size of the audience seems pitiful and sad. Everyone is ashamed that this music draws so little response. After decades of propagation, modernism still has a tiny constituency. But when Wally goes to hear John Ashbery read and only a hundred people turn up, it is remarkable how nobody is upset at all. There's nothing depressing. Poetry still works its magic, and disdains to have its spirits lowered.

I ask Wally how he explains this difference between music and poetry. He says maybe it's because if you write music you know that at least some composers do reach huge numbers of people. But almost no poets do.

At the next table was Arthur Schlesinger, who has spent his life as Camelot's secretary, defending the achievements of the Kennedy years. His presence prompted Wally to say there was not a single political commentator in America to whom you could now turn with any expectation of enlightenment or authority. Liberalism had lost its voice. I asked, 'What about Chomsky? When Chomsky went to Oxford, they had to have an overflow hall available so many students wanted to hear him.'

Wally agreed enthusiastically. 'Chomsky is a man I admire more than anyone. A measure of his greatness is that the *New York Times* refuses to print his articles on their op-ed page.' For the last week, the US has been bombing Serbian targets to try and stop Milosevic in Kosovo. So I ask Wally what he thought Chomsky would say about this. 'Well I can't answer for him, but I imagine he would say that the fox shouldn't be trusted to sort out the problems of the chicken coop.'

28 March Yesterday? I got up. Went to the theatre. Did a good matinée. Did an interview with the *Daily Telegraph* about the Brits on Broadway. Kipped for a while. Did an evening performance to a house which was heading for full. My voice held out, then croaked to a standstill offstage. Received a tremendous reception. Cancelled dinner, because I have to go on to 'vocal rest'. Came home blissfully. By 11 o'clock was having what Noël Coward called 'something eggy on a tray'.

29 March Since I got to New York I've been sleeping beautifully but last night, for the first time, I had a rotten night. It's my own fault. I went out to dinner on a Sunday. It was a foolish thing to do. I need the whole weekend empty in order to recover for the next week's shows.

I went to dinner because it was in honour of Richard Eyre. Judi Dench invited the cast of *Amy's View* to eat in a swanky restaurant to celebrate his birthday. I could hardly refuse. Richard has been my theatrical godfather for the past ten years, and he's been my friend for thirty. I first knew him when he was the hesitant and pause-laden director of productions at the Lyceum Theatre in Edinburgh. The actor Jack Shepherd used to say that, in those days, there was a moment when you could see a little flicker in Richard's eye while he ran what he was about to say through his internal computer to check it for possible problems. He seemed to think implications more important than self-expression. Your reaction concerned him more than his own proposition. As the years went by, he took more risks.

When Richard went to run the Nottingham Playhouse in 1973, I was supposed to be his literary manager. I persuaded Howard Brenton to co-author a satirical comedy called *Brassneck*, attacking corruption in local government. It caused a minor stir, not least when the rituals of freemasonry were performed on the stage. The masonic brethren on the theatre's board were not amused. The greatest tribute I can pay Richard is that *Brassneck* was only one of twelve new plays that he premièred in that season. Even then, it was an astonishing achievement. Now it looks miraculous.

I'm hoping that one day the story of Richard's years at the National Theatre, from 1988 to 1997, will be properly recounted. It's a matter of record that he expanded the classical repertory, introducing all sorts of little-known plays that earned their place beside more familiar classics. He brought on an exceptional new generation of directors who included Declan Donnellan, Katie Mitchell, Nicholas Hytner and Deborah Warner. He established the principle of integrated casting. But, most important of all, he managed, once more, to première a fair number of the best plays which were written in the period, including Tony Kushner's *Angels in America* and Patrick Marber's *Dealer's Choice*.

All this he did while setting an example of integrity and good management which made the National Theatre a cheerful place under his stewardship. As I said at his farewell party, some theatres are good, others are happy. It is almost unknown for a theatre to be good *and* happy. Many days, he was first into the building and last out. He was an invaluable script doctor. He would exert what I came to think of as his prime test of authenticity. He would check the claims of any work of art against his own knowledge of reality. If you think it sounds simple, try it. Richard always asked: would a person who really knows about this subject be convinced that you know as much as they do? Would they find your view true? Would they detect an element of skimping or posturing? If your play could not pass these tests then he was never slow to tell you to put it back in the typewriter.

In this sense, Richard enjoyed the enormous advantage of coming from an unartistic background himself. As someone who only took up writing in recent years, and who had been born into a philistine upper-class background, Richard always eyed the arts with a degree of suspicion which is unusual in a theatre director. He takes Othello's advice: 'Nothing extenuate.' That caution has informed his own work. He hates exaggeration.

He and I were clearly well suited, playing to each other's strengths. People usually said that it was because I was romantic and over-reaching, whereas Richard was careful and classic. The truth was far more complicated than that, as was proved when Richard directed *King Lear*. I had directed the play ten years earlier. It was interesting which scenes we each did best. Richard saw it as a play about a dysfunctional family. I saw it as a play about man's relationship to the gods. I made a frightful hash of the early passages, but thankfully I rose to the scene of reconciliation. When Tony Hopkins as the wasted Lear took the hand of Michael Bryant as the blind Gloucester on Dover Beach, it was one of the most moving things I've ever seen. But in Richard's production it was the terrifying moments of surrealist insanity – the Justicer's scene, in particular, when the king presides over a fantasy court – which inspired Ian Holm to his most unforgettable acting. Everyone thinks Richard is a rationalist. But against expectation, he could lead Ian to deliver the startling extremes of madness.

Now he's given up running the National Theatre, Richard is in that familiar state of free fall which marks a freelance director's life. One day, a TV series on the history of the theatre; next day, an opera in Aix-en-Provence. For any person of sensibility, this kind of itinerant existence can be either liberating or fatiguing. After quitting, Richard went through a bad period when he was like an exiled monarch forced to live in a hotel in Paddington. But, typically, he's come through. As you get older you instinctively divide people into those who are still interested and those who aren't. Richard most definitely is.

The meal itself was delightful, Judi looking beautiful and Samantha Bond full of the pleasure of having taken her family to the zoo in Central Park. As Tate Donovan said, New York's not as mad as it used to be. Perhaps people aren't taking so many drugs. But this morning, I bitterly regret going out. I wouldn't have done it for anyone but Richard.

30 March I slept badly for the second night running. Again, I woke at 4.30 a.m. This really pisses me off. The play had been taking no physical toll on me because I was sleeping so well. Everything will go to hell if I can't sleep.

In the morning I had been to talk on New York Public Radio. The host was Leonard Lopate. He had not just seen the *Via Dolorosa* on Saturday night, he had also checked up on some of my other plays. The interview lasted forty-five minutes. I was taken aback both by his erudition and the care of his preparation. He said that the novelist A. S. Byatt had told him that to get the kind of thorough and intelligent interview you once got on the BBC, you now had to come to New York. On this evidence, she's right.

Lopate had tried to read Lahr, and said that Lahr's objection to the play appeared to be that I was too covert about my own position. Political theatre should take a stand. It should come out boldly and pin its colours to the mast. I replied that this was something which is always said by people who know nothing about political theatre. They want plays to be 'positions'. They want them to be 'views', because they're uncomfortable with the human fallibility that lies beyond slogans. Good playwrights describe the collision between people and ideas. Intentions and ideals have to be embodied in inadequate vessels called human beings. Those intentions also collide with events. Therefore, not only is stand-taking counterproductive – the audience never leaves the theatre *en masse* converted to a single proposition – but it also precisely misunderstands the nature of the theatre. In good political plays you find an element of ambiguity, even of opposition. *Hedda Gabler* and *Mother Courage* circle their meaning, rather than knock handles into it. You no sooner feel you have understood something which you clumsily call the author's intention than it slips away from you again, teasing you, leading you on. A lover of W. H. Auden's once complained that he had expected a poet to be more romantic in bed. Auden replied, 'If you want romance, fuck a journalist.' My attitude is similar. If you want a view, read an article.

I had been warned that because it's Passover on Wednesday, business is going to be affected. Last night the stalls were completely full and the balcony was empty. But the audience were good, hanging on every word. Afterwards a great actor came to my dressing room.

Karen had tears in her eyes. I asked her why. She said, 'Because Jason Robards has told you that you're a marvellous actor.' She asked me why I didn't cry. I said, 'Because it's very hard not to laugh.'

In fact, of course, I was incredibly flattered – Robards is the best – and Karen at once remarked on what I had already noticed in London: 'Lesser actors don't like what you're doing because you commit the unforgivable crime of making it look easy. That's why they're not coming. If acting's that easy, why have they wasted all those years on training and experience?' I said, 'Karen, bear this in mind: I still can't *act*. I perform.'

I went off to a dinner party which was being given to celebrate Tom Stoppard winning an Oscar. Someone had been upstairs for a quick smoke and the bathroom was rumoured to be aflame. When challenged by the hosts, nobody owned up. Here in America this was probably not because the guilty person was ashamed of setting fire to the house. More likely, they don't want anyone to know they smoke.

I found myself talking to Stephen Schiff, who is now prospering as a successful screenwriter. He knows what he's doing until the end of 2001. This would not be unusual except that he used to be a critic. We groped for other examples of people who have made the transition. As a born-again creative, Stephen is now bitterly repentant about his former life. His conversation is marked with an almost religious self-laceration. 'I could never go back,' he says. 'Never!' It's quite touching.

I told him how much I had enjoyed *True Crime*, the new Clint Eastwood picture that Stephen wrote. He replied, 'I'll tell Clint.' I was taken aback. 'You'll tell Clint? Why on earth would you tell Clint?' 'Because the picture hasn't opened very well. It'll mean a lot to him that you liked it.'

I stood open-mouthed for a moment, thinking that Clint has surely never heard of me, let alone ever shown any interest in my views on his work. It reminded me of a night in Paris ten years ago when I had dinner with Brigitte Bardot's agent. As a boy, I had adored Bardot, and was profoundly impressed with a story Louis Malle told me. He was once filming with her in the street in Switzerland. The camera was already turning and the actors were playing a scene when an older woman in a fur coat walked into the shot and spat right into Bardot's face. She then screamed: 'You are destroying society!' It was thrilling, surely, that Bardot's sexuality was once that powerful. The fifties were meant to be a low point of repression in human history, yet they gave us Brigitte Bardot, Claudia Cardinale and Sophia Loren. The liberated eighties gave us Cindy Crawford.

Anyway, on that night in Paris, I told Bardot's agent that when we were at school, sleeping in a huge dormitory in Sussex, we used to have a game where we speculated on how many miles of freezing snow we would cover barefoot if we knew Brigitte was waiting for us at the other end. The agent looked at me and smiled. 'I'll tell Brigitte. She'll be really pleased.'

I remember looking a moment and thinking: Well, it'll hardly come as a great revelation to Brigitte Bardot that a lot of dirty-minded schoolboys in the early 1960s in England used to fantasize about ravishing her in a snow-covered field. And I can't believe that even if she did know that she could frankly give a tuppenny fuck. But, instead, I carried on eating and said casually, 'Sure. Tell Brigitte. Why not?'

31 March At last there were some Arabs in, and it made a big difference. Karen had said to me a day or two ago that she feels that the audience is at peace while we're in Israel because the subject is familiar. As soon as I go into Gaza you can feel them thinking: Oh my God, he's taking us into the other bit. Last night, on the contrary, I could feel the atmosphere quicken as I went on. When Hussein described his argument with George as a 'typical Palestinian conflict' there was laughter of recognition from one side of the house. It proved an exciting evening with lots of murmurs of agreement and dissent. When I got to the bit when Albert Aghazerin can't remember what animal the priests of the Third Temple will slaughter to precipitate the end of the world, someone helpfully called out 'calf' from the audience. They thought it was me that had forgotten the word. My acting perhaps a little too convincing for comfort.

I still can't do the scene between George Ibrahim and Hussein Barghouti in any way which satisfies me. I dread it every night as it arrives. Tonight I consoled myself by thinking of the French saying: *La maison qui est finie laisse entrer le malheur*. I sometimes think my *maison* will never be *finie*. So I'll keep trying.

Waiting for me outside the stage door was the *New Yorker* staff writer Daphne Merkin. I had recently enjoyed her book of essays, *Dreaming of Hitler*, so we were able to stand in Shubert Alley, enjoying the good literary sport of sincerely praising each other's work. I had particularly admired her book for its unexpected and graceful defence of the actor Richard Burton. Burton's gaze, she says, 'was an impenetrable as it was penetrating' – as good a description of an actor's mystery as I have read.

Merkin had been stimulated by *Via Dolorosa*, but she wanted to take issue with its politics. She told me she'd been provoked to want to write about it. I didn't tell her that since John Lahr reviewed the play in her magazine, I have now been approached by three separate writers from the *New Yorker*, all feeling they had something useful to add to the magazine's coverage.

1 April First the bad news. The great actress Irene Worth has had a slight stroke. She was due to start previewing tonight in the Lincoln Center's production of the Anouilh play, *Ring Round the Moon*. She's in hospital, and expected to get better in a few weeks. I certainly expect her to. She's still acting at 82 and as fresh and original as ever. She is one of the few people I know for whom old age has been a blessing. 'Nobody told me it was going to be so happy.'

Otherwise, we had the problem of Passover. I have forbidden all use of the phrase 'turning the corner' backstage, because for two weeks now we have all been coming in, looking at the size of the audience and quietly musing, 'I think we may be turning the corner.' The other over-used sentence is: 'The word of mouth is fantastic.' But if ever we are to do the forbidden thing, then Passover will not have helped. The theatre had incomprehensibly scheduled two shows for the most important Jewish holiday of the year. By nightfall, every Jew in New York is home with their family.

But what can you do? The balcony was closed for the matinée, but the stalls stood up at the end, perhaps in solidarity with me for having such a small audience. Between shows I went to talk to Ian Rickson, who is in New York directing a play which is due to open tomorrow. He had invited me for a cup of coffee to ask whether I would be interested in writing a play for the Royal Court for Stephen to direct. Ian described the debates they had had when they were given the lottery money to rebuild the theatre in Sloane Square. George Devine, the founder of the Royal Court, had always wanted to knock down the proscenium, so as to create a more embracing environment. When I worked there, I urged Bill Gaskill to move the company out of its home and on to an open stage in Covent Garden. Rightly, Bill took no notice.

Interestingly, it was Devine's closest friend, the designer Jocelyn Herbert, who swayed minds this time. She argued, simply, that the Royal Court is unimprovable. The relationship between the human figure and the frame is profoundly right. No amount of tinkering with the basic structure will make the theatre better. As a result, they resolved to improve the auditorium and the backstage facilities, but to leave the stage itself alone.

In folklore, Ian says, Stephen Daldry resolved to resign as Artistic Director on the day that this decision was taken. But to me they were right. I'm a fan of proscenium arches. One of the worst arguments I ever had with Richard Eyre was when he designed *Skylight* to be performed in a traverse arrangement. The audience would be on two sides and the action in the middle. I said, 'I don't go to the theatre to look at other theatregoers. I go to watch Michael Gambon and Lia Williams. Put them up one end of the room and then I can concentrate. Put them down in the middle and I have to watch a lot of other people crossing and uncrossing their legs. It doesn't interest me.'

It was John Osborne who said of the Royal Court, 'You can do anything on that stage.' John, of all people, surely proved his case.

I went back to do the second show, which wasn't as badly attended as we'd feared. Karen is taking today's show off because she is going to a Seder with her boyfriend's family. 'I'm so nervous,' she said. 'I've never been so nervous about anything.' I looked at her pitilessly. 'Try opening a one-man show on Broadway. I don't commiserate with anyone about nerves any more.' Karen laughed and said, 'Well, yeah.'

Alan Rickman had asked me to dinner and Lindsay Duncan was there. She's appearing in a Pinter play called *Ashes to Ashes*, which lasts forty minutes. Harold was delighted when Lindsay told him that she heard a man turn disgustedly to his wife and say, 'Calls that a play, does he?' Lindsay is a great Pinter player, and we talked enthusiastically about Harold's own acting. I had been lucky enough to see the author in *The Collection*. He came on stage as if he had just self-administered an electric shock in the dressing room. Lesser revivals of Pinter's work miss what Pinter had – a kind of eruptive mirth, bubbling under the mask of his character. Savage, suppressed humour made everything Harold said both very funny and terrifying at the same time. I have no idea how he does it, but I know it's precisely that mad comedy which makes his work so vital.

Judi Dench and Samantha Bond came on from their technical rehearsal. In *Amy's View* the outsider, Dominic Tyghe, says that what he hates most about theatre people is 'that they tell those boring stories all the time'. But there you are. A happy little community of actors, we sat round telling boring stories till midnight. Speaking for myself, I couldn't have been happier. When I got home, the company manager had left me a little bunch of flowers to thank me for doing two shows on Passover. I was touched.

2 April Tonight the old confusion returned. There was a larger audience. Perhaps this is the stupidest thing I can say, but in some way I think I prefer smaller ones. The sense of huddling together in the stalls can sometimes create an intimacy and solidarity which helps *Via Dolorosa*. Once it's fuller, a different kind of show seems to be demanded. I tried my absolute best to do the show as well as I possibly could. I came off thinking: I really do perform much better these days. But talking to guests afterwards, I didn't really feel they'd noticed. Doing it 'better' doesn't seem to make it any better. Is the greater part of an actor's effort directed to a 5 per cent improvement which nobody notices anyway? Is it 'the thing itself' which people respond to, and are all our obsessive efforts just on the margin?

I briefly considered accepting my destiny, giving in to my fate and becoming a Buddhist. But then I realized a Buddhist actor may be a contradiction in terms. Or Richard Gere.

So I was discomfited when I went on to dinner with Mary Selway and Aileen Mazel. Mary casts movies, and Aileen produces them. I said it was impossible to be happy and to be a serious film director. Every film-maker I know lives a life of anxiety and disappointment. The demands of money and commerce are such that nobody now goes from film to film with a sense of artistic development. These days you are out there without handholds. The more successful you are, the worse it becomes. Aileen told the story of Stephen Frears gloomily realizing after the success of *Dangerous Liaisons* that he had lost his freedom. 'What I hate,' he said, 'is that from now on all my choices will be significant.' I challenged them to name one serious movie director who was contented. They couldn't.

We talked about Martin Scorsese. *Taxi Driver* and *Raging Bull* stand comparison with the best films ever made, yet when you see the man on television, he radiates misery. Why? It isn't just temperament. It's predicament. Scorsese appeared this year at the Academy Awards in order to announce the Special Lifetime Award for Elia Kazan. The award was highly contentious because over forty years ago it was Kazan who famously ratted on his friends and named names to the House of Un-American Activities. He is also the director of *On the Waterfront* and *A Face in the Crowd*.

Kazan's own behaviour at the ceremony was unsurprising. People who had expected him to apologize or refer to his betrayals seemed to me extraordinarily naïve. He settled with Arthur Miller years ago and, for the rest, he feels he owes no explanation. I was much more impressed by my 27-year-old assistant Gabrielle saying, 'It frightens me that as Americans we're murdering our past.' So the true shock of the evening was working out what Scorsese, of all people, thought he was up to by putting his arm around Kazan in a gesture which plainly carried immense significance for both men. 'Marty! Where's Marty?' Kazan cried, and Scorsese scuttled, embarrassed, to his side. He seemed to be hiding behind Kazan, overwhelmed by an agony of contradiction and at the same time nearly throttled by him.

Watching Scorsese you could only assume that he was trying to say one of two things. I think we may dismiss the first possibility – that he was endorsing what Kazan once did. This leaves only a second interpretation. Scorsese was saying that the man's offences don't matter because art is more important than life.

Was that the message? And why on earth does that message mean so much to Scorsese? Odder still, why did he choose to convey it at the American Academy, an organization which has consistently overlooked him? If anything proves the stupidity of awards, it is that Scorsese's films have won so few Oscars. De Niro won for *Raging Bull*. Scorsese was nominated for the same film. Beyond that, nothing. You can't look at the Academy Awards without feeling they are used not only to honour but to punish. The Academy has gone out of its way not to pay tribute to its most distinctive film-maker. Yet there he was, in the place that has rejected him, rigid in some crazy armlock with a man who sent his own colleagues into poverty and exile.

Someone later told me that Marlon Brando had been asked to do the job, but that he had refused. What made things worse, Kazan is now so old that he barely knew where he was. Before the ceremony he was on his hands and knees under the table. When asked what he was doing, Kazan said he was looking for his cat. Scorsese had replied, 'Your fucking cat's in New York, for God's sake.' Scorsese had gone out on to the stage terrified that Kazan might go down on his knees saying, 'Puss, puss' during the presentation.

But beyond the comedy of the whole thing, the image of Scorsese's complex desperation and defiance has haunted me ever since.

3 *April* Being an actor is disarmingly like being in Alcoholics Anonymous. If you let your morale slip for a moment, if you experience one single moment when your attitude is not positive, then disaster occurs.

I was depressed yesterday. Nicole has gone to Japan for her regular trip to visit her shops there. For weeks I have enjoyed the illusion that, although Nicole is not with me, she could at any moment step on a plane from London. But now that she is in Tokyo, her absence seems more crushing.

I went to an afternoon dress rehearsal of *Amy's View*, which starts previewing at the Barrymore tonight. When it came to the fourth act where the actress Esme Allen struggles on in 'this hokey little play' after her daughter has died, I found myself not weeping discreetly at the beauty of Judi Dench's performance, but actually unable to control my great, gasping sobs. I had to run down to the rest room at the end to recover, in a state of complete Gwyneth Paltrow. The reason? The play will open without me being around. I will never get to be part of its encounter with a New York audience. I was overwhelmed, realizing I am not going to be a part of this group of people I admire.

I was in a terrible mood when I got to the theatre. I turned on the television and the centre of Belgrade was in flames, bombed to hell by Nato. There were pictures of refugees streaming across the border into Albania. All theatres have received a leaflet from Corin Redgrave who is appearing at a nearby address. This is the response of the organized Left. Hold a meeting. But it is a mark of the Left's confusion (my own confusion) on this issue that the flyer announced a meeting in the Helen Hayes Theatre on Monday. It boldly called for an end to the genocide *and* an end to the bombing. Well, yes. I mean, that would be nice, wouldn't it? But if someone in the world knows how to achieve both of those aims at once, why keep the answer to themselves? Indeed, why wait till Monday?

When I went out to act, a woman started the most terrifying, explosive cough I have ever heard within thirty seconds of my beginning. It became impossible for me to get a line out. Every time I attempted to speak I was drowned out by this astonishing noise. At first people grumbled, but by the time I had restarted three or four times, a man sounding like a Mafia hood from the fish and gun club yelled out from the back 'Get out! Get out of here!' The man was more frightening than the cough.

This situation could have turned nasty. I had made a mistake three weeks ago when I had shown my irritation at a cougher. So now I looked amused and laughed. I pretended it was all a big joke. As Karen said to me later, this put the audience on my side in a way they would never have been if I had shown my real feelings. Karen said, 'They instantly felt sorry for you. They were thinking that you were only a playwright, and you shouldn't have to deal with this kind of thing.'

The woman was hustled out by the house manager, protesting. 'I want to see the play,' she yelled, even as she went on racking her lungs and helplessly convulsing. Even when there were two doors between her and us, you could still hear her in the lobby, insisting on her right to attend. She was offered tickets for another night.

The audience, needless to say, had lost the thread. They'd missed the play's opening statements, without which it's almost impossible to understand anything of what follows. I worked like a lunatic for ten minutes, convinced I was too loud and too slow, but not knowing what else to do. I considered going back to the beginning, but decided it would depress everyone.

It's really the first time that the play has come skidding to a total halt. It wasn't for the expected political or religious reasons. At the end I felt I'd been wrestling with bears. But I'd learnt something important. Nothing's tougher than acting insouciance when you're panicking. The hardest thing to act? Being happy, when you're not.

4 April Nervous yesterday because last night was the first preview of *Amy's View*. I had brunch with Stephen Frears, who was extremely cheerful. He is here to make a film in Chicago but in three weeks he is going to Oklahoma for the day. He has won an award called a Wrangler for making his film with Woody Harrelson and Billy Crudup, *The Hi-Lo Country*. It has been chosen as best Western of the year. As Stephen points out, it is the only Western of the year.

I got through my two performances of *Via Dolorosa*. It still wasn't full – perhaps 650 of the 750 seats were gone. I have promised that everyone will get champagne when we finally fill the house completely. When I told this to Adam, the company manager, he let out a thoughtful little 'huh' which made it disarmingly clear that he didn't think I would be cracking open the bubbly too soon.

I was delighted to find a group of people at my stage door who were friends of Shulamit Aloni and Eran Baniel. They congratulated me on the accuracy of my impersonations. I would like to have talked longer but I had to hurry two blocks to the Ethel Barrymore Theatre on 47th Street to catch the last forty minutes of my other play.

I have said earlier in this diary that one reason for going on stage was to overcome my fear of the audience. Terror of what Peter Hall calls 'the great beast' is not unusual. Samuel Beckett sloped off after dress rehearsals and never attended public performances of his work. The moment I walked into the Barrymore earlier this week I knew that I didn't have a hope. All the hours I have piled up on the stage have been in vain. Even as I approached the golden doors of the theatre and entered its red plush auditorium, I knew I would be as tortured as ever to watch a live performance of *Amy's View*.

I find the Barrymore a hard theatre to deal with. Things, for me, are made worse by the fact that it was in this same theatre where, ten years ago, *The Secret Rapture* closed so precipitately. My father died in October 1989, in the week that the *New York Times* published its review. I flew back briefly to England, in grief, to bury my father, then returned to bury *The Secret Rapture* two days later. After the notice in the *Times*, it survived ten performances.

Last night the auditorium was charged with memory, so I crept round the back to the stage manager's office to listen to the play over the tannoy. The American audience always love narrative. They follow story much more keenly than the English. Even over the crackly drum backstage I could hear those satisfying moments of reaction where little waves of realization dawn and break over the audience. Crouched backstage, I loved the sound of it.

Amy's View, for better or worse, is what's called an audience play. Crudely, this means that a lot of people enjoy it. At the end there was tremendous crash of applause and the sounds of screaming. The actors came off pleased with their work. The principal producers, Robert Fox and Scott Rudin, seemed especially happy. One of the other producers said, 'It was good for a first preview.' This is always a lame remark, a fence-sitting remark. I wanted to reply 'It will never get better. That's all you're going to get.'

The only four people in the audience who seemed to have disliked the evening were, inevitably, in Judi Dench's dressing room, drinking her champagne and looking peaky in the reflected glow of Judi's faultless manners. There are a certain kinds of professional colleagues who are like heat-seeking missiles. They patrol the skies for happy occasions in the hope of spoiling them.

Robert Fox and I walked out on to the stage. I love that moment when the auditorium's emptied, but you can still feel the heat of the performance and of the departed audience. It's the most sensual moment in the theatre. Robert and I both dislike a sound effect in Act 2 when Richard runs a tape of Amy's children playing offstage. It's unnecessary and badly recorded. It jars with the flow of the play. It's an argument I often have with Richard. Like most directors, he likes what he calls a 'sound palette'. Like most playwrights, I don't. But from long experience Robert and I both know that there are times and places to bring up this sort of thing. At a dress rehearsal, the production was 95 per cent wonderful. When is the right moment to mention the 5 per cent? I have been working with Stephen Daldry, who is the least defensive of directors. But even collegiate Stephen might balk at having his sound effects criticized five minutes after his first preview.

So Robert and I decided to bide our time, and let Richard enjoy his triumph. He deserves it. It's the kind of trade-off you make when you're a playwright. As Howard Brenton once remarked to me, 'Knowing when to speak and when to shut up is nine-tenths of being a playwright in the theatre.'

The actors were going on to a restaurant, but I was too tired. This morning, I'm writing this account on the plane to London, where I have to go for just 24 hours. I had to get up at 6.30 a.m. to get to the airport. Matters were made worse by the fact that Daylight Saving Time began today and the clocks went forward. Trying to calculate when I would arrive reminded me of the Bette Midler joke about the backwardness of my homeland: 'When it's ten o'clock in New York, it's 1935 in London.'

6 April It's Tuesday morning and my insane trip to London is over. I flew out on Sunday morning from JFK, arrived home to sleep a single night in my own bed, went on Monday to a run-through of *Plenty* at the Almeida rehearsal room, then got on the 6.30 p.m. flight which delivered me back to my New York loft by 9.30 p.m. in time for a night's sleep. The management had generously cancelled Monday's *Via Dolorosa* so that I could make my journey. I have tricked my body into believing that it never went away, but at the end I am shaky and a little bit weepy as well.

It was upsetting to see my home so briefly. Nicole is away. She has recently designed a new collar for a cat who features in advertisements for pet food. She said she didn't want to be paid. They offered her some Arthur's. I came home to find 700 tins of cat food in the dining room. I woke on Easter Monday to see our garden in bloom. I was taken aback at how beautiful the English spring was, while knowing I wouldn't see the garden again till the middle of June. On Sunday night I talked to our dog Blanche, explaining why I had been away. But as we went upstairs, she looked at me reproachfully, then slunk away to sleep in another room. She wasn't going to risk getting attached to me by sleeping at the foot of my bed. She knew I would only desert her again. Blanche has me down as the leaving kind.

Plenty itself was both inspiring and upsetting. I had never met a lot of the actors. It was tough to have to walk into a run-through without ever having had a chance to get to know them. It was up to me to handle things as well as I could, but I don't think I managed to communicate my enthusiasm to everyone in the room. Cate Blanchett is playing Susan Traherne, and Jonathan Kent is directing. Understandably, Cate was so nervous at the idea that the author would only be over to see the play once that she fortified herself with a couple of vodkas at lunchtime before the run-through. She has a quality of vulnerability – what Jonathan calls her 'bruised' quality – which is overwhelmingly moving. Whenever she spoke of the war she reached right into your heart. She has the basic gift of playing Susan Traherne: the ability to be all things at once – both magnificent and infuriating, both alluring and mad. This woman who has a good war but then is disillusioned by the peace is the most demanding part I have written. Jonathan, who looks like a ghost, says he's directed *Hamlet*, and it's easier.

I spoke with the cast for half an hour at the end, then got in a car to go back to Heathrow. From the airport I called Cate, but I could tell she was in a sort of vortex of self-doubt. My words of admiration were no help to her. This left me feeling useless and clumsy. When I got on the plane my own melancholy overcame me. I felt bitter that this revival is going on without me. There is not a play of mine about which I feel more strongly. I will not be around to see Cate's performance grow into something remarkable. *Via Dolorosa* has robbed me of the experience of three other plays now.

I had a few glasses of wine, and tried to read a book about Rabin's assassination. I realized I was feeling blue because *Plenty*, which I wrote in 1977, is both worse and better than what I write now. The bad bits make me embarrassed by their awkward humour and shallowness. But the poetry of the play is the poetry of youth and I have lost it for ever. Susan Traherne stands on a French hillside and glows with the hope which is unique to being young. I cried as Cate played the scene. But perhaps I cried partly for literary reasons. There's a sweetness to the tone, a brightness I can no longer reach.

I thought of that passage in John Osborne's autobiography in which he remembers what it was like at the beginning. He gets into an open-topped car and drives south towards the Mediterranean in the company of a beautiful young woman: 'As we crossed the Italian border, I felt young as only the old can remember feeling: lean, lithe and swift.'

7 April Yesterday was frightening. I tried to do as little as possible all day, so that I could fight my tiredness. I ran a lot of the lines before I started. But I knew within thirty seconds of starting that my brain wasn't in gear. Somebody seemed to be speaking and I assume it had to be me. But it didn't sound like me.

A woman's hearing aid started making a high-pitched squeal and people were shouting at her to turn it off. I could no more deal with this moment than fly to the moon. I stood in the glare of the stage lights, scared to hell. I went, as Geena Davis would say, 'like, out of body'. The purpose of this diary is to make the reader feel what it is to be an actor. At this point I give up. You have to stand on a stage ravaged by jet lag and exhaustion to know what it is like. Only those who have stood there thinking: I do not know what the fuck I say next, in front of 700 people, can imagine the experience. You break into sweat. But, oddest of all, the more you panic, the more detached you become. I remember once being given an anaesthetic before an operation and it was the same feeling. You feel yourself going down. And you are disturbed by the fact you are going down willingly.

After half an hour I began to settle. I swayed a lot, thinking I was going to faint. My throat was tired, and I was croaking by the end. But I got through. Interestingly, we were nearly full on a Tuesday night. There was a very subtle shift in the nature of the audience. The applause when I walked on at the beginning was longer and more wholehearted. For the first time I felt that these were not people who had come because they were interested in the subject matter. They were coming to see *me*. Something in the event itself seemed to have changed. We shall see.

8 April No Broadway opening is ever trouble-free. However steady the ship, however experienced the hands, something always wobbles. I spent a full two hours this morning on the telephone to Scott Rudin and Robert Fox, making the minor adjustments they want to *Amy's View*. Richard and I made small changes in the text to make it more New York-friendly. Aqua Libra became San Pellegrino; a spanner became a screwdriver.

In some ways, Judi Dench gives you a false sense of security. One of the first people I ever watched working in the professional theatre was Paul Scofield. In those days, he was the hardest actor to direct that I'd ever seen. Not because he was difficult – far from it – but because he gave you infinite possibility. With most actors you are working to get them to accomplish one performance. Most of the time you know where you're heading. But Scofield was so fluent that he could give you fifty different performances, all of them dangerously alluring.

Judi not only gives you that technical freedom but also, in her personality, she soaks up all the usual shocks that a production undergoes. Because of her temperament, you suffer few of the normal anxieties and disagreements which mark everyday rehearsal processes. Judi's personality spreads warmth. There's a danger that warmth acts as a blanket, disguising real problems underneath. 'Oh Judi's wonderful,' everyone says. She is wonderful, but other things get overlooked.

I had two shows yesterday. When I arrived at the theatre a couple of strangers were measuring up the stage for the next show. This is a famous moment in Broadway legend. You think you're doing fine. Then you walk in one day and here are these gross intruders. Luckily, I am here for a limited season, so I was not shocked. But I still threw the interlopers out so that I could do my warm-up. When I made movies, I hated that moment when actors turned up carrying the scripts for their next projects. Fuck it. The Booth is my theatre, at least until 13 June. The gifted Australian drag queen who is bursting to come in and abuse his admirers can wait until then.

As far as my own public goes, I realized that my diagnosis from the previous day was depressingly correct. They've changed. They now know almost nothing about the subject. They have come simply to learn. I used to have a rapport with the audience which buoyed me up. By and large, they gave as much as they took. But yesterday I found myself at both performances mentally standing at a blackboard and pointing with a stick. The whole thing was like adult education class – with coughs. It was bloody boring and bloody hard work.

Amy's View ends forty minutes later than me, so I can go and watch a good chunk. The contrast could not be more startling. There is a rapturous warmth in the house at the Barrymore, a kind of toasty feeling which I will never get at *Via Dolorosa*. Judi's dressing room, with its air of the Chelsea flower show and its parade of famous visitors all coming to pay court, makes a vivid contrast with my own cell.

Let us be clear about one thing. At the end of five weeks of effort, I am still starring in the least popular show on Broadway. In the ebb and flow of this diary, let us never lose sight of this fact.

In Judi's room, people were saying the same things that they said to me a few weeks ago: 'We saw it in London, and it's even better here.' I happen to think they're right – in both cases. But the mantra has to be repeated. And it has to be believed, or else what the hell have you been doing for the last couple of months? Robert Fox is beadier about American audiences than I am. Beside him, I'm Pollyanna. Robert said, 'David, you may as well face it. They don't want plays on Broadway. They want actors. *Amy's View* gives them a very great actor. And that's what they want.'

Back home for a wonderful conversation with Wally. A young director rang him saying she had been looking for a Wally Shawn type for her new movie. Then she had the startling idea of asking Wally himself. However, she had then insisted he do a tape audition for the role. Which he did. I asked Wally why he had agreed to do the audition. Wally replied: 'Because I'm not sure I'm a Wally Shawn type any more.'

9 April This morning, the *Times* names *Sideman* as the play with the lowest attendance on Broadway. And Bernie Gersten points out that *You're a Good Man, Charlie Brown* still plays to a lower percentage of capacity. So whichever way you hack it, I am in the relegation zone, but I do not prop up the table. A false boast. I apologize.

I had a listless day. Lunch with Laura Pels to discuss the upcoming production of *The Judas Kiss* at the Atelier, her beautiful theatre in Paris. Then the strange ritual of being presented to the board of the Lincoln Center. You are expected to speak for a few minutes so that these business folk can get to hear the voice of the artist. It's a good idea.

I spoke briefly about my admiration for Joe Papp and William Shawn. Because I grew up in the sixties I took it for granted that good things always happened at the edge of society. I thought there was something called counter-culture. But when I came to America, Joe and Mr Shawn showed that the best place to be radical is at the centre. Joe didn't want to run a cult theatre way downtown. He wanted to mount challenging work and then move it to where as many people as possible could see it, either in Central Park or on Broadway.

William Shawn used his position as editor of the *New Yorker* to publish articles on the atomic bomb, on the environment and on foreign policy. Nobody gave a damn when the *Village Voice* opposed the war in Vietnam. But when the *New Yorker* began to call for an end to American involvement, it had an influence in Washington.

I said that at the Booth Theatre we were trying an experiment. We wouldn't know for some time whether it had worked. In my mind I couldn't help seeing a letter I've had from a madman, all green ink and underlining. It cut me to the quick. Among other rather shrewd questions, it asked, in huge letters 'Who's going to decide whether this play works? You? Or' – underlined five times – 'US?' It's a fair thing to ask.

Perhaps I was overly downbeat. Certainly Bernie Gersten was looking at me with a forced smile as if to say, 'Why is David running himself down in front of my board?' I've had a depressing run of shows, and have been beginning to lose heart. But last night, thanks be to God, my luck changed. The audience were a riot, and I came off the stage at the end singing my gratitude. John Gielgud said that once you start a run, you will feel that you only do one good performance out of ten. It may be true, but one good audience helps.

10 April Yesterday I was more tired than at any time since I arrived in America. I woke, groaning in disbelief that it was only Friday. I dragged myself four blocks to Dean and Deluca, bought some hot soup and crawled back to bed to watch movies on TV. By chance, they were showing an old Joe Mankiewicz movie which I'd seen in Paris only last year. I found myself watching *A Letter to Three Wives* for a second time quite happily.

If I ever write a book about the American cinema it'll be called 'The Study and the Street', because it's that opposition – between going somewhere or staying where you are – that provides many of the best American films with their essential framework. Behind their various stories lies one agonizing question: is it really such a good idea to leave the street you were born on? And, if you succeed in acquiring learning, money or class, will it ever really replace the authenticity and vitality of the street you left behind?

The classic American hero sits at the window of his study with a book in his hand, or in the big mansion with a cocktail in his hand, wondering whether he mightn't have been better off not making the journey. Particularly in the films of the forties and fifties (i.e. the ones I love best) you frequently find a central character who has been bourgeoisified. In the process of acquiring money, he or she has also acquired more rarefied manners, or even culture. Because of the exceptional mobility of American society, people are able to ascend very quickly. But they are also deeply suspicious of that ascent. In some way they suspect that the advance is a retreat.

I could fill the rest of this diary with examples. There are too many to list. Robert de Niro has made a career out of playing characters who are either unwilling or unable to make the trip. The conflict between Diane Keaton (gentry) and Al Pacino (street, aping gentry) in *The Godfather* is a classic playing out of the basic theme. She's too good for him, sure. But you could say she's also irrelevant. Pacino both loves her and knows that she doesn't have anything to do with real life. Joan Crawford (street) rises fast as *Mildred Pierce*, but there's always someone around to remind her that however fast she rises, she's still a tramp – and she knows it. She brings her daughter up to be gentry. She gives her all the piano lessons and posh clothes she never had. The results are predictably catastrophic.

In *Some Came Running* Frank Sinatra (gentry, now street) can't decide between the schoolteacher and the hooker. Of course he can't. No man in American cinema can. How does anyone choose between Ginny Moorehead and Miss French? The teacher tells him, 'I'm not one of your bar-room tarts.' He tells the teacher, 'I don't belong in your class. But you won't get a chance to flunk me again.' Citizen Kane (gentry) doesn't throw his life away on a débutante. He tries one of those, and the marriage goes quickly sour. Instead, he hands his life over to a showgirl (street). The reason's simple. She has something he doesn't. Naturally, she loses it the minute he tries to play Pygmalion. Pygmalion doesn't wash in America. 'We're different. We live in a castle,' says the showgirl bitterly, longing to be back among the hurrying crowds on the sidewalk in New York.

In the film of the Theodore Dreiser classic *Carrie*, Laurence

Olivier (head waiter to the gentry) helps Jennifer Jones (street) to acquire class, and then kills himself because she will never love him back. Pygmalion fails again. In *Love Me Or Leave Me*, Ruth Etting (played by Doris Day) has the ugly, vicious punk (James Cagney) tied round her ankle with irons. She can't walk into a room without him following. He's there to remind her that whatever airs she now puts on as a respectable face of show business, she will never escape the people she came from. Why can't she tell him to fuck off? Because Cagney blackmails her with the feeling that to throw off his malign vigour would be an impossible act of betrayal. Nice handsome Johnnie (gentry), who also loves her, doesn't stand a chance against the snarling, spitting, limping little ogre from Chicago.

Why else, for goodness' sake, does Burt Lancaster (street) refuse to run off with that lovely Deborah Kerr (gentry) in *From Here to Eternity*? Because Burt is the man everyone's looking for. The one who isn't willing to betray his roots. *That's* why Burt's sexy in the first place. If he went in Deborah's direction, he'd cease to be sexy.

Five Easy Pieces is the great seventies reworking of this essential theme of the American cinema because it has a conscious hero who is going the other way. Jack Nicholson (gentry, pretending to be street) has rejected the study – horrors! His family make classical music, so they must be phoneys! – and chosen instead to go off and work in an oilfield, because it's more real. And in a neat inversion of the usual story, a nice middle-class girl tries to haul him back up to the study – not, mind you, before he's told the working woman to stick the toast between her knees. As Deborah Eisenberg once said, 'If you've ever worked as a waitress, that scene isn't funny.'

In one of the first novels about an arriviste, *Le Rouge et le noir*, Julien Sorel doesn't question that ascent is a worthwhile aim in life. In French society, it may be taken for granted. In America the attitude is more complex. If you look, there's barely an American film of any value – *A Place in the Sun* springs to mind – which doesn't touch on this argument about acquisition and loss. Oh yes, the great American theme is class.

11 April As I was leaving the theatre last night, I knocked over a glass of wine. When I got home, I dropped a jar of honey. Just what I needed, trying to clear honey up off all the other groceries at 11 o'clock at night. Perhaps I'm getting Parkinson's. Or perhaps I'm just shattered.

I've paid a terrible price for that trip to London last weekend. We nearly had champagne tonight, but we were still twenty light. Karen was monitoring the box office till the last moment, dreaming of Veuve Clicquot. At the end of my two performances, I was due to go over to the Barrymore to catch the last half hour of *Amy's View*. But Danny and Gabrielle forbade me. They told me to go home. After a show the other night, Judi Dench said I looked like a cat which has been nailed by all four paws to a board. Last night I was a dead cat. I did as I was told and fled downtown.

12 *April* Against my wishes, I went to see the matinée of *Amy's View* on my day off. They play a Sunday matinée and I don't. It was my only chance to see the play before it opens. I sat in the middle of the audience in a fair degree of agony. The players seemed to me suspended at a half-way stage between the subtlety of the rehearsal room and the techniques they need to play an 1,100-seat house. You do have to take things very slowly and say them very loud. The Americans are less amused by the Ronald Pickup character, the Lloyds agent who claims to love Esme, but who loses all her money. Unlike the English, they don't think it's funny to be swindled by a man with a posh accent. Ronnie has adjusted his performance beautifully. As Esme, Judi works on a lethal slow burn, charming you, then eventually taking you in and playing havoc with your emotions.

Afterwards, Sidney Poitier pushed past me in his eagerness to congratulate Judi. As he flashed past, he looked as handsome as ever. I felt a thrill of pleasure at being irrelevant again. I realized how much I have missed it. I couldn't be happier than to be ignored. I long once more to be the man behind the clockface with the screwdriver.

The cast were all going on to an opening for which you had to wear evening dress. It all seemed part of some fictional way of life, a peculiar fantasy of show business which died in the thirties.

Instead I went home alone to roast a chicken. As I prepared it, I realized in horror that it came wrapped with an article from the *New York Times* about what a great bird it is. Has this town gone mad? The power of the press, indeed. Here, even the chickens flaunt their reviews.

13 April Fascinating morning being interviewed by Serge Schmemann. He has been due for two weeks, but because he is acting as foreign editor of the *New York Times* during the Kosovo crisis, he has been too busy to see me.

As usual, when you meet a first-rate journalist, you want to listen more than you want to talk. Schmemann was the correspondent in Berlin for the fall of the wall, in Moscow for the end of Communism and in Jerusalem for the assassination of Rabin. He eventually became spooked by the feeling that the big stories were following him round the world. To write about Rabin's murder four months after arriving in the Middle East was particularly daunting.

Schmemann said that there was a tradition of not sending Jews to cover Israel for the *Times*. Life had been much easier for him specifically because he wasn't Jewish. He said outsiders were always welcome in Israel. Everyone wants to explain things to them because it is assumed they are ignorant. But one of his successors, who was Jewish, was given a much harder time. People would bang on her car when she worked on the Sabbath. She would write articles making the same points he had. But she would get called a traitor.

This, he says, is the reason for the politeness with which *Via Dolorosa* is being received in New York. If it were by a Jew, it would be picketed, and there would be demonstrations. It's an interesting point.

At the theatre itself, I have a major problem. I opened nearly four weeks ago, but nobody has yet managed to post hoardings outside the building with the usual selection of quotations and photographs. We've had good reviews – it's crazy not to let people see them. I now understand why Bernie looked at me askance at the board meeting, because it turns out that last week we played to 82 per cent. But you wouldn't know it. From the outside, we look like a flop. Some people have even passed the Booth Theatre and enquired if it was empty. I am so sick of arriving every day at this desolate storefront that I am jokingly threatening to go on strike unless what they call the 'plastics' are up by the evening. I don't see why everyone else should be working so hard to make the show a success when the actual building looks disused. The Lincoln Center, where the play is not being presented, is festooned with huge posters.

It seems to be a problem of institutional theatre. There is a man whom I have never met who is in charge of these things. He's never introduced himself or picked up a phone. If you call him, he's on holiday. If the show were being presented in the commercial sector, his excuses wouldn't be accepted. A bracing encounter with Scott Rudin would sort the matter out.

The show itself was my forty-third in New York and it was fun. Everyone was in the stalls, so the empty balcony acted as a resonator. My voice sounded sharp. They were exceptionally intelligent and I enjoyed doing the show more than I have in weeks. I was in a good mood anyway because two of my children, Lewis and Darcy, are here for the week. My stepdaughter Candice joined us for dinner.

Today I have woken up tense because we are only two days away from opening *Amy's View*. I don't live in a corridor of uncertainty. More like, I dwell in its fucking palace.

14 April I arrived at the theatre to find there was still no display outside. Bernie Gersten wanted to come down to explain but I asked him not to. I said it wouldn't be helpful for me to get angry before the show. Being the playwright and the only actor is sometimes too much. You can't have raging arguments ten minutes before you go on stage.

The stage management knew how upset I was. So Donna and Karen had made a sandwich board and said they would be happy to parade up and down 45th Street on my behalf. The board was festooned with very funny made-up quotes. My favourite ones were 'I've seen it 42 times – Karen Armstrong' and 'His English accent is perfect – Meryl Streep'.

It was a scary night for me because Mike Nichols was in. I am always nervous when the audience contains either (A) people who know me well, (B) directors, or (C) people I have directed myself. Mike scores in all three categories. Knowing Mike was there, I was a little cautious, not wanting to make a fool of myself in front of him.

I would have been even more nervous had I known there was a person from category (D) present as well – people whose close relatives are portrayed in the show. Afterwards Shulamit Aloni's son came round and introduced himself with his wife and daughter. His response was electric. 'It's so important you do this. It's so important for American Jews. It's unique, for once, to see Palestinians presented as human beings, and yet, at the same time, for the work not to be anti-Semitic or anti-Zionist.' Equally gratifying, he thought my portrait of his mother perfect. 'It's exactly what she's like. Except, can I tell you? since you met her, she's a little happier. She really is a little happier since she left politics.' He said that his mother had asked him to apologize again for her rude behaviour to me at our meeting. I said it hardly bothered me, since it gave my play a striking climax. I told him that Shulamit is everybody's favourite character. 'Everyone tells her that. She's happy about that too.'

Mike and I went off in high spirits to eat at Joe Allen's. Mike understood the nature of the evening exactly, as I knew he would, and he insisted that what I did was indeed 'acting'. 'I don't know why you're questioning it. You do exactly what I teach my students. You convey the impression that you have something urgently important to say. You lay out the rules at the beginning and suggest that in order to receive this message, the audience is going to have to go down a certain route. And then you let no barrier appear between the audience and their access to your deepest self. That's acting.'

I asked him if he thought it was easier in a one-man show than in a play. 'It's not because it's a one-man show. It's because they're your own words. Only the very greatest actors can convince you that other people's words are their own, and that there is nothing at all between you and their feelings. They become not the instrument, but the author.' 'Who?' 'Judi Dench. Jason Robards.'

We were interrupted by Gabrielle, whom I had deputed to go to the press night of *Amy's View*. I had asked her to come and tell me the worst. She was cautious about expressing her own opinion, but she had talked to Robert Fox. He told her I should be very pleased. Richard Eyre had bolted in horror and spent the evening at the basketball instead. Mercifully, the designer Bob Crowley had stayed through the whole ordeal. A minute later Bob also appeared in Joe Allen's and reassured me that it had gone as well as possible, given the forty critics in the house. In fact, it was turning into exactly the kind of evening I have avoided since I started doing this play. It gave me a view of a whole other world. 'Ooh, look, there's Liza Minnelli' and 'Is that Liam Neeson?'

I ended up talking to Kevin Spacey. I hadn't seen him since the London run of *The Iceman Cometh*. Howard Davies' production has now opened here and has been rapturously received. Kevin was looking lean and happy.

KEVIN: People come too reverently to O'Neill. They behave like they're at a gala. Tonight I decided the only way to deal with it was to kick ass.

ME: (*taken aback*) Kick ass! Golly.

KEVIN: That's what I did. I just went out and kicked ass.

ME: Gosh! Did it work?

KEVIN: It certainly did. We had a great night out here.

ME: (*thoughtful*) Do you think it might work for me? Do you think I could kick ass in *Via Dolorosa*?

Long pause. Kevin looking at me closely.

KEVIN: Maybe. Maybe. Why not try it and see?

15 April I tried it at yesterday's matinée. Someone was coughing during Benni Begin, so I kicked ass. The effect was pretty exciting. The audience fell silent, awed. When I came off Karen, with a big grin on her face, said, 'Don't get addicted.'

I did the evening performance, then went to a nice, mellow dinner party over on the East Side. A mixture of journalists and folk from my line of work. The first person I ran into was Harrison Ford, who said that *The Designated Mourner* was one of the most perfect things he had ever seen – the design, the direction, the play, everything. Naturally, because we both know Mike Nichols, I began to talk to him about acting and what we had learnt from watching Mike. I have always admired Ford. I found him more forthright and clear-headed than almost anyone I have spoken to, with a note of defiance.

'When I'm offered a part, then I'm aware I bring a certain amount of baggage with me, in terms of how the audience view me. So the first thing I question is whether that baggage is going to be helpful to the picture or not. If it isn't, then I tell the producers so, and turn the picture down. The audience see me in a certain way, and there's no point in pretending they don't.

'I only get as far as page 7 of most scripts. If I get to the end of the script, I'll almost certainly do it. I have to feel an emotional connection to it at once. From then on, most of the time I'm asking to cut the script down. I get rid of the talk. Most dialogue in films is what I call action-talk. In other words, it's talk about action. That dialogue is always unnecessary. It's more satisfying to show the action, not to talk about it.

'I don't do any of that stuff about character. I hate it when people say "My character this" or "My character that". I believe that my character is there to tell the story, and it's the story that's important, and the feelings the story raises. The pleasures of film-making are the pleasures of craft. I love it. I love hitting a mark. People think having to hit marks is boring, but there's a real pleasure in doing it well. I was a carpenter, and dovetailing wood is a beautiful thing. My most important relationship after the director is with the dolly grip, the guy pushing the camera. Because he and I have got to have an understanding. He needs to understand how my body moves, and I need to understand how he moves. Once you have that rapport, you're away.

'Years ago I was a contract player for Columbia earning $150 a week, and nobody took the slightest notice of anything I said. I was very, very unhappy and frustrated. I was fucking angry. I knew I would have to earn $1,500 a week before they started listening. I'm now paid enormous sums of money because I know that's what my value is. That's what I'm worth to them. And the advantage is that people now listen to what I say. I only go to work once a year. It's my work. That's what it is.'

I said, 'You must be heaven to make films with if those are your attitudes.' Ford grinned. 'I am.'

16 April Another opening. A day of horrible foreboding. *Amy's View* had been going far too well. The audiences were coming. They were loving it. So you're just standing around waiting for that moment when the boot goes in.

Jonathan Kent rang from London to describe the first preview of *Plenty*, which also happened yesterday. *Plenty* starts in 1962, then flashes back eighteen years earlier to when Susan Traherne was behind the lines in the SOE during the war. Unfortunately, last night, they put up the wrong caption. The 1962 scene was announced as being set in 1944. When Susan's friend came on carrying a plastic bag of food, someone in the stalls said, 'But they didn't have Chinese take-away in 1944.'

After that, things went well enough for a first preview. There was not just a queue for returned seats but for the chance of standing places being returned as well. It's slightly bewildering. A whole generation has not seen this play, partly because it's so expensive to put on. It's like an opera without songs. Jonathan was very tired, but also nervous. He feels that both Cate Blanchett and the whole company are on the brink of greatness. Cate had left the theatre pleased to have begun, but with a burden of responsibility on her shoulders. She's preternaturally adult, and aware of her own quality. She knows how good she can be, and how important it is, both for herself and for everyone else, that she fulfils the potential. There is something moving at the heart of this young woman's relationship to her own talent.

Jonathan noticed how shocking the play still was to a modern audience. People gasped at Susan's ferocity, but were also repelled and annoyed by parts of the play. It really irritated them. Sometimes you forget how much stronger medicine the theatre used to hand out. When I saw Lindsay Duncan in a brilliant revival of Pinter's *The Homecoming* a couple of years ago, I was shocked by it. It was written in 1965. There are moments in it when you reel back. Human contact is represented as transactions of violence and violation. It wasn't 'bad language' shocking. It was deep down shocking. People around me were horrified by its apparent amorality. But then, to be honest, so was I. I loved it.

Jonathan's call to my dressing room set me off into a state of distraction. I wasn't helped by going over to the Barrymore to give the actors their presents. The marquee was surrounded with TV crews and reporters. I stayed fifteen minutes, then slipped back to the Booth, where my backstage team had decorated our theatre with balloons and presents to give me some sense of my opening two blocks away.

It was weird to miss *Amy's View*, and weirder still to be out on stage trying to do my own show, while knowing what was going on elsewhere. It wasn't a pleasant experience, and the audience were determined not to help. It revived my theory that, for some reason, for *Via Dolorosa*, Thursday nights are the worst.

Amy's View started last night at 6.30 p.m., so when I finished my own performance, a small group of people who had been at the other event generously came to my dressing room to tell me about it. They were glowing with the experience. It had been 'transporting', 'extraordinary' and so on. It was pretty much the same story at the party which was a couple of blocks away in some peculiar red-velvet night club. I took Lewis, Darcy and Candice, and we were met by a wall of people telling us that it was one of the best first nights they had ever attended. They had never known an audience seem so unforced in their response.

None of this was washing with me. I was beginning to have a really horrible time. It was my honest intention to get drunk, but I found, in Brendan Behan's words, that 'one drink is too many and a thousand not enough'. I saw my director a couple of times on the dance floor, and was happy to see that Richard had drunk enough for both of us.

The press agent came over to inform me that the first television reviews were terrific – one said, 'If *The Blue Room* was pure theatrical Viagra, then *Amy's View* is pure theatrical Ecstasy.' I was handed from person to person, and found myself talking to the director Nick Hytner, whose own thoughts chimed weirdly with my own. He said, 'I sat there watching *Amy's View* thinking that the play was so bold. You never get boldness in the theatre any more.' I agreed with him, thinking about *The Homecoming*. 'We've lost something, no question. Our theatre's grown anaemic. It's weak.' I repeated what I had thought about the Pinter and Nick made a brilliant reply: 'Yes, plays should be sour. It's actors who should make them sweet.'

It became apparent that we weren't going to get the print reviews before we went home, so I headed off at midnight for a reasonable night's sleep. This morning I have woken to everything I expected in the *New York Times*. The general tone could be summed up as: It doesn't matter what sort of rickety vehicle she's in, at least you get to see Judi Dench.

Arts journalists have often had a problem with *Amy's View*, because it contains a rather mistrustful portrait of an arts journalist. The English reviewers gave disproportionate space to the impact of the second act, which is centred on an argument about the media. It's set during the time when Esme's son-in-law, Dominic, is working as a critic. Not surprisingly, real-life critics tend to see the whole play as an attack on their profession. They find it hard to see past some particularly abrasive exchanges on the subject. As Candice said when she came out, 'Goodness, I wouldn't like to have been a journalist at that play.' This is a feeling some newspaper critics manage all too successfully to convey. They tend not to notice that, in its later acts, the play explores rather more profound moments of loss and love, what Joyce called 'those big words which make us so unhappy'.

Ben Brantley's review this morning is the apotheosis of this trend. Everything which is not Judi Dench is damned. Tate Donovan, he says, hasn't settled yet. Samantha Bond is lumbered with the worst part. Ronnie Pickup is a stage drunk. Richard's direction is merely 'likeable'. My own work is 'verbiage', 'annoying', 'heavy sledding'.

Grudgingly he does admit that the play itself has a quality of 'transcendence'. But Brantley tucks the word away, as if 'transcendence' were something you get every night at the theatre, handed out with the programmes.

For the rest, Brantley praises Judi, as she deserves to be praised, but at the expense of everyone else. In a calculated aside he remarks that the play is not as good as *The Secret Rapture*. I must admit that I found even my jaded old eyes popping at that proposition. As it was the *New York Times* which ensured the closure of *The Secret Rapture* in one of the more publicized stand-offs between a newspaper and a playwright in recent years, I think we may take this posthumous elevation of the work to be some bitter kind of a joke.

Brantley also seems peculiarly disturbed that we have sold seats before the bench has handed down its judgment. The whole review embodies a nakedly political sentiment about the power of the *Times*. The critic dislikes the idea that people have already booked without the benefit of the *Times*' advice on whether their money will be well spent. His argument eerily echoes the words of Dominic Tyghe in the play: 'A book costs what? £12, £13. We're here to say, "Hang on, is this thing as good as it's cracked up to be?"' Brantley is piqued by the play's popularity into accusing us of bringing Judi to New York to exploit her new international film stardom. He's factually wrong. We've been planning this season since long before her two films were released. Believe it or not, we've admired her as a stage actress for quite a few years now.

Of the four plays I have had in New York in the last twelve months, the *New York Times* has attacked three and admired one. Normally, at this point, I would fly back to England and throw the newspaper out of the window at 35,000 feet. But the problem this time is that I am condemned to stay in town. I am not looking forward to it. For all of us, the purpose of bringing *Amy's View* to New York was to let the American public see Judi Dench and to vindicate the play itself. In the first, we have succeeded. As of this morning, in the second, it feels like we have failed.

A passage from John Osborne's autobiography, about New York

theatre: 'The astonishment of writers like Arnold Wesker and David Hare when they find themselves its sacrificial victims is hard to understand. It was ever thus . . . I felt that the odds were much the same as punting at The Sands in Las Vegas.'

17 April My mood passed like the weather. By 3 p.m. I'd eaten a steamed fish in Chinatown. I realized I'd opened three plays this season on Broadway without anyone involved sustaining any damage. The ground had shaken a little from time to time but all three buildings were still standing. And so were the people who lived in them. I was sent a selection of quotes for the *Amy's View* ads, and they confirmed what the press agents had told me. The other reviews are very good. Tom Erhardt, my London agent, said, 'Some of them appear to think that Judi Dench is so brilliant that she must have written her own lines.' I laughed and said, 'Not much we can do.'

I did the best *Via Dolorosa* I've done in weeks. Because I'd been distracted the night before, I was determined to get back on track. When I reported Danny as saying that America was a place with no spiritual values and where life was completely empty and meaningless, a man called out helpfully, 'He's quite right.' Later, when I got to the terrible pun about 'sects and the single church', the audience groaned and hooted so much I couldn't continue. The show was a lovely mix of serious and funny. A man was heard by Lewis and Darcy to get up at the end and say, 'Wow. Well that's given us something to talk about.'

Eva Marie Saint came round afterwards. I couldn't believe I was meeting the star of *On the Waterfront* and *North By Northwest*. For me, it was a privilege. She said, 'It can't be true that you're going to give up acting?' I said I was only doing this one play. 'But you're so brilliant. You can't give up,' she said. 'You can't.'

Robert Fox was giving a dinner in an Upper East Side restaurant for the casts of his two shows – *Closer* and *Amy's View*. It was heaven. Steak and chips, and a lot of friendly faces. I managed to provoke Judi Dench by telling her that Eva Marie Saint had told me on no account to give up acting. She had said I was too good. Judi exploded at this news. 'She didn't say that! She can't have! Does she have no taste at all?'

18 April A Saturday of ridiculous contrasts. When the house manager called backstage to tell us we could start the matinée she said, 'I've let in the halt, the lame and sick. And good luck.' A full inventory of destructive effects detonated throughout. One man had to be taken out in a state of advanced bronchial crisis – again, loudly protesting that he didn't want to go. What is it about coughers in this city, that they believe they have rights? Other people rattled tins of sweets between fits of tubercular hacking. One man kept up a running commentary on the play for the first fifteen minutes. I glared at him, and when he resumed five minutes later, my mind went blank. I was so upset that I came to a complete halt. I stood like a goldfish, blowing air into my cheeks. After a torrid silence, I managed to grapple again back up the cliff face. For the subsequent five minutes flop-sweat ran down my spine. I gave a horrible performance, right through to the end.

Afterwards I was told that we had broken a Broadway geriatric record. The cloakroom had issued precisely 150 listening devices for an audience of 500.

The evening was a different story. This time the house manager rang through half an hour before the show to tell us that every seat was sold, and to ask what our policy was on standing. We laughed and said we had never had the opportunity to formulate one. I said, 'Let 'em come in. The more the merrier. We're hardly going to turn them away.' This was one show I was determined not to fuck up. Soon after I got into the settlements, the lights suddenly faded on me. The board operator had hit the cue button twice. I stood there in total darkness for five seconds, and then the lights came back up. I carried on as if nothing had happened.

Afterwards we opened the Veuve Clicquot. It was intensely moving. It has taken us exactly fifty shows (fifteen previews, thirty-five full-price performances) to reach this point. Not one day has gone by in which my little team wasn't working flat out for this moment. Nor has one cross word ever been spoken between us. It has been an impeccably conducted campaign, and all the sweeter for being so difficult. All the appeal of working in the theatre was there in that moment in the dressing room when Karen, Donna, Gabrielle, Danny and I stood, glasses in hand, no less proud than NASA scientists or wheel changers in the winning pit. We raised our glasses of champagne – in relief, yes, but also in love. We drank to the next fifty.

19 April Off to Connecticut for a Sunday in the country with the dance/theatre director Martha Clarke. Arthur Miller came to dinner with his wife Inge, and we found ourselves discussing the origins of American theatre. Much to his surprise, Arthur had recently discovered that there were shows of some kind even during the Civil War. David Belasco later wrote melodramas. A man about to be killed throws the American flag over his face, then challenges his enemy to shoot him if he dare. The American theatre only finds its first true playwright in Eugene O'Neill. Miller never met him. O'Neill was in hospital in 1949 when he read *Death of a Salesman* and asked to meet its author. But O'Neill became too ill and died.

What I like about Arthur is that he tells the story of plays with an almost child-like pleasure, as if they were true. He tells of a Dostoevsky adaptation which he saw in Moscow. A handsome young prince was undressed in his beautiful bedroom by four servants. The prince, who appeared to be tall and well built, was first taken out of his elaborate military costume. Then he reached into his eye socket and took out of one of his eyeballs. Then his teeth. In front of your own astonished eyes, you saw a big young man becomes a tiny old man. The four servants picked him up in a sheet and carried him, like a crow, to bed. Most astonishing of all, when Arthur and Inge met the actor afterwards, he was young and tall.

This story reminded me of when Michael Gambon played *A View From the Bridge*. It was the most brilliant Arthur Miller performance I ever saw. When he read the text, Michael made one basic decision. Eddie Carbone would start out a big man. But by the end of the play, he would be small. That's precisely what Michael achieved in the role. I have no idea how, but Carbone shrank in front of your eyes. 'Great actor,' said Arthur. 'Like a Russian.'

20 April Good news from London. *Plenty* is still proving to be offensive. When, on Saturday night, in the second act, Susan Traherne met the Foreign Office apparatchik and he warned her, 'I have to tell you, Mrs Brock, it is more than likely you have met your match,' a man in the audience, excited at the prospect of Susan finally being squashed, burst into applause. In his review of *Amy's View*, Ben Brantley called the play 'annoying'. It did not seem to occur to him that 'annoying' is something the author might *want* a play to be.

In one way, it's sad that *Plenty* is said not to have dated. Twenty years later, it is still rare to see work in which women take charge and make no concessions to gender. Jonathan says that he usually goes up to the upper circle for the scene beside the Embankment when Susan goes to proposition a young working-class man with the aim of asking him anonymously to father her child. Jonathan sees the young women in the audience leaning forward, watching jealously as a taboo is broken. The men, he says, fall silent.

The allied bombing of Yugoslavia has plainly helped us. The lines in the Suez scene about 'the British becoming the cowboys of the world' are received with particular attention. Partly, you may say, it's fluke. Partly it's context. This is the fascination of the theatre. It tells you as much about the audience as it does about the play. *Hamlet* works wherever you do it, but it was lit up with a special urgency when it was presented in Berlin, in Prague or in Bucharest. In the fifties and sixties, in the worst days of the Cold War, it was seized on as a kind of encoded manifesto.

This question of why certain plays speak to the spirit of the time is the most elusive theatre puzzle of all. There's no predicting what will appeal and what won't. I always used to argue to Richard Eyre when he was running the National in the nineties that it was risky to do the Jacobeans because you could tell they didn't mean anything to the contemporary audience. In the 1960s there was a tremendous vogue for the revival of Jacobean work. Everyone found their decadence topical. Webster was everywhere. But thirty years later, the same playwrights were resolutely unperformable. Or rather, you could perform them but nobody gave a damn. Although there was a theoretic parallel between their age and ours – programme notes used words like cynicism, sexual corruption and mercantilism – the audience didn't feel it. Every time the National attempted a Jacobean play, I was proved horribly right.

For all the publicity, I was never really sure anyone was very interested in Oscar Wilde. I mean, yes of course, they were *interested*. A play in New York called *Gross Indecency*, which deliberately eschewed interpretation of Wilde's life and chose simply to lay out the facts, proved hugely popular and moved its audience deeply. It was better received than the fictional play I wrote with the same hero. But for all the articles in the papers claiming our affinity with the supreme playwright of the previous *fin de siècle*, did the audience feel that Wilde's special quality spoke specially to them? The passion *The Judas Kiss* provoked was in response to elements other than Wilde himself. The first-rate Australian production, which I saw in Sydney (with Bille Browne as Wilde) managed to erase all feeling of biopic. It became a play on its own terms, and the better for it. But it was odd. I was left feeling that a figure who everyone said embodied the Zeitgeist turned out not to.

21 *April* Howard Brenton says he hates it when he hears people say, 'Oh, I love theatre.' What is there to love? Theatre is tat, Howard says. It's a few pieces of canvas and wood and some lights. What you can love, he adds, is what the theatre can do. For myself, I love the theatre's unpredictability. I was beginning to get bored last night, at least in the first half. I was thinking how tired I was of doing what Scott Rudin calls 'laying pipe', i.e. bedding down exposition which you know will only pay off sixty minutes later. The pleasure of the evening now lies in the moments when I can stop explaining and start feeling. But when I got to the end, I found that Maggie Smith, of all people, had been in the audience and that she was waiting to come to my dressing room.

A difficult moment. My first job in the professional theatre was as an usher at the Old Vic during Laurence Olivier's famous early seasons. I watched Maggie Smith in *Othello* and *The Recruiting Officer* many times over, trying to understand the sharpness of her mind and her technique. When she came into my room I warned her that I had made some progress towards becoming an actor, but I still hadn't mastered the rituals of the dressing room. She said, 'Nobody has, except Judi.' I said how nervous I would have been had I known she was there. As it was, I'd had several moments of wondering what the hell I was doing out there on stage. 'Yes, that does occur to one.'

I told her that in England when people didn't like the show they told me how brave I was. 'They no longer say that. Now they tell me how beautiful the Booth Theatre is.' Maggie Smith said that one-man shows drive you crazy. When Alec McCowen used to tour round reciting the whole of St Mark's Gospel, he found the loneliness so overwhelming that he began to worry he was going off his tree. He found himself one night before the show looking into the mirror and saying, 'Why are ye nervous? Thou knowest thy lines and thou hast no reason to worry. Thou willst be all right when thou gettest out there.'

I laughed when Maggie Smith told me this story. But it was the laughter of recognition and fellow-feeling. It has a hideous plausibility.

22 *April* If an actor starts laughing on stage in England it's called 'corpsing'. In the States they call it 'going up'. Whichever, you might think it impossible to do in a one-man show because there's nobody there to laugh with. But I've proved the contrary.

Yesterday at the Wednesday matinée, I was overcome with a sense of absurdity and found myself shaking in an effort to keep control. The noise the audience made in response to my best jokes was so lame, so half-hearted, so fundamentally *inert* that I wanted to burst into gales of healthy laughter in return. They sounded like dead fish whose stomachs had been cut open to let out a little gas. I at once imagined Karen in the stage manager's corner and how she would be laughing. I played whole sections with an inane grin on my face.

Over at the Barrymore I was in time to meet Samantha Bond coming off the stage in floods of tears. I asked her what was wrong. 'Nothing was wrong. I've never done the third act better. That's why I'm crying. And I realized I've wasted my best performance on a Wednesday matinée.' She had met Judi Dench briefly at the side of the stage, doing a quick change. 'This lot are never going to laugh,' Judi said, 'we might as well try and move them.'

This morning I have written a letter to the management saying eight performances a week is too much. It's not because I can't do them. If I have to, I will. But Wednesday afternoon in the graveyard of laughter is a bummer. As Richard Eyre says in a fax from England: 'Even Hamlet doesn't talk non-stop for ninety minutes, and certainly not eight shows a week.'

Yesterday, twelve students and one teacher were killed by two fellow-pupils in a school in Littleton, Colorado. Everyone came into the theatre having spent the morning watching television. In 1996, 30 people were killed in Britain with guns. In the same year, 9,390 were killed in the United States. The answer to America's problems lies in its own hands. But everyone knows that, for reasons of political cowardice, gun reform is not on the agenda. Instead, visiting Poo-Bahs are dispatched from media headquarters to televise the locals in extreme states of grief. We are all forced to watch Katie Couric and Dan Rather stick microphones up the noses of people who have just lost their children.

The dead bodies had to be left in the school library for 24 hours for fear that the place was booby-trapped. The most intrusive pictures were of parents waiting in agony, in the near-certainty their children were inside. I had to turn away. What the fuck do these television people think they're doing? They transmit pictures of orgiastic grief purely to compensate for national impotence. Emotion is put on display as a substitute for action. A lot of people on TV invoked God, knowing that God is unlikely to pass a good, sensible gun law.

23 April Stephen Daldry flew over from England to see the show. As you might have predicted, it wasn't very good. It's always the way. Directors come on the wrong night. I was trying too hard at the beginning, partly because I'd had such a huge success the previous evening. I imagined I could carry over the air of that success into the next performance. Fatal.

What Stephen saw was a Broadway show, not *Via Dolorosa*. Only in some degree is that my fault. For the rest, it's the audience. If they want to turn the whole thing into show business, I seem powerless to stop them. I didn't feel they were engaged. Afterwards Stephen and I had no time to discuss it because Liam Neeson was also in. The release of the new *Star Wars* film next month is about to blow through his life and turn it upside down. He's such a gracious, sweet-natured man that I left the theatre less depressed than I deserved to be.

I was also amused by Tony Roberts, the American leading man. When Danny asked him what he thought of my acting, Roberts looked at me pitilessly and said, 'Let's just say if you promise to lay off the acting, I'll lay off the playwriting.' It was a deal.

24 *April* Stephen and I worked together for nearly an hour at 6.30 p.m. He suggested about twenty-five little changes of emphases and intention that he would like effected during the performance. It was stimulating, and just what I needed. I was desperate for input. I have lost sight of so many passages, and Stephen reminded me of their purpose. It made me realize that when, as a director, I have gone back to performances late in the run and told actors they were all wonderful, I was not, in fact, being very helpful. At this stage an actor needs and welcomes dialogue.

As soon as I began the show, I knew Stephen's changes would have to be made in front of an unhelpful audience. Not only was I work-ing to do things differently, but I was also fighting to win the hearts of a doubting public. Sweat started to run down my face and I was aware of my diaphragm aching with exertion. About two-thirds of the way through, I became more tired than I believed possible. In the middle there was a noisy walkout. Two people were offended by my account of the settlements and banged their chairs as loudly as they could, to make sure nobody missed their departure.

At the end Stephen was euphoric. He said it was the best show I had ever given. He had intended to take notes but instead he'd sat back and enjoyed it. I said it had been good on Wednesday too, but then it was because the audience inspired me. Tonight I was having to fight them. These nights involved much, much harder work. 'But great work,' Stephen said.

It was satisfying that this particular performance was the fifty-seventh in New York. I am exactly half way through the American run. I have finally grasped the simplest truth which most actors learn on the first day, but which somehow has eluded me. You have to run to keep still. You have to change all the time to stay where you were.

By chance, a letter had just come back from the management refusing my request to go down to seven shows a week. 'We firmly believe that the cancellation of a performance results in a loss of revenue and that it is an over-simplification to hold that anyone desiring to purchase a ticket will purchase based on availability . . . If it were true, then the logic would be that a show playing at 50 per cent of capacity would be better served by playing four performances a week at capacity rather than wearying their actors by playing eight shows in half-empty theatres . . . There is some unknowable dollar amount that is the value of the remaining Wednesday matinées. We would estimate it to be $100,000.'

Something in the letter's tone seemed completely unreal. It arrived like a paper dart across a canyon of incomprehension. However good the management, producers can simply never know what it is like to expend the amount of effort involved in a one-man show. How could they? The accountant-like prose made an amusing contrast with the figure of the man whose task is to help them recoup their investment. I was flopped out in my big dressing room chair, too tired even to take off my costume. I told Stephen that there was no chance that I would be able to do the play to this standard more than twice a week. Karen nodded. 'You usually do two. You do two a week like that.'

By chance, Wally Shawn rang me from England, where he has gone for rehearsals of his play *Aunt Dan and Lemon*. The previous night he had seen *Plenty*, which is still previewing prior to its opening next Tuesday. It had brought him up short. 'I had forgotten that plays don't have to be about how we live. Once they were also about how we might have lived.'

25 April It is famously said that when the Lincoln Center presented

Chekhov's *Ivanov*, Kevin Kline became so enraged by the coughing in the first act that he took advantage of his character's absence from the opening of the second act to appear in full nineteenth-century costume in the circle. He proceeded to distribute cough sweets to an astonished audience. I do not know if it is true. I certainly know that he insisted pastilles be handed out at the entrance to the auditorium.

The highmindedness of this diary sometimes seem more than a tad ridiculous. Yesterday afternoon I arrived at the theatre in a mood of despair, unsure where I would find the energy for two more shows, and beginning to be really angry with the management for having dismissed my plea for fewer shows so summarily. To prove my point, the Saturday matinée was destined to demonstrate the demoralizing pointlessness of matinées.

There comes a moment when all you can think about are the interruptions. I think we probably had about twelve persistent coughers in an audience of 600, but they certainly made it impossible for me to do any serious work. They were even planning to cough through the excerpts from Himmler's letter about the extermination of the Jews until I stopped for a full ten seconds to make it clear that even if I didn't deserve silence, perhaps the dead did. That didn't stop them getting back into full hack mode for the last two words of the play. 'Via Dolorosa,' I said, attempting to sum up the entire passage of the play. Someone coughed loudly, bang on target. It was the rudest thing yet.

The lesser distractions seemed routine. Somebody's hearing aid developed a high-pitched whine. Ushers roamed, torches flashing to try and deal with it. Sweets were unwrapped throughout. Beyond the behaviour of these selfish and inconsiderate arseholes I could feel bunches of ordinary theatregoers trying to listen to what I had to say. My homilies about the fundamental seriousness of Broadway audiences seemed particularly inapposite.

Theatre, when it's bad, leaves everyone in a foul temper. People hate bad theatre more than they hate bad anything else, because they can't escape. You can walk past a bad painting and move on to a better one. You can throw a bad novel against the wall, skip the bad poem and turn off the bad CD. But at bad theatre, you're trapped.

But, for me, bad performance also raises questions about art itself. I choose to work in the performing arts because the audience is part of the experience. The play is not the play. It is the interaction between the audience and the play. At the turn of 1998, Nicole and I went to Australia. We attended a recital given at the Sydney Opera House by one of America's most distinguished sopranos. I had looked forward to it for weeks. From the moment the singer came on, it was clear that she had lost what had once made her great. Not only was her singing thin and inadequate, but she also acted out emotions with a cynicism and staginess which was consistently contrived. A wrap was snaked and re-snaked round her shoulders, supposedly to express voluptuousness. She produced not one single feeling all evening which convinced you either of its reality or of its sincerity. She had become a faker.

We might have written the evening off and forgotten it, had it not been for the audience's reaction. To my disbelief they treated this fool's gold as if it were real. They cheered paste as if it were precious stone. They wept. They sat in profound silence, moved. I found myself thinking: How can a group of people sit together and receive something so false as if it were true?

Fundamental to my faith in the theatre is my trust that the audience *knows*. It knows true from false. The whole purpose of public art is that an act of communal discernment be made.

The unique claim of the performing arts is that there is some collective instinct for 'the truth'. We believe something special happens in the dark. So how do we account for that special something being specially false? If the audience does not know, if the audience cannot discriminate, if the audience can be sold an obvious pup, then what virtue is there in public, rather than private art? Is theatre one big Nuremberg rally?

Devotees speak all the time of the pleasure of being in an audience with six or seven hundred people and realizing that you are all experiencing something together. You learn together. Great plays seem to be both personal and shared. Yet against this elevated view of our calling must be set all the godawful nights which were not *Saved*, which were not *Long Day's Journey Into Night*, which were not *Top Girls*, but which were received, and then written of, exactly as if they were. It is one thing to know that some lazy or specious piece of work is popular. It is another thing altogether if the quality of the attention brought by the audience to that work seems exactly the same as that brought to *Hamlet*.

I remember once meeting the Irish playwright Brian Friel. I told him that I had attended a performance of his play *Dancing at Lughnasa* and that I had been even more moved by the audience than by his excellent play. At one point I had looked along my row and seen the faces of the spectators, lit from the stage, reacting to every line and gesture like a field of corn. It was an achingly beautiful sight. Friel replied that, by coincidence, he had had a similar experience at my own play *Racing Demon*. He had spent most of the evening turned away from the stage. Everyone had told him that England was now a secular country. Yet here was an audience drinking up every word, eager for mention of a subject in which they were meant to be no longer interested. If the British had ceased to be a spiritual people, then what was this thirst? Theatre performed its crucial function of uncovering something he had not known was there.

The easiest thing for a playwright to do is to hate the audience. If you decide they're a bunch of tasteless ignoramuses then, frankly, life becomes much easier, because you cease having to listen to them. A couple of my loftier colleagues regard reaction as irrelevant. The only thing that matters is what they have to say. If it's ignored or misunderstood, so be it. But I am more at peace trying to keep faith with the audience. I have lately reached the rather Catholic conclusion that there's very little point in having a faith unless it's tested. From time to time, to destruction.

27 *April* An extraordinary day. At 3 p.m. Karen rang me at the apartment to tell me that Yitzhak Rabin's widow Leah was coming to the show tonight. My first reaction was to recall an agreement I had made with Stephen. We had resolved that, should Leah Rabin attend, we would cut two passages which we thought needlessly cruel. In the settlements, Mrs Rabin is despised as the wife of the

man who signed the Oslo agreement. As soon as her name is mentioned the settlers disparage her by claiming that she is 'ugly, a very ugly woman to look at'. Later, they repeat the rumours that Rabin was unfaithful to her.

I was nervous when I walked on, but when there was a round of applause at Judi Dench's name, I stopped dead, realizing it was Judi's day off. I was facing a double whammy. That said, I did feel inspired when I reached the passages about the murdered leader. When I got to the moment where I describe Shulamit Aloni as a woman whose life 'has been destroyed by Rabin's assassination', there was an extraordinary calm in the house. I was vibrating like a tuning fork. I knew I had hit home.

I changed quietly in my dressing room. Leah Rabin came in with a friend who had seen the show before, and a man whose name I missed. She shook my hand gravely, but her first words unsettled me. 'You cut some lines tonight. Usually you say that I'm an ugly woman. Isn't that right? Don't you usually say I'm ugly?' She was looking right at me. Her dark eyes are deep set, her hair is black, her nose is strong and she has a hawk-like dignity. She was dressed entirely in black. I said: 'I'm not going to talk about it. I refuse to talk about it.' She said quietly, 'But you do, don't you?'

She had spoken to Judi in the corridor outside and asked her if she thought I favoured anyone in the show. Judi had said that my whole strength was that I allowed everyone their point of view. Mrs Rabin had said, 'I don't think so. No, I don't think so. I know who he favours.' Now that she was in the dressing room I told her that I hoped that she could see that the play had a hero. Every night, I could feel the audience's love for her husband. Again, she looked at me very hard. 'The audience? I don't know about the audience. But I can feel your love for him.'

I remembered that on the night Rabin was shot down at a public meeting, a journalist had asked Leah whether her husband was wearing a bullet-proof vest. She had replied, 'What kind of question is that? What does he need a vest for? Are we living in a banana republic?' Now, as we discussed whether I should have taken the show to Israel, she shook her head and pointed at the man beside her. 'You would have had to live with one of these.' The man whose name I had missed was a bodyguard.

She took my hand again. Her grip was steady and she was completely focused. 'I can't thank you enough. What you are doing is a valuable contribution to the whole story of our part of the world. There is one thing I am sure of and I can say it to you with utter certainty. My husband would have loved it. Yitzhak would have loved it.'

When she was gone, Judi and I opened a bottle of wine. I sat down in relief. Judi said, 'I'm never going to joke about your acting again.' I asked if she thought what I was doing was acting. 'No. It isn't. It isn't acting.' For weeks now, Judi has been telling me that she wants me to write a play in which she and I would appear together. It's been a running joke. So I asked her if she now thought that I could come plausibly into a room, pick up a cup of tea and ask someone how they were. 'I honestly don't think you could. I don't recognize anything you did tonight as what I do for a living. It's not in the same family. There's not a single movement or intonation which an actor would choose. At one point you do some funny little step – no actor would choose it. Or you address a line in a completely peculiar direction. And yet whatever it is you're doing, it is so moving. What you are doing is new. It's a new genre. You speak something and we believe it's the truth.'

Judi told me she had been offered many one-man shows but has always turned them down. 'I couldn't do them. When I was getting ready, I wouldn't know who I'd be getting ready for. I have to believe I'm going down there to meet someone.' Judi was horrified that I was doing eight shows a week. 'You can't. It's not even at issue. It's not even to be discussed. You'll kill yourself if you go on doing this.' I said the management had said I had to. 'Who's the management?' 'The Lincoln Center.' Judi looked at me, that surprisingly fierce look she sometimes has. 'Huh.'

She asked me to eat with her and her friend. 'But you can't,' she said, 'I know you can't.' I said that, after tonight, I needed to go home and be quiet. 'Quite right. Of course you do.' She said she was going to write to me. I said I would like that very much. And then Judi turned and left.

28 *April* This was the most melancholy day for months. Gabrielle was giving me a computer lesson at my apartment in the afternoon when Jonathan Kent rang from London at the end of the press night of *Plenty*. He felt Cate had overpitched the first act. She was wonderful in the second. I could tell the evening had not been what Jonathan had hoped for – what we all hope for when we work on a play. He had reached that moment when, expecting everything, we arrive at something.

Nicole rang to reassure me, as only she can. It was true, she said, that in the first act Cate had lacked a sense of progress. But you still could feel the power of the play. Then my son Joe came on the line. 'I know this is going to sound wanky,' he said, 'but I can't see any difference between your young work and your mature work. It's the same voice.'

I had to go off and have my photograph taken to publicize *Via Dolorosa*. I found myself spinning off into a terrible mood, distracted, lost, swept away with the sadness of having missed my own first night by a full 3,000 miles. It was one thing to miss *Amy's View*, but at least it was two blocks uptown. The little sense I have of *Plenty* is gathered from scraps, shouted from a phone box in St Martin's Lane.

It's the passage of half a lifetime. Twenty-one years ago *Plenty* was produced in a flush of creative excitement and ardour which is still red hot in my memory. I can still see the production scene by scene, recall the first time Kate Nelligan read it and the passion of her reaction. Now I sit in some fucking featureless hotel room, a mile high in the sky, on some random photo shoot, wondering what's happening on the other side of the Atlantic. I'm an absence.

I went into a slump of morbid self-pity in my dressing room. In the afternoon I had banged my knee against a desk and the pain was raging. It occurred to me that it used to be Thursday or Friday before I got really tired. Now it seems to be Tuesday when I start to feel the week's already been going on long enough. There are still seven more weeks of this punishing schedule.

Bernie came to talk to me about making a film of *Via Dolorosa* at the end of the run in New York. But my heart wasn't in the conversation. I went out to do the show and felt again that maddening mix of power and powerlessness, order and disorder that I now recognize as being the characteristic condition of acting. Then I went home and sulked. I could feel my spirits sinking. A part of me asks: What have you got to be upset about? But on nights like this, it's the journey which seems precious, the event disillusioning. You always believe that art will give your life shape, that somehow the production of a play will give it a climax it would otherwise lack. A play will open, you think, and everything will change.

I turned on the TV and there was *Repulsion*, as vivid as when it was first screened in the early sixties. In my terrible mood, its assurance seemed cruel. Polanski, like Bertolucci, has had the toughest career an artist can have. In youth, by instinct, he effortlessly exhibited a power which he has spent the whole of his life searching to imitate by experience.

29 April I have come to the entirely rational view that it's impossible for me to judge *Plenty* until I see it in late June. This may seem obvious, but the confusion of kindly voices from London had thrown me for twenty-four hours. I spoke to Cate Blanchett. She detailed the same experience Kate Nelligan and I had twenty-one years ago. In an eerie replay of the National Theatre opening, the leading lady, walking out to do work she believed in, was taken aback by an openly hostile first-night audience who were willing the play not to work. As Jonathan says, the play hits a subliminal tone which a certain kind of male receives at the pitch of a dog whistle. At the sound of it, the male bristles involuntarily and cocks his little tail.

This morning I got up to go for a massage. Someone had weeks ago given me a voucher as a first-night present. As I walked towards the so-called urban spa on 16th Street, I realized what a pleasure it was to be doing something which had nothing to do with show business. I have been in New York for eight weeks. I realized that my tally for the last two months is as follows:

Museums visited	0
Concerts attended	0
Friendships forged outside theatre	0

Last week, when Nicole was here, we did go to the Metropolitan Museum but the exhibition we wanted to see had closed. Day after day, I wake up with the feeling that I have little time. Each day I am on a grid, counting down the hours until the evening comes, never feeling free until the performance is over, and even then thinking that I must get to bed soon. I rarely stray further uptown than 45th Street. My intention to finish my half-written screenplay while I am here seems particularly idiotic. What have I actually done?

It takes me all day to get down to Dean and Deluca for a pasta dish or to buy orange juice. How do actors ever marry, pay taxes, grieve?

The pleasure of walking to my massage was that the world started to seem real again. It was a beautiful morning. The sun was at that angle which means summer is coming. The sky was the clear blue of the Eastern seaboard. The spa itself was a little Balinese fantasy, with wooden duckboards and Buddhas, cups of weak tea and soft-spoken women. People moved around silently in robes and smiled dreamily at each other. I lay there, letting Thea dig in as hard as she liked. For months everything has been to a purpose. I can't wait to finish acting and once more have whole days to spend, enjoying the bliss of the irrelevant.

30 April Last night I invited the art critic Robert Hughes to see *Via Dolorosa*. I have only met him once but he is a hero of mine. I admire intellectuals whose gift is for popularizing complicated subjects. Hughes' two television series *American Visions* and *The Shock of the New* are masterclasses in the genre. I was slightly worried that Hughes might talk above my head. But you forget. Really clever people are always lucid. It's stupid people who obfuscate.

By coincidence Hughes was sitting near George Stephanopoulos,

*Ross McKibbin, *Classes and Cultures in England 1918–1951*.

the ex-Clinton aide who has published a book about his days in the White House. Stephanopoulos was concerned because he couldn't work out where I had hidden the plastic screen from which I was reading the lines. He refused to believe I had no electronic assistance. It tells you all you need to know about the Clinton ethos. Interested in the how, not in the what.

I specially wanted Hughes to see my play because I knew he would relish the argument about art. He would understand the artistic choices I made after recoiling from the falsity of the artworks in the Holocaust Museum. As we walked across to dinner Hughes said, 'It was sad that you gave so little time to that argument, but then of course mine is the perspective of an art historian. I agree with everything you're saying. All Holocaust art is terrible. There are certain subjects that are so monstrous, so huge that art needs to keep out of them. I was asked what artwork should or could be put up at Dachau to commemorate the dead. At once I could visualize one of those bloody awful statues of a burning body. I said, "The ovens themselves are perfect. With their simple brick lines and their metal mouths, they are the supreme images of what was done to the Jews. How is an artist ever going to improve on the eloquence of the place itself?"'

As we sat down for dinner, I said that the only good Holocaust art was in a museum in Prague. Exhibited there are the sketchbooks of children who were in the camp at Ravensbrück. As a way of passing the time, these children had simply drawn what they saw, in crude crayons, on lined paper. The naïve images of bunks and showers, of huts and of Nazi guards, transcribed with the eye of innocence – as *fact*, as nothing but fact – had a power which no grown artist could simulate.

Hughes said that a distrust of iconography is equally important to Christianity. In the early days it was forbidden to make or worship images of Christ's death, because it would be degraded by being represented. The crucifixion had more power if it existed solely in the imagination. But the badness of Holocaust art is part of a more modern problem. In the twentieth century, photography becomes the dominant means of representation – the one that is felt to be true. At the same time, the war memorial is changed by the scale of the carnage. By the time of the First World War, the heroic statue seems inappropriate.

It is Lutyens, Hughes says, who first overcomes this difficulty. At Thiepval he designs his famous Memorial for the Missing, to remember the numberless dead in the mud and the trenches. Lutyens understands that it is the scale of the event, not only its nature, which must be commemorated. He comes up the idea of three simple arches and, behind them, a never-ending field of crosses. When he visited, Hughes said he wept like a child at the clarity and sweep of the image. I said that the Vietnam memorial in Washington, which simply engraves the name of every American who was killed in South-East Asia, is presumably an extension of the same idea.

By the time food arrives, I am asking Hughes the unanswerable question. Why is Goya the only artist who has ever come up with images which are consistently adequate to the nature of war? Hughes roars with laughter, as if he'd known this was coming. 'There's no real answer to that. Goya is the exception. Why is he the exception? I don't know. Except he's the genius. Like Mozart. What really helped him was that he didn't work to an idea of classical art. He was a sketcher. He represented what he saw. You could also say that painting is not suited to representing this kind of modern experience. Painting is there to convey ideas of tragedy, and the ennoblement that comes with tragedy. In these terrible disasters of the twentieth century, there is no ennoblement. Painting stands to one side and can only look on.'

We shared a car home, swapping stories of people we both admire. We ended up, however, talking about Albert Speer, Hitler's architect. Hughes had met Speer while making a television series. Speer had hero-worshipped Hitler. 'You mean, like the captain of the cricket team?' 'Exactly.' Hughes said surely it must have been more than that. Speer had replied, 'Have you never loved the captain of your team?'

They were filming at Nuremberg, the stadium Speer had built fifty years before. Some hardy weed was pushing up through the steps. Unfortunately, although the camera was turning, the lens flashed and the moment was unusable. The 70-year-old Speer bent down and ripped the weed athletically out from between the cracks. 'The Führer would be furious if he knew the concrete was letting weeds through.'

2 *May* The end of the best week I have ever had on this show. We had seven responsive audiences out of eight. Each night I played to sensitive, intelligent and discriminating houses.

Only the Saturday matinée was tough. By Saturday night, I was senseless, wiped out. I could barely stand up. I said to Karen that I thought things had changed because we have worked our way through the Lincoln Center subscribers, and are now playing to real members of the public. Karen warned me not to raise my hopes. 'It's been extraordinary. I've never seen audiences like these on Broadway. You may never get a week like this ever again.'

Friday was the hundredth performance: thirty-six in England, sixty-four here. I drank a glass of champagne with the team and with Arthur Miller who, by chance, was at the show. 'You should be very happy,' he said. 'Thank God you didn't write a regular play.' Amen.

3 *May* God help us, it's awards time. The whole month of May in New York is studded with awards, like cloves in a ham. As far as I understand it there are six different sets available:

1 *The Fany Awards*
2 *The Drama Desk Awards*
3 *The Outer Circle Awards*
4 *The Critics' Circle Awards*
5 *The Tony Awards*
6 *The Drama League Awards*

Of these, it is generally held the Tonys are the most publicized, and therefore the most prestigious. *Via Dolorosa* has already won two of these awards – the Fany and the Outer Circle – and is nominated for the Drama Desks which will be given out next Sunday. However, this morning came the news that all three of my Broadway plays – *The Blue Room*, *Amy's View* and *Via Dolorosa* – have been passed over for the Tony nominations in favour of . . . well, in favour of every other serious play presented on Broadway this year. Judi Dench, mercifully, has been nominated as Best Actress, and Samantha Bond as Best Supporting Actress. So haste to the wedding, boys, and the fastest runner gets the garter of the bride.

There is very little I can do about my own exclusion. It is an insult and I shall take it as such. The Tony people are telling me to fuck off back home. It means that a couple of other outstanding performances, by Ronald Pickup and Tate Donovan, have been ignored. People think directing consists of showy effects, so I had realized that Stephen Daldry and Richard Eyre might be overlooked. But I was disappointed that even Rick Fisher, whose lighting Mike Nichols called the best he had ever seen for a straight play, was passed over in the general vote against my work. A couple of people rang asking if they should protest. I told them not to be silly. Someone used the word 'injustice'. Surely, injustice is what happens in Kosovo, or when Congress refuses to vote hurricane aid to Nicaragua.

I once saw David Puttnam on TV bemoaning the fact that Roland Joffé had not won a British Academy Award for *The Killing Fields*. Until that moment, I had always believed that Joffé had won. By protesting the outrage, Puttnam succeeded only in drawing attention to it. People don't remember who won what, and they care less. One person has already congratulated me on winning the Tony. I said, 'It wasn't the Tony, it was the Fany.' They didn't seem any the wiser.

Awards ought to be gifts. They should be bestowed as an acknowledgement of admiration for a piece of work. They should be an expression of generosity. The minute the competitive element is introduced, all the wrong chemistry starts. For years in England, I've made a rule of refusing to attend dog shows. It has stood me in good stead. If you really respect someone's work, why not tell them? Why invite them to Crufts with the express aim of disappointing three or four other people in the process?

That said, there are good reasons for my *amour propre* to be a little damaged this morning. I have always thought of New York as a place which is friendly to me. Joe Papp welcomed me here and made the place feel like home. In 1982, *Plenty* was received with a warmth and understanding that I had never known before. Somehow the deliberateness of today's exclusion has brought home to me how much the feeling has changed. I am simply one of the more conspicuous British playwrights of whom American professionals are sick to death. Audiences welcome our plays – they don't care where they come from – but the profession doesn't. There is no reason why the Tony nominators, who are, by rumour, American theatre workers, should be aware of my romantic notion of my place here. For them, my history means nothing. Why should it?

Beyond that, there is the larger problem of being a 50-year-old playwright. I embarked on this particular decade knowing full well that the water was likely to get rough. It always does at this point. In his book *99 Plays*, Nicholas Wright remarks on how many playwrights' lives end badly. 'Molière coughing his lungs out . . . Bulgakov unperformed . . . Farquhar starving, Horváth on the run, Kleist in despair.' But what is also observable is a period in late middle age when all playwrights go out of fashion. You can't avoid it, unless you're truly second rate.

I knew Tennessee Williams quite well during the days when he could not get his plays produced in New York. His hurt and bewilderment were unbearable. It was often agony to be sitting helpless in his company, while he described, once more and at length, the conspiracy against his work. He would be amused by the rise of his posthumous reputation. It would tickle him pink. Nobody changed the British theatre more for the good than John Osborne. But I knew John best when he had retired to a country house whence he brooded over what he saw as the eclipse of his work. He was left with a frightening bitterness. He thought the struggle had not been worthwhile. 'It wouldn't have mattered if I hadn't lived.' I heard of Arthur Miller's terrible prickliness at being dismissed by his fellow countrymen at the very time when he was being fêted abroad. And I have seen the film of Noël Coward folding his tent and going to live on a hilltop in the West Indies.

To actors and writers contemplating a career in the theatre I often say: 'You think that you are going to go up there and do things. Wrong. You are going to go up there, do things and then be judged. Have you considered the question of whether this continual scrutiny is something you wish to endure? Are you sure you have the right temperament for a lifetime of being judged?'

In *Amy's View* Esme Allen says that the theatre is a young person's game. There comes a point where its continual disappointments and humiliations cease to be dignified. As a young writer or actor, your own work is the cause. But by middle age it becomes tedious and shaming still to be battling on your own behalf – the cause goes stale after so many years. The answer for many actors is to go into films or television where the contact with the audience is indirect and less bruising. The answer for many playwrights is to go to some place – for John Osborne, Shropshire; for Noël Coward, Jamaica – where animals are kinder than human beings, where nature makes some allowance for everything you have risked.

Philip Roth says that there is one epitaph suitable for the tombstone of a writer. 'He came here to be insulted.'

5 May I have enjoyed a rare two-day break. Up till now *Via Dolorosa* has been presented Monday to Saturday. I've done six evening shows and two matinées. But now, with the arrival of summer, we are going over to a new schedule: Tuesday to Sunday; five evening performances and three matinées.

On Monday evening there was an official British reception for Judi Dench. The consul managed to inject a note of distinctively tepid English ambivalence into Judi's triumphs here. He spoke about how much he admired her in *Winnie the Pooh*. Other British actors appear not to have been invited.

I ran into a British journalist who told me I have precisely misunderstood the massacre in Littleton. Visiting Colorado, he found the place full of kids in BMWs. Their first instinct, when under attack from schoolboy killers, was to reach for their cell phones. They called the media, not the police. I had imagined the television coverage intrusive. But it seems I am an anthropologist who does not understand the tribe. These people grieve by taking their once-in-a-lifetime chance to appear on television. The startling thing, says the journalist, is how easily everyone takes to the conventions of grieving on television, as if they had prepared for it with the same thoroughness as the boys had prepared for the massacre. One kid is quoted in the paper today as thinking: Hey great! I'm talking to *Time* magazine. Then I realized, no, I should be sad, because I'm talking about the death of my best friends. Katie Couric and Dan Rather are not, as I had thought, intruders. They are priests.

In the same paper, I read the words of Charlton Heston, the spokesperson for the National Rifle Association. 'We cannot let tragedy lay waste to the most rare and hard-won human right in history.' I love the resonance of his phrasing – 'hard-won', 'lay waste'. He's talking about the right of kids to buy guns. Chuck even belches like Ben-Hur.

At the theatre, the team seemed traumatized having spent almost three days apart. They were like grief counsellors. Donna had brought me lilies. Sweet Adam Siegel gave me a photo of my name in lights above the Booth Theatre. And when I told Danny Paul that I'd turned down Gerry Schoenfeld's invitation to extend my run beyond 13 June, he let out a heartfelt 'It's so sad. I can't believe it. Only six weeks to go.'

I was extremely nervous because the two Israeli settlers I stayed with had insisted on coming to see the show. All their friends had told them to go. I can't say I relished the prospect. While writing *Via Dolorosa*, I consulted many of the people I proposed to portray. I felt a duty to send them pages of dialogue to ask them whether they felt I was being fair. I had no right to stand on the stage and pretend to be Eran Baniel unless I first asked Eran Baniel. In the case of some Palestinians who never appeared in the final text, I was aware that I could endanger their lives were I careless enough to attribute things they had said about Arafat and the Palestinian regime.

When it came to the settlers, however, I had been so taken aback, and so keen to convey the sharpness of their attitudes, that the only available route was to change their names. I knew that if I sent the authors the text of their remarks they would deny having made them. Settlers live, necessarily, in a bubble of ideological conviction.

They mingle with the likeminded. I was reporting them from across a cultural gulf. I believed one thing. They believed another. By protecting their anonymity I felt free to portray exactly what I had seen and heard.

When I have worked as a journalist, I have sometimes practised self-censorship. Covering the 1997 election for the *Daily Telegraph* I decided not to report one first-time candidate who told me that she had only got married to her longtime boyfriend in order that she could claim the expenses he would be entitled to when she was elected an MP. This remark seemed so stunningly naïve ('I Married to Claim Expenses') that it would be a kind of violation to put it in print. I also refused to report some disgusting racist language from a Conservative constituency chairman in a northern city. I knew it would unfairly reflect on his candidate. The editor backed me up. 'I'm not having that Alf Garnett stuff in the paper.'

In the case of the Weisses, however, I felt very strongly that they had made a choice. They have decided to make their ideology their lives, and their lives their ideology. They live where they do in order to make a political and religious statement. They are *not* naïve. They know that many view them as provocateurs. When they invite a writer to stay with them, they can expect that he will want to present what he sees.

I knew that their visit would not be a comfortable experience. None of us, in the dreaded phrase, enjoy 'seeing ourselves as others see us'. Still less do we want to listen to an audience who may well find us amusing. When I wrote my play *The Absence of War*, about a failed Labour electoral campaign, Neil Kinnock told me that he found the parallels between himself and my fictional George Jones so haunting that the three hours in the Olivier Theatre were among the most painful of his life. When I pointed out that the play is intensely sympathetic to the Kinnock-figure, and lends him the dignity of tragedy, Kinnock was not comforted. The experience was well nigh unbearable.

On this occasion, I insisted that the play's press agent, Philip Rinaldi, stayed on for the end of the show in case things turned nasty. I was more worried about Sarah than Danny. How could anyone not be uncomfortable at hearing themselves retailing low gossip about Yitzhak Rabin's private life in order to justify their political prejudice against the murdered leader's wife?

After I had changed, I met them in the small waiting room. I could tell at once they were not happy. The Danny-character said to me: 'You do the show brilliantly. You're brilliant. Like a demagogue. And how many people see it? I'm told 600 a night. It hurts me to think that every night you are telling people about Israel, and that they are hearing about it from a man who has entirely missed the point of it. It's such an opportunity. And you get it so wrong.'

I did not ask him what he meant, because I had decided in advance that an argument was not going to get us anywhere. Danny bent down to pick up his raincoat, but the Sarah-character was still shaking with anger at his side. As I had anticipated, there was a certain respect between me and Danny. But Sarah had no respect. She hated me. 'You come into our house and then you portray us like this. You misrepresent and distort things we said. It's an abuse of hospitality.' I pointed out that I had changed their names. They could hardly challenge the truth of my report, even if they disliked the interpretation.

Philip led them to the stage door. The idea of having Philip there had been a good one because I saw Danny give him his card and say, 'He's your man. I understand that. Your job is to represent him.' Sarah said to Philip, 'The English always betray you.'

Karen was upset for me but, in truth, I would only have been disturbed by Danny and Sarah if I felt I had done something wrong. I knew that Sarah was never going to soften. 'Bad man' were the last words I heard as they disappeared down the stairs.

6 May Something very peculiar is happening. I had been warned by actors that in a long run things suddenly go to ratshit. The words cease to make sense. You have done it all so often that it becomes gibberish. I have certainly had that feeling, more than once. But no actor warned me of the opposite. There is also a point where you feel you are doing the show as if for the first time. I'm 105 shows in, and think: This is the first time I have ever done this properly.

For nine days now, I have felt inspired at the theatre. A slightly alarming clap-happy sense of well-being has begun to infect me. I put it down to two things: the help Stephen gave me and the improvement in the quality of the audience. I throw myself into the show. I work harder than I had ever believed possible and I come off exhilarated.

Inevitably, I have considered the possibility that I am going mad. If I am, how would I know? It's a one-man show. I have no reality check. I was therefore disproportionately pleased to run into Zoë Caldwell last night as I was leaving the theatre. I had heard a roar at the curtain call. There was a shout of bravo which seemed to come from a US marine, or a particularly raucous stevedore. 'That was me!' Zoë was back at the show for a second time. 'You're extraordinary! You're extraordinary!' she shouted across 45th Street. 'It's better! It's even better!' Putting away the possibility that maybe Zoë Caldwell is as mad as I am, I was reassured.

A consequence of this happiness is that I'm desperate to do a film. In London, I turned away an offer from the BBC. But it now seems a mistake to close when we know it can never be revived. Nobody else can play the part. It is my intention never to play it again. Therefore I must get it filmed. The project is being budgeted as I write. We shall have the figures by the end of the week. Pray God it goes ahead.

7 May Great news from London. *Aunt Dan and Lemon* has had excellent reviews at the Almeida, fifteen years after its première. Nicole saw it and said that both Glenne Headly and Miranda Richardson were remarkable. Not only is Wally Shawn my friend, he is also one of the finest contemporary American writers. He happens to work in the theatre but, really, his work is literature. That's why the regular theatre doesn't always know what to do with him. I walked around in a glow of pleasure all day.

On stage I'm sweating a lot. It's May and things are beginning to get hot. I don't want the air conditioning on because it makes such a racket. I was drenched by the end. Peter Shaffer came round to see me afterwards, white-haired and gentle as ever. I asked him if he had ever considered acting. He smiled his sweet smile. 'Oh yes,' he said. 'Oh, yes, yes, yes. But I resisted the temptation.'

8 May An update on awards. I have now won four. Yesterday I went to a lunch in a hideous hotel in Grand Central Station in order to collect the Drama League Award, which is given by an admirable organization dedicated to the spread of live theatre. The whole thing is a glorified media bash. The other night, when I went to a Mike Nichols tribute at the Lincoln Center, it never occurred to me that the lines of photographers who were shouting 'David! David!' could possibly be referring to me. When I finally realized who they meant, I wanted to say: 'Don't you know I'm giving up acting in six weeks?'

I've got wiser now. Nothing throws me. At yesterday's occasion I even answered the person who thrust a camera at me and demanded to know who my favourite *Star Wars* character was. I said, 'George Lucas.' We were then all made to stand on a dais for a group photo. Forty actors from the current Broadway season posed in some strange parody of those MGM photos where Louis B. Mayer boasts about owning 'more stars than there are in the galaxy', and then hands them all a bowl of chicken soup. I felt a bit like Zelig. Someone yelled out 'Actors, stop talking please.' I said to Kevin Spacey, 'I suppose you're used to this sort of humiliation.' He said, 'Is it more humiliating than standing in line at Hampstead Post Office?'

At lunch, I was sitting between Glenn Close and Uta Hagen. Hagen surprised me by telling me how unhelpful Elia Kazan had been directing her when she took over from Jessica Tandy in *A Streetcar Named Desire*. 'I'm bored with the play and I hate Blanche DuBois. Play her how you like.' Harold Clurman had then arrived to take over the direction. Things looked up at once, she said. Kevin Spacey, whose courage has a touch of recklessness, then told how all the coughing and sweet papers have driven him to a point where he simply stops acting, looks at the guilty party and waits for as long as it takes to get silence before he resumes. He has even stopped the show and said, 'This is our professional space. We're trying to do our work here. Can you please respect that?' Kevin uses *The Iceman Cometh*'s two intervals to send messages to particular coughers via the ushers. Uta Hagen, who is held in high regard here as a teacher, replied forbiddingly that she always told her students that people only coughed at the theatre when the acting wasn't good enough.

Any first-rate actor can impose silence on an audience by the authority of their performance. Kevin and I said nothing.

When we'd eaten, a representative of nearly every Broadway and off-Broadway show said a few words. This gave me a welcome opportunity to put faces to names I'd known all my life. 'Oh, that's Gwen Verdon.' 'Ah, so that's what Bernadette Peters looks like.' Judi Dench then got up to introduce me. She made some suitably fulsome remarks. My own speech, however, was mispitched. I paid proper tribute both to Nicole Kidman and to the cast of *Amy's View*. But when I began to make jokes about the awfulness of my acting, nobody laughed. I realized it was a breach of manners. *Via Dolorosa* means something to at least some of its audience, and they don't want to hear it put down by its own author. I felt stupid. They have grasped the basic point that my sense of my own shortcomings doesn't matter. Why can't I?

I think I am just beginning to realize that I am the only person on this continent who thinks my acting peculiar – or even the *fact* of my acting peculiar. As before, there are differing responses to the text of this play. But since I made landfall at Kennedy, almost no one has said a word against the manner of its performance. My acting is simply a given. 'Here he is. He acts. Let's listen to what he says.' As someone who took up this sport somewhat late in life, this seems a confounding state of affairs. But the oddness of it all passes everyone else by.

In the afternoon I did a book signing at Barnes & Noble. This was lovely. If this is what my public looks like, then I couldn't be happier. An 80-year-old woman said she loved all my plays, she'd seen *Via Dolorosa* twice, and was there any chance I'd marry her? I said I was already deeply married.

My Booth Theatre team had warned me they'd be there in disguise. Danny didn't fool me for a moment. He had a baseball cap and a wig and had shaved his beard, but I still signed his book and said, 'Haven't I met you somewhere before?' Donna, on the other hand, had a complete triumph. A rather spaced-out hippy girl approached me in a lot of denim. She had very long hair and dark granny glasses. She asked me to sign her book for her friend Nina. I did so, looked straight up, smiled at her full in the face, and still didn't recognize her as my deputy stage manager.

At the theatre, Donna was exultant. 'You looked straight at me!' she said. The show itself was OK, except for one determined hacker in the front row who sprayed her germs at me throughout and did everything possible to destroy the play for everyone else. I came off and said, 'Send for Uta Hagen. I'm not good enough, it seems.'

9 May I've been exhausted before, but there has been nothing like this. The feeling that I am, at last, doing the show properly means that I come off the stage every night in a skeleton-racked fog of fatigue. I had no idea it was possible to be this tired.

After two Saturday performances, the second to a rather white-bread audience, I came home and scanned the Internet for a London Sunday paper. Dirk Bogarde has died. When I was first went to the cinema, I didn't want to act like Dirk Bogarde. I wanted to *be* Dirk Bogarde. When I got to meet him, it became obvious you had to be careful. He was a mass of grievances. He never recovered from the moment when his favourite director, Joseph Losey, abandoned him in favour of the glamour of Richard Burton. Thirty years later, it still drove him nuts: the betrayal. I shall silently dedicate this afternoon's performance to his memory.

10 May Something new. I wanted to vomit. This is one more rite of passage which actors have warned me about. Judi Dench told me that John Neville did eleven *Hamlet*s in one week in Moscow. On the Saturday night, going back to his room, he projectile-vomited over the walls of the elevator from exhaustion. That's how I felt at my first Sunday matinée yesterday. As I reached the passage about the Museum of the Holocaust, I was convinced that I was going to throw up all over the stage. I'd had an egg sandwich and a Caesar salad. It was tiredness, nothing more.

I went on to dinner at John Darnton's. Having spurned dinner as if it were contagion during the London run, I now accept like a shot. Two reasons. One, I'm so tired it makes no difference what I do. And two, I want to talk about anything besides the Middle East or the theatre. John used to be London correspondent of the *New York Times*. His wife told me how shocked he had been to discover in what low regard reporters were held in England. The English take columnists, who express opinion, terribly seriously. But they treat as scum people whose job is to marshal facts. In the States, she says, it's the reverse.

While I was at dinner, I was winning another award – this time from the Drama Desk, who are Avis to the Tonys' Hertz. I have now bagged five. It all makes no sense. The ceremony was on television but I missed it.

11 May Monday off. Sprawled in bed with videos, more or less insensible. Last week I'd snuck off to see Truffaut's *Tirez sur le pianiste*. There's a retrospective of his work at the Film Forum. I was disappointed. A film I had loved when I was young now seems to be silly, romantic tosh about low life and genius. So today I got *Les Deux Anglaises* out from Tower Video to see if Truffaut's whole oeuvre is decomposing. I admit to a prejudice against the myth of Truffaut. When he was a critic, he attacked previous generations of French film-makers, and called them old hat. His article in *Cahiers du cinéma* was so violent that the editors prefaced it with a disclaimer. When he went on to make films himself, he changed his tune, but not before he'd done some harm. He had savaged Henri Clouzot, but did Truffaut ever make a film as good as *Le Corbeau*? The young clambering over the bodies of the old in order to advance their own agenda.

Truffaut is presented by his admirers as a *cinéaste* to his fingertips. I wonder if he isn't a frustrated *littérateur*. Young film-makers who now hope to start a *nouvelle vague* may notice how steeped in written culture Truffaut is. Voice-overs are used for the opportunity of quoting from leading French novelists. *Les Deux Anglaises* has an absolutely spanking script about a young Frenchman's confusion over which of two English sisters he loves. But what you notice is that it's not very well directed. The acting is stiff and the images of the Welsh countryside are surprisingly lame. For some reason, it was shot in Normandy. Neither Kika Markham nor Stacey Tendeter look sure what to do with their roles.

Truffaut isn't helped by Jean-Pierre Léaud, an actor incapable of playing love towards anyone but himself. Léaud's relationships with women seem intended only to decorate and enhance his own character. Woody Allen suffers from a similar limitation but he makes a big joke of it – and has sustained the joke for more years than anyone would have believed possible. Truffaut is more alive to the literary ideas in his work than he is to their realization through acting and image. Again, how odd it is that Truffaut, as a critic, originally attacked France's *'films de qualité'*. He accused them of being more literary than filmic. Yet he himself sometimes seems to be addressing us from a stuffed armchair in a library.

I scarcely dare go to this week's revival of *Jules et Jim*.

12 May At 5 o'clock I had to go to Sardi's to pick up my Critics' Circle Award. My relationship with critics has not always been smooth, so I was moved by their generosity. I wanted to go because I wanted to say thank you. The most unexpected figure there was Margaret Edson, the author of a play about cancer which has had a big success off-Broadway. Wally's play *The Designated Mourner* imagines a world in which everyone who has read the poems of John Donne is dead. By coincidence, Edson's play, *Wit*, imagines an expert in the poems of John Donne dying. Edson had flown up specially. She is a schoolteacher in Atlanta, and she is taller than I am. By the time I write this, the following morning, she has flown back home and is teaching class once more. Her intention, she says, is not necessarily ever to write a play again. She wrote *Wit* when she was thirty-two and had something particular to say. Now she's thirty-eight and she's said it.

I had forgotten what a pleasure it is to do *Via Dolorosa* when I'm not exhausted. The break had restored my voice and my spirits. The house was the fullest I'd seen on a Tuesday night. It crackled with goodwill and humour.

To my amazement, Shulamit Aloni was in the audience. I knew the former Israeli Minister of Education whom I portray with such reckless aggression would come to the show some time. But I had not expected her so soon. She's on her way to Montreal to speak at a conference about Israel which, she says, 'is now balanced between fear and hope'. That, she says, will be theme of her speech. 'But you'll be back in Israel for the elections on Monday?' 'Of course.'

The whole of our team gathered on the stairs to greet her. Karen said, 'You are the person in the world I most wanted to meet.' Shulamit seemed dazed. She was softer, prettier, more nuanced than I remembered. I describe her in the show as 'a manic depressive Melina Mercouri'. There was no sign of the manic depressive. I trotted out my ritual remarks about how the whole audience loves her. Shulamit just smiled, as if overwhelmed at finding herself the centre of attention.

She had loved my portrayal of Haider Abdel Shafi. 'It is wonderful how you do him. It is beautiful. He is the most principled man in Palestine and everyone respects him.' What did she feel about the way I did her, though? 'Everyone had told me about it. Everyone had told me I had to see it. I was very violent to you that day, and I am sorry. I am calmer now, even though the situation is even worse. Even I can see the joke against myself.' I said that the joke wasn't against her. Not at all. Her feistiness was inspiring and spirited, rooted in the pain of Israel having lost hope when it lost Rabin. Shulamit smiled at me. I felt it would take a long time for her to absorb what she'd seen. I'm not sure she knew what she felt. She neither expressed hostility nor did she offer shallow words of praise. I admired her for that.

When she'd gone then I sat down with a glass of wine to talk with Michael Brandman, the producer who is trying to finance the TV film of *Via Dolorosa*. He is expert at trying to get a bit of gristle into the American stew. In the present climate, his work is getting tougher and tougher. He has got some money from the BBC, but it is not enough for the whole film. But he cannot find an American partner. The obvious candidate is public television. A woman called Rebecca Eaton is resisting like hell. She has the likeable air of a woman who knows what she ought to be doing, even if she doesn't fancy it. The other cultural channels have a drearily 'heritage' idea of what culture is. A&E is short for Arts and Entertainment. Someone who works there said, 'We now do an awful lot of E and very little A.' It's all bonnets and blazers. They look as bored as we are. HBO is in the ratings business and has a resolutely American tilt.

Bernie Gersten had promised me that, if necessary, the Lincoln Center itself would make up any shortfall in the budget and take a gamble on an American sale. The Lincoln Center has had a tough year, losing a lot of money to an outfit called Livent, which went bust while co-producing their musical *Parade*. So it remains to be seen whether the film happens. An inexorable law of life is that the person who most wants something ends up doing most of the work to make it happen. In this case, that looks like me.

13 May After the Wednesday matinée, a meeting in my dressing room to firm up the TV film. The Lincoln Center will offer a bridging loan of $50,000 while we try and make up the shortfall. The budget will then be shaved in the usual manner – i.e. by asking creative people to take deferrals. Stephen and I won't be paid unless we make a sale to American TV. At this news, I didn't even raise an eyebrow. In show business, there is always a new reason for not paying the creative people. I've heard some crackers in my time. My favourite was when I wrote a long article about Schnitzler for the *New York Times* (the world's richest newspaper). They then rang me up, saying, 'We must talk about the honorarium.' They told me it was such a privilege for a freelance to write for the *New York Times* that they couldn't pay a fee. I'd love to see the editor of the *New York Times* getting get out of a yellow cab and saying to the driver, 'Now, about the honorarium.'

At the evening performance, I found myself thinking about Shulamit Aloni, and of how she had stood the previous night with such warmth and sadness on the stairs. The memory of her infused my performance, and I felt myself raising my game at the end of a very long day. I came off both satisfied and frustrated.

The frustration is this. I am now in a very long run. As Karen says, 'It becomes a job.' I have a deep sense-memory. For the most part, my diaphragm guides me more accurately through the evening than my mind. How I breathe expresses what I mean. Last week I felt in the grip of revelation. Now I feel dull again. Unless I am handed the gift of something as striking as Shulamit's visit, I am unable by force of will to lift myself to that level which makes the work fresh.

Deep in the run of *Amy's View*, I visited the Aldwych Theatre unannounced and found Samantha Bond and Judi Dench playing Act 3 as if the ink were still wet on the page. How do they do it? Where do they get it from?

14 May A dangerous note of hysteria is beginning to enter the proceedings. Last night, I was trying so hard not to fall into a rut of routine that I threw myself into the performance like a man chucking himself defiantly against a brick wall. God knows what it looked like, but it felt desperate.

Afterwards, I went off with the team to a raucous bowling alley for jugs of Samuel Adams ale and a good deal of misdirected bowl-throwing – on my part, at least. Danny and Adam were the champs. I went to bed at 1 a.m. without having eaten. I woke up this morning feeling as if a steamroller had passed over me. I went out to get groceries. The sun was shining. As I walked back, my mind was in its customary daze of 'How do I make the play better? How do I do it better?' At a cross street, a man was lying dead in the middle of Broadway, knocked down by a taxi a minute earlier. He was in blue jeans and a check shirt. They were slapping his corpse on the tarmac as if he might come to life.

15 May Scrub the rude remarks about Truffaut. Once when I lectured at the University of North Carolina, a professor told me that nothing annoyed the students as much as when the world's greatest expert on *Hamlet* began his lecture with the words 'The thing you have to understand about *Hamlet* is that it isn't a very good play.' Even the farmboys and girls from Carolina groaned. They knew that this kind of iconoclasm is often self-advertisement. There is now a queasy sub-tribe of journalists in England who say stupid things and call it controversy. When Anthony Burgess pronounced in an obituary that Graham Greene wasn't a very good novelist, it was Burgess who looked silly, not Greene. Nabokov's intemperance towards Dostoevsky has left Dostoevsky read, Nabokov unread. Shaw never laid a glove on Shakespeare.

It's a relief to be able to report from an afternoon at the Film

Forum that *Jules et Jim* hasn't rotted in the can. If anything, it's deepened. From its release in 1961, we thought of it as a charming essay on troilism. 'Isn't it the one where two men are in love with the same woman?' You certainly remember Georges Delerue's ravishingly bold score. But now it seems effortlessly to embody what I always think of as the Shakespearean ideal – passion and distance, held in balance. In the light of Jeanne Moreau's overwhelming performance, the film comes across as a study of doomed femininity. It makes no difference who loves this woman, or how. She's going down.

After the film, I strolled up the forty blocks in the sunshine and fell asleep in my dressing room. The performance was torture. I am now so dog tired, bone tired, gut tired that it is agony to contemplate performing again, let alone do it. Athletes call it 'the wall'. I reached the point where I meet Muna Khleifi in Gaza and had to rack up the energy till the end. I thought: Get me out of this. Somebody get me out of this hell.

The audiences have been consistently attentive in the last three weeks. But I couldn't read this lot. At one chilling moment, I thought: 'They are looking at me, and what they are feeling is pity.'

I was shattered when I came off. Karen said, 'Perhaps we shouldn't have gone bowling.' I said, 'Perhaps I shouldn't have agreed to do 114 performances.' I cancelled dinner with Wally and Deb because I knew I had to go home and sleep. I said to Wally, 'The minute hand's swirling like crazy, but the hour hand's not moving. Do you know that stage when you have to work yourself stupid in the hope that you can keep the thing alive at all?' Wally replied, sadly, 'Oh, I know that moment very well.'

There was a lovely letter waiting from Kirk Douglas. 'I don't approve the men who write plays being able to act them that well, but what the hell?' I wanted to write back: 'Kirk, if you want to take over, please do.'

16 May I am in the tunnel and I must get through. Life is pared down to lying in bed and doing the show. Thus, yesterday, Saturday: bed, matinée, bed, evening performance, bed. All impression of the play's effect gone. Only the fact of doing it. Then doing it again.

17 May At 4.45 p.m. yesterday I finished my hardest week yet. Perfectly good audiences. But mentally, I'm on the ropes. Nothing left to give.

Reg Gadney says he is always nervous at the theatre because he is convinced that something terrible is about to happen. I know exactly what he means. Every day I wake up terrified I will get ill, fall over, forget my lines, make a fool of myself, be booed. I can't wait for the day this tension is lifted from me.

People knew Richard Nixon was completely bonkers when the disgraced ex-president used to take people on a tour of San Clemente, point to his desk and announce: 'This is where Nixon wrote his books.' I knew I was in trouble at the Sunday performance when I found myself on stage thinking: If I can get through this paragraph, then the other bloke can do the next bit. It was a shock to realize that, definitively, there is no other bloke.

18 May I took to the stage on my night off, but only to pay tribute to Judi Dench in an evening at the Barrymore Theatre organized by the Shakespeare Foundation. They presented her with something called the Gielgud Award. It was the nicest gala audience I've ever seen. They showed clips from Judi's films and a whole lot of good actors like Christopher Plummer and Ronald Pickup read bits of Shakespeare. Hal Holbrook gave five minutes of his upcoming Shylock which he is about to do in Washington. As he came off, I said to him, 'Well, you've sold at least one ticket.'

I was too tired to face the dinner. These days, I find meeting strangers even more exhausting than standing on stage. Instead I went off for a quiet meal with Robert Fox. He had just flown in from Melbourne where he has a musical running called *The Boy from Oz*. I am fond of Robert. In conversation, you do have to watch out for the swish of his *épée*. I've stepped sharply backwards myself on the odd occasion. But his wit is forged from his heartfelt belief that putting on plays should be fun. With Robert around, it is. He is here to re-cast *Closer*, so the conversation turned to the frustration of having to close *Amy's View* when Judi finishes in July. No actress who attracts audiences is willing to take over the part. They feel they can only suffer by the comparison. The play is breaking records at the box office, as *The Blue Room* did, and *Skylight* before it. They all closed full. But I'm not complaining. Fourteen weeks of Judi is worth fourteen years of most actors.

This morning I have woken to the news of yesterday's Israeli elections. It was always clear that in the wake of Rabin's assassination Benjamin Netanyahu was the man least qualified to heal his country, or to advance understanding with his Arab neighbours. He was a media talent and he's overseen a cynical interregnum. The Labour Party leader Barak has swept to power, but not before performing the Tony Blair-like trick of renaming his party One Israel. Benni Begin, whom I portray as the most principled opponent of the peace process, has resigned from politics altogether in reaction to the result. The *Times* carried a photo of him hanging out his washing.

As I read the news, I couldn't help thinking of the Weisses in their encircled camps in the Palestinian territory. History seems to be moving against the settlers once more. Their trip to my play will only have confirmed their sense of righteous persecution. Meanwhile, it will be fascinating to see whether *Via Dolorosa* will play differently, now there's an outbreak of hope in the Middle East.

19 May A massage in the morning, then lunch with Richard Eyre, who is in town for forty-eight hours. He spends as little time here as he can. He seemed wistful, envying the humour and intensity of the experiences all of us are having here, but unsure whether he wants to be part of it. If you hate exaggeration, New York is never going to be the city for you. Richard's mind is on his impending television series in which he will encapsulate the history of twentieth-century theatre in six hours. If anyone can do it, Richard can.

I then did an interview for CNN. *Newsweek* had asked me to write 800 words on the Israeli elections by Friday but I said, truthfully, that there wasn't a chance I could do it. I arrived at the theatre dreading the show. It was the beginning of the week and I was already shattered. But half way through, for no reason, energy came upon me, like divine grace. Barak's election had sharpened the audience's interest, not dimmed it. For the first time in many shows, I began to enjoy myself.

Afterwards Donald Moffat came round to congratulate me. I'd never met him before, but I felt very honoured. In the 1985 revival of *The Iceman Cometh* with Jason Robards, he was the finest Larry Slade you could ever hope to see. By chance, two days earlier, Josef Sommer had also come to the show. It was a coincidence to have these two fine actors visiting within days. The public knows both their faces without being sure of their names. In England they would be valued. They would have worked steadily in the subsidized theatre, and they would be knights by now. The very best American actors, like Moffat and Sommer, must practise their craft intermittently between bouts of playing the president or the local fire chief in dumb TV series. Do British actors know how lucky some of them still are?

20 *May* Interviewed by CNN, I was asked whether anything I had read about my work had ever helped me at all. I said that the *Observer* critic's remarks about my gestures on the first night in London had done me good. In thirty years of playwriting, no literary comment from a critic had ever affected me.

This isn't entirely true. Yesterday the ex-editor of *Time* magazine, Henry Grunwald, wrote a piece in the *Wall Street Journal* headed 'The Power of the Word'. In it he argues that we live in a visual culture, where pictures are meant to inform us about what is going on in the world. But *Via Dolorosa*, he says, is proof that we still need words. 'Journalists should go to see *Via Dolorosa* to learn and be humbled . . . Mr Hare does not exactly mimic the people he tells about; he only suggests their tones, accents and gestures. Their passions speak through him as though he were a medium . . . The addition of film or tape-recorded conversation would not only not help but actually destroy the effect. I found myself not missing pictures at all because I kept seeing them in my own mind. Mr Hare resembles but surpasses Ed Murrow on radio drawing word-pictures of the Blitz in London . . . What journalists can learn, or relearn, from Mr Hare is the power of the word and the virtue of accurate and convincing observation . . . One leaves Mr Hare's performance with the conviction that one word can be worth a thousand pictures.'

I may safely say that I have not been so pleased by anything written about my work in a long time. This is for two reasons. First, because Henry Grunwald has so precisely understood what it is Stephen and I have been trying to do. We could not describe it better ourselves. But secondly, because there was no need for this article to be written at all. When a professional critic writes, then I can't help myself seeing their words as part of theatrical game. What they write is only rarely from the heart. But Grunwald had no *need* to write. He did it because he was moved to. The piece came upon me like a gift. Grunwald has spent his whole life considering the problems of news and photo journalism. So I admit, with a little shame, that I was deeply grateful.

21 *May* I don't share Judi Dench's horror of the one-man show because, for me, the audience is the person I'm playing with. Last night they were eerily quiet. It disturbed me. If I don't get into a dialogue, then I have nothing to think about. I found that I was only remembering certain words at the very last moment, because I was working in a scary sort of void.

However, at the end, the audience suddenly leapt to life, as if they'd been held back for an hour and a half. They cheered like lunatics. It bewildered me after such a quiet show. Paul Newman came round to see me with Joanne Woodward, who said, 'You reminded me of my three-year-old grandson. Believe me, it's a compliment. This kid just gets up and does what he wants to do. He doesn't give a damn what the adults think. Everything was real. You acted like a child.'

This morning I am in a filthy temper. We have been turned down by some more US buyers in the last few days. The American television industry is poised somewhere between chicken and chickenshit. I am now being told that if the film is to happen, I am going to have to do it for free. I had expected only a token sum, but there is something peculiarly annoying about being expected to work for nothing at all. In England, the BBC is paying for the film. Once, it would have been inconceivable for the BBC to film a one-man play and not pay the person who wrote and acted it. But by the marvels of freelance culture, they are free now to admit no obligations. They simply buy a 'product'. They don't care if it's made in a sweatshop. It's not their business, they say. Highly convenient for a public broadcaster. Jenne Casarotto says it happens more often that you would believe.

The rational part of me sees that the person who gets most joy from *Via Dolorosa* should expect least money. But the irrational part has to face the fact that 'least money' may here be taken to mean 'zero'.

22 *May* After a certain amount of violent negotiation, Jenne has secured $5,000 for me and for Stephen, and the film is going ahead. Stephen is a hero in all this, because he will put in most work for least personal advantage. As always, his commitment is exemplary. When Hollywood film-makers ask how the British still manage to go on making the odd decent film, I always reply 'By taking so much less money than you do.' In the US even the director's salary can be more than the cost of an entire British film. Jean-Luc Godard was the first person to predict the effects. In the sixties, he was prescient enough to say, 'Once you start paying people these huge sums of money, you will destroy the movies. The actors will take your money but they will behave badly because they will despise you for giving it.'

A PBS producer in Washington rejected us for the most brutal reason yet. 'He's too old.'

Nicole is with me for five days. She came to the show for the first time in eight weeks. She said it was the best yet, the clearest, the most articulated. As an actor, I was now much more skilful. I knew exactly what effect I could have by smiling, by angling my body, by twisting a phrase. 'Like a whore,' she said, looking me in the eye and laughing.

We went off for dinner with Wally and Deborah at the Union Square Café. We chose a really good Bourgogne. It spread warmth as only good red wine can. Wally was already glowing from his experiences in London. He is a rare playwright who enjoys watching his own work. We did *The Designated Mourner* twenty-four times, and he was certainly there for nineteen. Soon he is hastening back to *Aunt Dan and Lemon*, so as to catch the end of its run. What he had admired most about the English critics was that they had praised Miranda Richardson and Glenne Headly equally. 'Here, they would need to say which one they preferred. There'd be an edge of competition. You'd have to have a winner. In England, it's still possible to say you like both.'

I asked him if he got the part of the Wally Shawn-type in the movie. 'No,' he said, 'they gave it to Steve Buscemi.'

23 May Jonathan Kent was passing through, so we had brunch. The Almeida Theatre, which he helps run, is a gravity-defying phenomenon. Jonathan and Ian McDiarmid manage to present a repertory of Jonson, Pinter, Beckett, Albee, Lorca, Shaw, Chekhov and Brecht at their theatre in Islington. In the West End, meanwhile, they have just presented two plays by Racine, one by Gorki, and *Plenty*. Yearly, they provide Malvern with its Summer Festival. Jonathan is also talking of next year filling another space in London with two plays by Shakespeare. This bewildering range of work is offered on a subsidy of £461,559. The National Theatre gets £12,569,000.

This refusal of the funding authorities ever to recognize vitality is killing our theatre. They give money to institutions, not talent. The Almeida has a high international reputation. Alastair Macaulay said in the *Financial Times*: 'The Almeida sets standards higher than those of our larger national companies.' In fact, it hardly matters whether they're higher. They're at least comparable. So why is there no one in British arts funding with the imagination to answer energy with energy? The bastards never look. Nor do they care.

Jonathan is undimmed by this neglect, though he admits that private fundraising is the most depressing aspect of running a theatre. He is used to living on the knife edge. I have never seen him not looking harassed and windblown. At any moment, he says, 'the Almeida is three flops away from extinction.' Because Jonathan came to directing late, he is both generous about other directors and sunny about the way his life has changed. His work is a tantalizing mix of the flair for display which he learnt at the Glasgow Citizens Theatre, and mastery of the more austere traditions of text-based English theatre. His convulsive enthusiasms can be a little on the puppy-like side – I keep wanting to say, 'Yes, Jonathan, you don't need to persuade *me*' – but is there anyone else this good-hearted, this kindly, this committed to serving others in the theatre?

Sometimes I look at Jonathan and remember what Lindsay Anderson said about the founder of the Royal Court. It was running the theatre to the philistine indifference of the Arts Council which killed George Devine.

Brunch was the usual sweep of subjects. Jonathan was drinking disgusting-looking carrot juice in an effort to make his unhealthy life healthier. We spent a lot of time, as we sometimes do, telling each other what we already knew. It's like a play by Ibsen where characters review events with which they are thoroughly familiar. It's reassuring. But in between we laughed about friends, planned whether we could one day follow our *Ivanov* with a *Platonov* and discussed whether Jonathan will ever find a suitable American actor to play Chance Wayne, the young hustler, in his planned revival of *Sweet Bird of Youth*. As always, I left his company feeling happier.

At the theatre I sailed through a couple of shows. I tried to do the matinée at record speed (which, up till now, is 1 hour 29 minutes 51 seconds) and was alarmed to find that by making a *Chariots of Fire*-like effort I still only breast the tape at 1 hour 31 minutes. Cue Vangelis. Obviously I have got slower and more self-indulgent without realizing. I resolve to give future shows a firmer beat.

One good thing. As I get more tired, my voice mysteriously gets stronger. I have become a turtle – more prized for longevity than for finesse.

24 *May* The whole principle of American democracy was that the good life should be available to everyone. That is the reason it is said to have caught on. Capitalism, in the famous image, was the great tide which would lift ocean liner and small craft alike. But you can't

spend three months in New York without seeing how, in this city, the principle has been eroded. Nicole has been here for the past five days and is more shocked than I am. 'This city is run for the rich,' she said.

The cliché is to say that celebrity has replaced birth as the indicator of class in America. At one level it's true. At lunch the other day, as a transient and distinctly minor celebrity, I was given a card with what I was assured was the restaurant's *true* booking number. I was asked not to share it with friends. Last night, taking Judi out to dinner, we were sent elaborate desserts without having ordered them, on the grounds that to those who have shall more be given. Whether they want it or not. Nothing in the small gradations of fame seems to me as powerful as the apartheid of cash.

Manhattan has always been the gilded heart, fed and supplied by four darker boroughs which have existed to service it. But it used to be cheap, at least compared with Europe. In the last couple of years it's become dazzlingly expensive. I shall leave New York without a penny of my acting salary. It will all have gone on the cost of living here. I can't count the number of people who say that they have to work every hour of the day for the privilege of remaining in a city they have no time to enjoy. My assistant Gabrielle, for instance, has three jobs to maintain her share in a two-bedroom apartment in the Lower East Side. For people trying to stay here, the whole thing is like the Japanese film *Woman of the Dunes*. Sand blows into your house every day to a point where you no longer know if you are shovelling sand in order to live, or living in order to shovel sand.

In 1996 we came to New York with *Skylight* imagining that audiences would identify principally with the character of the energetic entrepreneur played by Michael Gambon. To our amazement, their sympathy instead seemed to go out to the woman played by Lia Williams who had abandoned the private sector for an ill-paid job teaching in the East End. The anger of those in the caring professions who have been left behind by those in the pampered big-business sector seemed to strike as deep a chord in the States as it did in Europe.

Somewhere downtown, on Wall Street, people are earning huge

sums of money as lawyers and financial analysts, and they are fucking up the ecology of New York for everyone else. It's not romanticism alone that makes me remember my SoHo of twenty years ago when rents were low and you never knew what was round the next corner. The mayor boasts that the city has been cleaned up. Crime is down and there are fewer homeless in sight. Opposite my apartment is New York University, and the young look wonderfully various, purposeful and happy. But in the everyday transactions of life, at least at my level of society, there is the strong sense of a club with only one serious qualification for membership. It seems a shame. Is this what European capitals were like in the nineteenth century?

26 *May* John Bailey is to help Stephen conceive the TV film of *Via Dolorosa*. Last night he came round after seeing the show for the first time. He is rather a baggy, thoughtful man in his fifties with that engaging seriousness good cameramen have. I liked him immediately. When we had done *The Designated Mourner* as a stage play at the National Theatre, we closed on a Saturday night and began shooting at Pinewood Studios at 8 o'clock the next morning. We shot thirty-three minutes a day. By Tuesday night we were finished. I've never been happier making a film.

John's head was spilling over with ideas of how he might shoot *Via Dolorosa*. John previously filmed Spalding Gray's monologue *Swimming to Cambodia*. At the time, he said, he and Jonathan Demme had no inkling of how the film would endure. It is popular to this day because people respond to the notion of one man being caught up in the movement of history. In his enthusiasm, John wanted to discuss his ideas with me, but I felt that it would be far better if he waited till Stephen arrived. I know only one thing. The play only works if the audience feels me to be an honest reporter. Somehow that same sense of honesty has to be there in the way the film is made.

When I got home, there was a fax from John Darnton, the arts editor of the *New York Times*. Serge Schmemann has just delivered the interview he did with me on 12 April. I make that six weeks. John says the piece seems a little dated. Is there a chance I can give

Serge a follow-up interview so that it may appear before the play closes in three weeks' time?

I do sometimes wonder if the *New York Times* is, apart from the Chinese Post Office, the only pre-*glasnost* institution left in the world.

27 May New York performances numbers 92 and 93. The audience seemed over-reverent again. I wanted to shout out: 'Lighten up!' It may be a result of the burst of favourable publicity we've had lately. I like this play best when I sense a lot of people would be happy to climb up on stage and argue the toss. Now, we are back to the listeners and learners. Brian Cox, the Scottish actor who came round to see me said, 'They seem awed.' I'm not sure I like this word. There's a good reason 'awed' rhymes with 'bored'. I'm beginning to feel like a monument – the Man Who Tells You About the Middle East on Broadway.

28 May Last night it got worse. I was warned that Memorial Day weekend is a bad time for the theatre. Even so, I was shocked to walk out to a half-full house. With just over two weeks to go, it was a depressing sight. Once again, they seemed to go quiet on me. I couldn't work out if it was because I was bad or if they were. My words disappeared into a void of incomprehension. I went back on for a thoroughly confusing standing ovation. It depressed me. Are they applauding the show's reputation, rather than the show itself? Karen said, 'You shouldn't start changing your performance on the basis of two bad houses.' To be honest, I don't know how I *can* change it. I feel as if I've done it every which way. The last two nights, none of them seemed to work. I felt forced and insincere.

My self-confidence has gone. I'm not convincing myself, so nobody else convinces me either. Stephen Daldry is due to arrive today for the first time in five weeks. He will arrive like the cavalry. Not a moment too soon.

29 May Things cheered up at once. Just having Stephen in the audience meant I did the play better.

It turned out that he and John Bailey had spent the afternoon in some disagreement. The three of us went off to Joe Allen's for a quick supper to plot the film's strategy. In the week after we close we will film two special performances to invited audiences. Earlier in the day, Stephen had apparently been arguing that we needed to film the event in its full theatricality – sort of David Hare in Concert. But by sitting in the stalls next to John, Stephen had realized how close the cameras were going to be. He had come to agree with John's belief that if I go on acting for a 750-seat house, I will seem to be playing beyond the cinema and television audience, rather than towards them.

I received this news with some dismay. I have already once re-conceived my performance for radio. The prospect of having to do different things again on film doesn't thrill me. I asked them to make sure that we had proper rehearsal time so that we could all be sure we were talking about the same thing. Corny instructions like 'bring it down', or 'do less', or 'centre it more in yourself' are useless unless they are applied to specific parts of the text.

I remember once directing an actor who had hitherto only worked in the theatre. He was standing in the shot looking like a plank. When I asked him why, he replied that he'd always been told that film acting consisted of doing nothing. I had to say, 'Yes, but nothing doesn't actually mean *nothing*. You are meant to *think*, you know.'

Behind the argument between my two directors, I sensed some confusion about how exactly the work is going to be divided. When Michael Brandman first proposed a film, he spoke a little hopefully of 'making a record' of what I already do. He even implied that per-haps only a cameraman would be necessary. I had to remind Michael that without my director I'm nothing. The production has become invisible in just the way Stephen hoped. But because it's invisible, you mustn't take it for granted. Stephen came to *Via Dolorosa* with a reputation for flamboyance, for brio. His best-known productions blazed with animation and colour. But in this play, his presence is so tactful that few in the audience remark it. I said to Brandman: 'As an actor, I'm the pot. Stephen's the potter.'

It's true that when I first met Stephen Daldry I entertained all the usual suspicions. Do we all feel that someone who is charming must necessarily be shallow? In the last year I have understood how much Stephen's habit of flying from a room is related to the deep quality of loyalty and commitment he gives you while he is there. When I chart his recent departures and arrivals then I realize he has come and gone exactly as I have needed him. Whenever I have asked anything of him, he has given it, without a moment's pause. Probably he takes on too much. But why is he always in a hurry? Because he wants to go to the next place and give of his best.

When I casually asked Karen which American directors excited the theatre community, she thought a moment, then said, 'To be honest, people are mostly excited about Stephen.' I can see why. Nicole said to me the other day 'You don't even realize. You walk differently. A year ago, you didn't even move the same way. You don't see it. I see it. Stephen taught you to walk.'

30 May Yesterday was around 88 degrees, today it will be 91. It's Memorial Day weekend. Most New Yorkers have left the city and been replaced by the 18,000 sailors who are in town for Fleet Week. They walk the streets in dazzling white, creating an erotic force-field for man and woman alike. The rest of us look soiled and sweaty. Karen watched a seventeen-year-old matelot picking up a hooker on 8th Avenue – an eternal scene. She wanted to say, 'Don't do it. It's a mistake. Go home.'

It seems extraordinary that thirteen weeks have passed already. I arrived in New York wearing a thick winter coat. Now even a T-shirt seems oppressive. On days like this, watching the kids frying in the parks, verbal theatre seems a Nordic sport. It's no coincidence that Ibsen and Chekhov came from chilly climates. There are 'sweltering' playwrights – Lorca, Soyinka, Walcott – but they're in the minority. As Voltaire says in the play, you must choose between countries where you sweat and countries where you think. Theatre is vaguely unnatural in the heat.

A handful of sailors came to the matinée. It was very quiet. I modified the performance to a pitch where Stephen could begin to imagine it on film. He'd given me a pack of new ideas, most boiling down to a note I have myself given to actors in long runs a thousand times. He reminded me to discover the text as if for the first time, rather than to retail it as if it were already familiar. It's Page One. But how hard it is to remember.

Stephen also asked me to take various passages slower. I did, and yet the running time was shorter. Only Einstein could explain why it's clarity which shaves time, not speed.

In the evening, when Stephen was gone, I had a serious alarm. In the heat of the day, I'd forgotten to eat. After twenty minutes, I was in danger of fainting. The bank of top light which shines down throughout the first forty-five minutes had me swaying, I didn't dare go near the edge of the stage. I could feel sweat running down the inside of my thighs, like my legs were gutters. I thought that if I could get to Gaza, then the lights would change and the stage become cooler. They did, it did, and I calmed down. But it was a scare.

31 *May* The film *Brief Encounter* was first previewed in Rochester, Kent. When the working-class audience roared with laughter at the absurdity of the middle-class antics, the makers left the cinema convinced their film was a flop. Yesterday, when I went to see the British romance *Notting Hill*, one member of the audience, no longer able to endure Hugh Grant's stuttering gentility towards Julia Roberts, shouted out, 'Get on with it!' The whole audience burst out in gales of mocking agreement.

I have had a film of my own laughed off the screen, so I know how painful it is. *Paris by Night* was jeered at a preview I attended in Seattle. I never catch the stench of that toxic primrose butter-slime they squirt onto popcorn in American cinemas without recalling the moment when my film was loudly given the bird. *Notting Hill*'s screenwriter, Richard Curtis, is a clever fellow. He understands the power of myth. But the audience is so familiar with the textbook strategies of the UCLA writing courses that they cannot take them seriously. They know by now that when the hero encounters the apparently insuperable difficulty in Reel 10 (Julia Roberts withheld) he will overcome it in Reel 11 (Julia Roberts attained). They weren't born yesterday.

In the last weeks, the conviction behind *Via Dolorosa* that we must find new ways of telling stories has occasioned some reaction in the American press. In the *Times*, Ellen Brockman has argued that my cry in the Holocaust museum – 'It's the facts we want! Give us the facts!' – chimes with a decisive moment in American culture. She believes that the play is part of an artistic movement towards the real. Because people now watch so much reality, they also expect reality from art. I think this is quite wrong. For me, television rarely rises to representing the real complexity of 'reality'. I'm sure that people still long for fiction. They just don't want it rattling, driverless, along artificial tracks which it's rattled along five thousand times previously. We should all aim towards Chandler's obituary for Hammett: 'He did over and over again what only the best writers can do at all. He wrote scenes that never seemed to have been written before.'

In *Newsday*, Linda Winer has raised a parallel question. She asks whether my play has been spoilt by Barak's election. A specific moment of deadlock and despair is described in *Via Dolorosa*. But a new Israeli leader may end that deadlock. Does that mean my play is now out of date?

Winer called me on the phone. I argued that if my aim had been to rabble-rouse, if the play had been a piece of anti-Netanyahu propaganda, then its moment would indeed have passed. There are such plays. A producer here is currently trying to present our 1985 satire *Pravda*, in which Anthony Hopkins brilliantly played a mad South African media mogul. But my co-author Howard Brenton has insisted that the play was of its time. The problem of a media dominated by nihilists answerable to no one has hardly gone away. But sadly, Howard says, the satire comes wrapped in all sorts of arcane and transient detail about regional British papers which would now seem laboured. We're refusing its revival.

Via Dolorosa is not such a play. Yes, it's a piece of reportage. Yes, it describes a historical moment. But the larger themes embedded in the collision of Palestine and Israel will not go away simply because history is making the play shine at a different angle. There are always going to be arguments about whether stones matter more than ideas. The division between those who believe in causes worth dying for and those who don't is not one which is going to be healed by a single election.

When I first went to the Royal Court I was influenced by its artistic director, Bill Gaskill. As well as passing on to me his hatred of plays where life is depicted as a circus, or in which characters are called Little Chap, or, worse still, Man, he also taught me to mistrust that sixties style of production which used rock music and gangs of actors advancing towards the footlights, wreathed in smoke. Hysteria, Bill said, is always the easiest emotion to get going in the theatre. It's as easy as shouting 'Fire!' on the tube. For a political writer it's about as useful. From Bill I learnt the valuable lesson that a slight touch of distance is needed if we are going to be able to think and feel at the same time. That distance, naturally, is provided by form.

It has been my ideal of theatre ever since. *Via Dolorosa* is inside the events it describes, but one step back from them as well. Whenever I meet students they ask me the same question. Can art change society? In one sense, the answer is obvious. Art has changed society, just as technology has, and plague has, and accident has, and politics has. The Dreyfus case led Herzl to believe that anti-Semitism in Europe was so endemic that only a national state could address the problem. The modern idea of Zionism is launched in his play *Das Neue Ghetto*. Zola's reaction to the same case, *J'Accuse*, is not only an example of the French conscience being roused by a writer. It also disproves the cliché that great polemic cannot be one-sided. Oscar Wilde's *De Profundis* is unashamedly one-sided, and it's one of the most stirring letters ever written.

Most art may not change very much. But the idea of its potential to do so gives it powerful allure. I am aware that for many people such a belief is self-deceiving. I have been corrected a thousand times, more or less politely, for holding to it. Art, people claim, should exist only as a leopard exists, to make the world more beautiful and various. I know well what the Hungarian novelist Dezsö Kosztolányi means when he writes in his diary that, for him, death is the only subject. 'I have nothing but disdain for those writers who also have something else to say: about social problems, the relationships between men and women, the struggle between races etc etc. It sickens my stomach to think of their narrow-mindedness. What superficial work they do, poor things, and how proud they are of it.' Yet Kosztolányi surely overlooks the fact that, in writing the story of human progress and the obstacles to it, great writers have touched on the only subject as powerful as death itself: human courage and imagination in the face of death.

There's a fair chance – we already begin to feel this – that although Brecht is certain to be pulled from the wreckage of the twentieth century, Shaw and Sartre may not yet be so lucky. Just as likely, people will take witness from the aesthetes – from Beckett, from Proust, from Kosztolányi himself. It bothers me not at all. Given a second chance on Parnassus I wouldn't change my loyalty. It would be a sad sort of writer who chose their team because they were going to win. 'I'll play with the losers, thanks.'

3 June The Wednesday matinée was our hundredth performance in New York. Adam celebrated by offering home-made ice cream sundaes, with lots of broken nuts and cream squirted in a foam from a can. We had champagne at night. There are now only thirteen to go. I had expected that as the end came in sight, my burden would lighten. But I have checked with other actors and my experience is typical. I feel as if I am running through sand. Every step becomes heavier.

The audience celebrated the occasion by letting off their mobile phones in a cheery chorus of abandon throughout the performance. The distinctive squealing of the hearing apparatuses was back, too. As Judi observed of Wednesday matinées, 'You have to conclude that either the audience is stone deaf or a hundred admirals are being piped aboard.'

4 June Nicole is back in town. I didn't want to go to the theatre at all. I started with the utmost reluctance, then did the best show I have done in weeks. For no reason. About twenty minutes in, I realized it was going well and I thought: I'm going to hold on to this. I was delighted Meryl Streep was there and saw the play at its best. She was glowing. I told her, 'If you hadn't liked it tonight, you would never like it.' At the height of her popularity as a young actress, Meryl helped a series of difficult projects to get made, including *Plenty*. You can say of her as of very few people in her position: she used her power for good.

We went off for a lovely dinner at Gabrielle's Lower East Side apartment. The food was excellent. The company was our usual gang plus a few friends. For the first time in a long time, I went to bed pleased with a day's work.

5 June Last night, tried twice as hard. Was half as good. Infuriating.

6 June After my two shows, Nicole took a group of our friends to a Vietnamese restaurant to celebrate my being fifty-two, though there isn't much to celebrate – fifty-three is the dangerous age for playwrights. It's when David Mercer, C. P. Taylor and Kenneth Tynan all died. I'd better get my skates on.

7 June I came off after the Sunday matinée to find myself being doorstepped by the *New York Times*. A vexatious litigant has filed a suit against the Royal Court Theatre in a Manhattan court claiming that Stephen Daldry sent me to the Middle East after having read another play on similar themes which had been posted to the theatre. These suits are a familiar problem for film studios and have given them a perfect excuse for not reading unsolicited material. The Royal Court has affidavits from two of their play readers saying they never even passed the play on to any of the directorate at the Court. Stephen cannot have known of the other play's existence, let alone have read it. I sent Gabrielle downstairs to say, 'No comment'.

However, the truth never got in the way of a good story, so I had to pass an hour in calls to Philip, the press agent. There is no accusation of plagiarism against me, nor does the suit even name me. But the *Times* knows that they can only make things sound sinister if they stretch the story to attach my name to it. Vikki Heywood, from the Royal Court, rang them to point out that the litigant is careful not to claim that I knew of his play's existence. This has not stopped them trying to make bricks without straw. This morning the paper has gone big and silly under the headline 'A PLAYWRIGHT LAYS CLAIM TO PARTS OF HARE'S VIA'. They are setting quite a precedent. They are telling their readers that if one writer makes an baseless allegation against another, then the paper will guarantee them 800 words of publicity. As someone said to me this morning, this is a new low. The *Times* has become the *Post*.

I had to do all my telephoning yesterday in my dressing room while Danny was tying my bow tie for me to go to the Tony Awards. I picked up Nicole, who turned out in a wispy number which made her look like a particularly ravishing fairy in *A Midsummer Night's Dream*. We headed for the Gershwin Theatre where it was to be my job to join Judi Dench in presenting the awards for Best Director and Best Director of a Musical.

The Tony ceremony, as I know from having been once before, makes for a crushingly long evening. You have to be in your seat at 7.30, and you don't get out till past 11. The highlight was a speech by Arthur Miller. He pointed out that *Death of a Salesman*, whose revival was winning a succession of awards, had once been a daring new play by a new American writer. He pleaded for Broadway once more to take the risks it had forty years ago. Where was the courage which once made Broadway important?

The awards themselves provided an all-too-vivid demonstration of Arthur's complaint. They had all the glamour of a Rotary Club night in Cleveland. With a few brilliant exceptions, any decision which might have endorsed growth or radicalism was rigorously avoided. Nearly everything was tossed into the lap of the reactionary. As Arthur pointed out, we all know that outstanding American plays are still being written. But because producers do not risk them on Broadway, they are not eligible. Howard Davies' revival of *The Iceman Cometh* was completely shut out.

The evening was close to a disaster. Angela Lansbury and Carol Burnett are remarkable people. But they hardly represent the spirit of a Broadway season where audience have craned their necks to see Anna Friel and Nicole Kidman. At the end of three and a half hours, the much-advertised problems of the American musical looked near-fatal. Some mugging and simpering from *Annie Get Your Gun* brought back the kind of stuff that used to struggle on the end of Hastings Pier in the 1950s. Traditional show business had its head cut off years ago, but it's still running around, squawking. When I attended the Tonys in 1983, the atmosphere was markedly different. At least in those days when big cheesy shows won, they got big cheesy cheers. People still believed in Tinkerbell. What was remarkable now was the indifference with which the winners were received. They met with only tepid applause. Tony voters will die rather than acknowledge the new. But even they have lost all faith in the old.

This morning the television ratings for the ceremony are down again, and everyone says the whole thing must be re-conceived. Nicole and I set an example by re-conceiving our evening. We skipped the ball afterwards and sped downtown to eat toast together in our kitchen. It was a relief. We had both watched the whole event awed that this gruesome fiddle-faddle had travestied or ignored the great theatre which we have so often seen in this city.

8 June Yesterday a dinner party was given in my honour at an Upper East Side apartment adorned with Picassos. While the New York theatre was thinking about awards, peace broke out in Kosovo. The peace turned out to be illusory. Last night the bombing was resumed.

I love the tradition at an American dinner party that if you have a great authority on some subject at the table, they may be asked a few questions at the end. By good fortune we had Richard Holbrooke, who negotiated the peace deal in Bosnia four years ago and who was therefore asked to comment on the present crisis. Holbrooke is Clinton's choice to be Ambassador to the UN, and is about to face some difficult Senate hearings. The most surprising aspect of his answers was the degree to which he stressed Tony Blair's decisive influence over Bill Clinton.

Nobody else seemed as surprised as me. They took it for granted that Clinton was in thrall to Blair. I'd always assumed it was the other way round. For the whole of my life I have seen Britain as a place of diminishing power and influence. When Margaret Thatcher bragged about providing the brains for Ronald Reagan's brawn, I always found the spectacle farcical, and ultimately humiliating for the British. Who was she kidding? If she was that powerful, why did she have to boast all the time? But it does seem that, in this war, Clinton comes off the phone from Blair feeling chastened. Clinton feels that 'under him, my genius is rebuked, as it is said Mark Antony's was by Caesar'.

People gave various explanations. Blair was loyal to Clinton through the Monica Lewinsky scandal, and so Clinton owes him a special debt. Blair enjoys a level of domestic popularity that Clinton envies and admires. But beyond that, I was assured, Blair is deemed to possess a quality of 'moral authority'.

I left the wealthy apartment block, said goodnight to the doorman and strolled out into the steamy night. It was chilling to walk past Central Park knowing that something is happening which I had never thought to see again in my lifetime. Large numbers of civilians are living and dying at the word of a British prime minister.

10 June The vexatious litigant is giving us a major pain in the neck. In order to make the film our producer Michael Brandman has to take out insurance against lawsuits. But, of course, he now can't get that insurance because there is a lawsuit already pending. It's potentially disastrous. No insurance, no film.

People have been running around screaming for days. I'm sorriest for Michael because he is working out of the noble feeling that the film deserves to be made. For his pains, he has to spend all his time on the telephone to lawyers from the Royal Court, the Lincoln Center and the BBC. As he says, 'No good deed goes unpunished.' John Bailey is already in town with his gaffer, and working as if the whole thing is going ahead. It makes no difference that the suit is worthless, and will be thrown out in a couple of weeks. It happens to have arrived at the worst possible moment. Stephen, who is the real target of the suit, is threatening to countersue for defamation of character. But it isn't going to solve our problems. We need insurance now.

All around us, shows are closing in post-Tony despair. There are seven plays and musicals which have waited before deciding to fold at the end of this week. This is a tough town for the theatre. There is always a seasonal cull at this time of year. On the one side the *New York Times*; on the other, the Tonys. In the month of May, only the most robust craft navigates between the two and sails on.

11 June A couple of days from closing, and a Shakespearean diaspora is being planned. My team are breaking off from the mother ship, with orbits and missions of their own. Gabrielle is preparing for flight to Pittsburgh, where she will play Nerissa in *The Merchant of Venice*. Danny is strolling the corridors, preparing to go back to his old college cross-gartered, playing Malvolio in *Twelfth Night*. Nothing is more touching in American life than this passion for putting on Shakespeare when the summer comes. The Booth, meanwhile, has been full for days as people cram in for the last performances.

I made my film acting début by walking down Shubert Alley, opening the stage door and going in. It passed off effortlessly. The line producer told Karen, 'He's very good, the way he opens that door. Like a proper actor.'

13 June The theatre is now full of activity. Everyone is flying in for next week's film-making, in spite of the fact that no contracts have been signed. The BBC is behaving atrociously, demanding all sorts of extra clauses to protect itself from our rogue litigant. You'd think it had never been threatened by a lawsuit before. It even wants to charge us for the time its in-house lawyers take to write a letter.

Stephen came in and was taken aback by the matinée. 'I couldn't believe it. It's so bloody good. It's unbelievable.' If I am to be honest, I wasn't surprised. It's something I've known for ten days. After 149 performances, I've finally cracked it. That's why I've found it harder and harder to get on to the stage. I've had to be pushed on by Karen and Danny, protesting loudly, because I am no longer motivated. I am more tired than I could ever have imagined. The other night I crawled back up the stairs to my dressing room on my hands and knees. Up till now, it was failure that kept me out there. It was incompletion. But when Louis' widow Candice Bergen came the other night and told me what a great actor I was, for the first time ever I did not demur and say, 'Don't be ridiculous.' I just smiled and said, 'Thank you.'

'I can't believe it,' Stephen kept saying, shaking his head, then laughing like a maniac. 'I just can't believe it.'

Later. The beauty of theatre is the beauty of transience. Its profound correspondence with life lies in the fact that it is there and then it is not. Literature, they tell me, lasts. Literature, they say, is a bulwark against the shortness of our lives. Freud says that man builds in order to protest against mortality. But theatre is the ultimate and most beautiful metaphor of that mortality. It is intended not to defy nature but to express it.

I did my last public performance. As I came to the epilogue, the description of my return from Israel began to merge in my mind with the journey I know I shall make in five days' time – the journey up the hill to my home in Hampstead. As I spoke of it, I began to lose all control, croaking my way through the words, groping, tapping my white stick insensibly against walls, suppressing feeling as best I could. When I went out for the curtain call, the whole house rose, cheering. Gabrielle, Candice and Danny threw flowers on to the stage from the aisles. I ran fast into the dark, weeping like a child. A lock was opened. I sat in my dressing room, crying uncontrollably. The whole year's effort became a river.

John Bailey said of the impending film performances, 'Can we just have two more like that one, please?' And Bernie was shaking his head and saying, 'It's crazy to close this. It's crazy. It's never been better. How can it be closing?'

In the evening we all went for a meal in a restaurant. We ate good French food and told stories, fourteen of us down a shadowy table, all related by a common experience.

I once read a book about the high incidence of suicide in the game of cricket. An extraordinary number of ex-cricketers have killed themselves. The book was called *By His Own Hand*. The ability of the game to make you forget everything else, its absorbing nature, the beauty of the summers, the pleasure of answering to the rhythm of the seasons; all these combine with the comradeship to offer a way of living which can never be matched and after which everything is for ever a disappointment.

14 June Later still. So that's it. How weird. That's the experience. A couple of days' filming and then I go home, eighteen months of my life packed away and put to bed.

I'm sitting in the elegant apartment they gave me. It's 3 a.m. and the traffic is still pounding, the sirens are screaming, the pulse of Manhattan life is banging inexorably against my many rattling windows, and I'm dreaming of Hampstead, of my wife, my dog, my children, my garden, and of living the rest of my life with a book in my hand and a tartan rug pulled up over my knees.

What have we attempted? What have we achieved?

The American surrealist Man Ray had a favourite story which ran as follows. Two wise men are sitting by the riverbank with their fishing-rods. One of them hooks a beautiful girl's head from the water. As the full figure is pulled out, she is revealed as a mermaid, with a full tail covered in scales. The man looks at her a moment, then lets her sink back into the water. One sage turns and utters one word: 'Why?' After a moment's pause, the other wise man replies, 'How?'

It is painful to disagree with one of our century's greatest pranksters, but my sympathies are always with the person who asks why. Everything else in the theatre follows from that question. The practical lessons that I learnt from Stephen, from Natalie and from Patsy in August last year have remained important. Anything I have intuited since has been the fruit of these lessons, but has never replaced them. Their teachings were blows from the sculptors' chisels, aimed to make the block beautiful. But the block itself was forged in need, in will. Patsy Rodenburg, from London, describes to me the frustration of regularly auditioning young actors who arrive to see her, well turned-out, presentable, competent, assured. Yet they lack the element that would make sense of their choice of profession. They do not convince you of their need to speak.

Patsy also tells me that there are actors in her classes sidling nervously up to her and asking, 'Do you think David Hare would let me do *Via Dolorosa*?' I wonder why. *Why* do they want to do it? More importantly, do they even ask themselves why? For its formal demands? For the challenge? For the giddy idea that they will be alone on the stage? Is it therapy? Or do the young dream of performing *Via Dolorosa* because they agree with what it is saying? Because they, too, want to say it? Does the news from the Middle East hit them as hard as it hit Stephen and me?

I have no idea.

Once I had a play on in Holland. I asked my agent, 'How did it go?' 'Well,' he said, 'it went as well as a play can go in Holland.' I asked what on earth he meant. He said, 'They don't really like plays in Holland. It's a puritan tradition. Plays are distrusted because they tell stories, and stories are lies. And it's wrong to lie.' The most popular form of theatre in Holland, he explained, is performance art, because what the artist puts on display is him- or herself. The avant-garde has always thrived in Holland because the Dutch are more comfortable with the baring of the soul or the body (essentially truthful) than with storytelling (essentially untruthful).

At the height of Thatcher's ascendancy, twelve years ago, I sat in the Place de la Concorde in the middle of the night, eating dinner in a striped tent which had been put up for the crew of the film we were making. It was December and the coldest night in Paris I've ever known. The French sat on one side, the English on the other, all of us eating *coq au vin* with a good green salad. Some of the actors were lazily mocking the young focus-puller, who had hitherto worked only in commercials. But he did not take their banter in good part. 'What's wrong with commercials?' he asked, his voice rising suddenly. 'Why are you all so snooty? Commercials are no different from feature films. They exist to sell you something. And that's what feature films do, regardless of how artistic they may claim to be. In this film, David is trying to sell you his view of the world. He's a salesman. He's trying to persuade you of his point of view. He may call it art. But I call it selling. He's selling his ideas and he's selling his talent. And David's just looking for people who will buy.'

269

I can still hear him. His name was Simon. I can still remember him. I can see him now, his passionate young face burning red as he was baited during the crazy row that followed – voices raised, raging in English and in French. For two minutes there was the unlikely excitement of a film-crew given over to violent, personal dispute about the nature of art. And then, at the climax of the argument, the near-fictional moment of Simon pushing back his chair and overturning the naked-flame industrial heater behind him. Next, all of us scattering and the sight of the little striped tent burning brightly on the Place de la Concorde.

If only all such arguments could end so neatly.

Sitting here now in the cool of the New York night, I am convinced that I will never act again. Why would I? What purpose would it serve? Mostly I have had the pleasures of acting and few of its cruelties. I have not known the waste of unemployment nor the agony of working with colleagues I disrespected. I have not had to endure stupid directors, nor have I watched parts I coveted be distributed to folk with faces prettier than my own. I have not felt the anger of low status nor the humiliation of being overlooked. Only with a spirit that overcomes these trials does the element of the heroic attend the actor. Mine has been a cosseted existence, sharing time only with people I admired, and cradled, for the most part, by the expertise of professionals who were dedicated to supporting me. Nor have I had to speak someone else's words as if they were mine. What I have been doing, Simon Callow observes, is 'somehow the antithesis of acting, which is about an abandonment of one self into another'. In a memorable phrase, he describes my time on the stage as 'almost a war with acting'. And, whatever else I have done, praise be to God, I have not had to embark on the uncertainties of an actor's life.

Is my respect for actors increased? Of course. How could it not be? Until you've tried it on for yourself you can have no idea what it is to dress in a threadbare suit sewn in equal parts out of error, terror and hope. How could I wish again to reach 8 o'clock every night, nothing achieved, nothing remarked, nothing absorbed, because all my attention has been centred on the mere two hours which will follow? Why would any soul who has tasted freedom wish to be welded to a track which leads inexorably every day, every night, to the same steps, the same patterns, the same demands? 'I didn't like *him* much, did you?' Who could want this and be sane?

How then, I wonder, to explain this joy – a joy I have never known as a writer nor as a director? Everything feels right. Why? How to explain the feeling that something is resolved, something is despatched? It is the middle of the night as I write. The glass of water is to one side. The typewriter is in front of me. A carrier bag of correspondence – from the angry, the grateful, the needy, the confused – sits unanswered at my feet. Across Great Jones Street, a large spotted Doberman lies sleeping in the window opposite.

Something new, this calm. Fascinating to see how long it will last.

15 June The fag end of the award-giving season. For the last time, I have to give an award to Judi because she is Woman of the Year. Quite right, too. The event at the Tavern on the Green, sponsored by The Women's Project, is significantly sincere and affecting.

A man approaches me to ask if I have heard about the close-captioning of the Charlie Rose Show. A month ago I appeared on television to talk about *Via Dolorosa*. The deaf are provided with a print-out which they can read at the bottom of the screen. It must be voice-activated. When I said, 'My wife is Jewish,' a legend underneath me appeared reading: 'My wife is George Bush.' The man's mother, who is deaf, rang her son from Florida excitedly to break the news. 'David Hare has just said his wife is George Bush.'

Bloomsday When I arrived at the theatre on Tuesday for the first of my three days of filming, I was shocked to see that my plastics had been removed. The marquee was already festooned with testimonies to the brilliance of Dame Edna Everage. Apparently they went up on Monday at 8 a.m. The show does not open until October. One part of me, of course, was admiring. But the other part felt like a rejected British prime minister forced to carry the Chesterfield out into Downing Street on the morning of his defeat. The beauty of transience, yes, but its pain as well.

Earlier, I had been for a medical for the film's insurance. The man opposite me in the doctor's waiting room looked at me and said, 'Aren't you David Hare, the actor?' I said, 'The very same.' It is the first time I have ever been asked this question.

The filming was very light – just bits and pieces of me preparing in my dressing room. So last night I went to bed early to prepare for the more serious work which begins today. I woke at 3 a.m. and lay awake for hours, feeling fear again for the first time in months. Tonight I have to give, for the cameras, an altogether different performance from the one I have given on the stage. I am refusing to rehearse. I said to Stephen, 'Either it will happen or it won't.'

17 June Yesterday morning I went to look into the toothache that has been bothering me. After an hour's investigation, the dentist told me that I would need immediate treatment on my return to London. Judi had already warned me that actors' bodies collapse at the end of intense experiences. She had put me on a course of ginseng to prepare me for the process of decompression, but to no avail. I am completely predictable. Root canal surgery, on cue.

When I arrived at the theatre for a walk-through, I was greeted with the frightening sight of four cameras, three of them on platforms in the middle of the stalls, and the fourth roving the auditorium on a Steadicam. We are shooting film as if it were television. Downstairs, in what is normally the audience lounge, John Bailey sits in front of a huge bank of monitors, giving orders through cans to camera operators in the auditorium.

For the filming itself, there was an invited audience of about 300. For months now my primary relationship has been with the public. From the moment I walked on last night, it was clear that the people in the auditorium could have no chance of access to what I was doing. Most of them were either in the balcony, which I could no longer play towards, or else scattered in hopeless corners of the stalls where they couldn't see past the cameras. I had asked Stephen to make a speech in advance to the audience, releasing me from the obligation to entertain them. Their job, he said, was to witness an act of filming, not to see *Via Dolorosa*. For a start, large parts of it would be inaudible. He also mentioned that it would be helpful if they didn't cough. They didn't.

However much he had primed them, I still felt rude and vaguely dishonest, effectively ignoring the public and playing purely for the cameras. But mercifully I had little time to think about it. This was one of the most intellectually demanding ninety minutes of my life. Almost every line, every gesture and every eyeline had to be altered on the spot so that it would seem to belong on the screen. The lighting was different, so a whole series of familiar landmarks had gone. We had made some cuts in the text to reduce the length of the piece. And just ten feet in front of me camera assistants were loading and reloading at regular intervals.

My heart was ice cold. There was no question of my being able to put any real emotion into the reading. I kept remembering Saturday's and Sunday's performances which had seeped effortlessly with true feeling. I had been so genuinely moved. But now, in adapting my performance for cameras, I had so much clinical brain-work to do that it was impossible to engage any other part of my being except my strategic faculty. I thought of Howard Davies' words about his profession: 'My job is to help actors to access certain emotions and then to replicate them.'

A lone mobile phone went off in the last thirty seconds of the show, just to give me a reassuring sense of returning to normality. 'Via Dolorosa.' BEEP-BEEP! When I finished, I felt that we'd filmed about 60 per cent of the text to a standard by which I would wish it to be remembered. I refused to meet friends afterwards in my dressing room on the grounds that, in my view, they had not seen the show. Today I have to try and knock off that other 40 per cent.

18 June Actors tell you that the last performance is always an anticlimax. My last *Via Dolorosa* was to an invited audience for a second filming. Overall, it wasn't as good as the first. Most of the afternoon's audience were theatre professionals. They roared too loudly at the jokes and then didn't follow the story.

It was hard going and I was not a very happy boy. I found the words quite hard to remember. My brain was letting go of them, knowing that after today it would no longer have to retain them. They were slipping away from me, melting like ice cream on a hot day.

When evening came we had four hours of pick-ups to do, including some alternative versions of lines where I wasn't to say 'fuck'. Apparently Michael Brandman can't sell the film in the Bible Belt if I do. Speaking for myself I find 'Tel Aviv is the fornicating capital of the world' much more shocking than 'Tel Aviv is the fucking capital of the world', but each to his own criteria of offence.

I could tell Stephen was in a bad mood. All this technology had overwhelmed him. There were cameras on cranes, cameras on stilts, cameras up ladders. I don't think he liked working in a medium he doesn't yet understand as well as his own. While John Bailey called shots, Stephen was sitting grumpily in the stalls, saying nothing. When I asked what he thought of a particular take of some line we needed to redo, he just muttered, 'I can see it's hard.' I said, rather wearily, that this remark wasn't much help to me. I was asking his help because I needed it. The moment I said this he stopped sulking and was transformed into his usual, purposeful self. It's one of the oddest things about Stephen. He's so alive that you get all the more alarmed when he does his trick of suddenly going dead on you, for no reason, as if they've taken his batteries out.

Towards 9 o'clock he wanted me to do the epilogue in a new way, just for the cameras, without raising my voice at all. For the first time, there was proper film lighting and we set the shot up with intense care. When I'd done one take, I said the emotional effort of re-conceiving it was too great. It was pointless to try and get another out of me. I was certain not to do it as well. Stephen said I might as well try a second, just for cover. I did. At the end, the crew burst into applause. I was deeply grateful to Stephen for letting me do some proper acting in what was otherwise a frustrating and bitty sort of day.

Afterwards I joked with my gang that if I was to make my début as a film actor, it was nice, at least, to do it in a film where all the shots are of me. None of that needless sitting around while other actors do bits. The backstage atmosphere was quite subdued.

Danny had a long face all day, and Gabrielle was working quietly, getting my new computer ready for the idea that it will one day live in England. Everyone had a task and no one looked up much. We didn't know how to bring things to an end. There was to be a wrap party at John's Pizzeria, but when I passed Karen on the stairs, she said she couldn't face coming. We burst into tears in each other's arms.

It is a Russian custom that before a friend embarks on a long journey everyone should first share two minutes of silence before they part. That's how it was at the theatre. Without Karen, the rest of us walked along the street to the restaurant. We passed a theatre where they were loading up a big traditional musical called *The Civil War*, which had opened a long time after us and closed almost immediately. René, our house manager, looked at the guys working on the trucks and said, 'There goes another ten million dollars.'

Inside there were hefty slices of pizza, and I knocked back a gimlet twice the size of my fist. The restaurant used to be a chapel, so it's cavernous and gloomy, with a lot of stained glass. Like me, Stephen had to be at JFK next morning by 7.30. Neither of us felt like hanging around. From Heathrow Stephen was going to have to take a plane straight to Newcastle. 'I'm in trouble,' he said. Stephen's first feature film is meant to be about a ten-year-old working-class boy at the time of the miners' strike in 1983 who is discovered to have an extraordinary gift for classical ballet. 'What's the trouble?' I asked. 'We can't cast it,' Stephen said. 'I'm thinking of backing out.'

Stephen was frowning, in the way he does. He told me the financiers were furious. They'd spent a lot of money on this project and now Stephen was saying that it was impossible to cast. He and the casting director Patsy Pollock had been in Newcastle for weeks now and they'd auditioned over a thousand boys without finding someone who was right. 'The whole film is about this boy's unique talent. If the boy isn't unique there isn't a film. After all, working-class Geordies who can dance like Nureyev aren't easy to find.' 'Do you have a back-up?' I asked, 'Is there anyone you could go ahead with if you have to?' 'There's someone I could do it with, yes. It's just . . . they're not perfect.'

Now we were looking at each other, right in the eye. I've worked for eighteen months with Stephen now, and I think I know him quite well. Or as well as anyone knows him. And he knows me. That's presumably why he was smiling. He could tell what I was going to say.

'Stephen, consider. You really don't want to get a reputation as the kind of person who backs out of things. That's not in your own interest. Who wants to be known as a person who always backs out? On any film, there are a thousand reasons for not going ahead. If a director or a producer or an actor needs an excuse, believe me, they aren't hard to find. At any one moment, you can sit in the production office and find ten thousand. As in life, there are always ten thousand reasons for not doing something. And there's usually only one reason for doing it. But, to me, you see, that ratio itself is the most compelling reason for going ahead. You go ahead for that very reason. The very fact it's ten thousand to one.'

Stephen was grinning now, boyish, as when I first met him. 'Do the film, Stephen. Just do it.'